FIASCO

FIASCO

The Break-out
of the German Battleships

by

JOHN DEANE POTTER

STEIN AND DAY/*Publishers*/New York

For Lucinda

Contents

Illustrations

For permission to reproduce copyright photographs in this book the publishers are indebted to the Imperial War Museum. The publishers are also grateful to Admiral Sir Mark Pizey for permission to reproduce the painting of himself, and to Commander Paul Schmalenbach for those on the first and third pages of photographs.

Acknowledgements

This book is based mainly on information supplied by survivors of the action, both British and German. It is impossible to thank them all, but those to whom I am most grateful for their help include:

Royal Navy

Admiral Sir Mark Pizey, Captain Nigel Pumphrey, Commander Colin Coats, Commander Anthony Fanning, Commander Hugh Griffiths, Mark Arnold Forster, Douglas Ward, Ted Tong and Charles Hutchings.

I also wish to thank Rear-Admiral Peter Buckley and Miss Lindy Farrow of the Naval Historical Branch for their kind co-operation.

Fleet Air Arm

Edgar Lee, 'Mac' Samples, Charles Kingsmill and Donald Bunce. Also, Commander Mike Nicholas.

Royal Air Force

Air Commodore Constable-Roberts, Group Captain Tom Gleave, Group Captain Bobbie Oxspring, Gerald le Blount Kidd, Brian Kingcombe, Roger Frankland, Bill Igoe, Cowan Douglas-Stephenson, Norman Nicholas and Tom Betjeman.

For further help, especially with squadron reports, I am indebted to Eric Turner and Miss A. N. Marks of the Air Historical Branch.

Army

Brigadier Cecil Whitfield Raw, Lieutenant-Colonel Stewart Montague Cleeve, Major Bill Corris, Mrs Nora Edwards (née Smith), Dennis Hagger, Albert Mister and Ernest Griggs.

On the German side, I am indebted to Admiral Gerhard Wagner, Admiral Karl Smidt, Vice-Admiral Kurt Caesar Hoffman, Vice-Admiral Helmuth Brinkmann, Captain Helmuth Giessler, Captain Hans Jurgen Reinicke, Captain Wilhelm Wolf, Captain Johann Hinrichs, Captain Erwin Liebhart, Commander Paul Schmalenbach, Professor Friedrich Ruge and Frau Ruth Fein, widow of Captain Otto Fein.

I also wish to thank Dr Maierhofer and his staff of the German military archives at Freiburg, who produced so many documents, including those of the Führer's conference.

I must acknowledge my debt to H.M.S.O. for the use of material held in Crown copyright, mainly material from the Bucknill Report (Command 6775).

These acknowledgements would not be complete without special mention of Cyril Morton for his German investigations and translations, and of Mrs Patti Clapp, my secretary, for her immaculate typing and eagle-eyed enthusiasm.

Author's Note

The *Scharnhorst* and the *Gneisenau* were referred to as 'battle-cruisers' by the Royal Navy, but I have used the more popular term 'battleships', which is also a literal translation of the German Naval expression for them – *Schlachtschiffe*.

North

North Coates
407 Sqdn.

WALES

ENGLAND

Coltishall
42 Sqdn.

Lowestoft

Harwich

16th & 21st
Destroyer
Flotillas

LONDON

Swordfish
attack

Manston
825 Sqdn.

Ramsgate
5 MTBs
Dover

MTB
attack

Bristol

Thorney I.
217 Sqdn.

Portsmouth

Straits of Dover

Calais

Boulogne

St. Eval
86/217 Sqdn.

Portland
Bill

I. of Wight

Channel

Identified
by Spitfire
10.42 am

10.45
am
Le Touquet

Dartmouth

English

5.15 am 12th

8 am
12th

6.30am

R. Somme

Dieppe

Plymouth

8.55 pm 11th Radar
failed 9.56 pm
returned to base

Alderney

Guernsey

Cherbourg

Fécamp
Le Havre
R. Seine

1.14 am
12 th

Jersey

Ushant

Brehat I.

Brest

FRANCE

N.S.H.

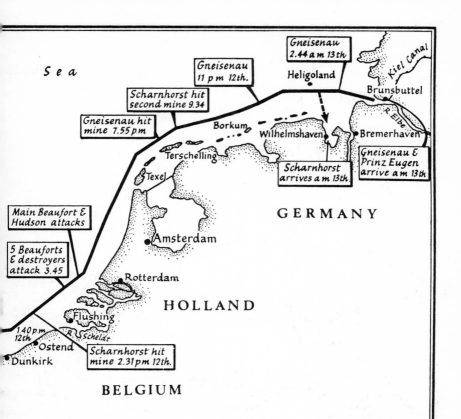

Sea

Gneisenau
2.44 a m 13th

Kiel Canal

Gneisenau
11 pm 12th.

Heligoland

Scharnhorst hit
second mine 9.34

Brunsbuttel

Gneisenau hit
mine 7.55 p.m

Borkum

R. Elbe

Terschelling

Wilhelmshaven

Bremerhaven

Texel

Scharnhorst
arrives a m 13th

Gneisenau &
Prinz Eugen
arrive a m 13th

GERMANY

Main Beaufort &
Hudson attacks

Amsterdam

5 Beauforts
& destroyers
attack 3.45

Rotterdam

HOLLAND

Flushing

1.40 p.m
12th

R. Scheldt

Ostend

Scharnhorst hit
mine 2.31 pm 12th.

Dunkirk

BELGIUM

The Break-out of the *Scharnhorst, Gneisenau, & Prinz Eugen*
12th - 13th February 1942

-------- British aircraft patrols
———— Route of German squadron

0   20   40   60   80   100

Miles

I

Hitler Decides

The two great grey ships appeared off the entrance to the French Atlantic port of Brest just after dawn. They were Germany's 32,000-ton battleships, *Scharnhorst* and *Gneisenau* returning from marauding raids against Allied shipping in the Atlantic.

They had sailed from Kiel at the beginning of 1941. Evading the British Home Fleet based at Scapa Flow, they had broken through the Denmark Strait into the Atlantic. For the next two months like gigantic pirates they roamed the Atlantic shipping lanes sinking more than twenty ships totalling over 100,000 tons. It was the first – and last – successful foray by German battleships against Allied merchant shipping in the Second World War. Then in early March they seemed to disappear into Atlantic mists.

At 7 a.m. on 22 March 1941, as sullen French dock workers watched, they tied up at the quai Lannion in Brest. It was nearly a year since France had fallen and the French Naval base had been taken over by German dockyard workers from Wilhelms-haven. They had returned to Brest because they were badly in need of repairs. The two-months' cruise had revealed serious defects in *Scharnhorst's* boilers. The tubes of the super-heaters, especially, had given constant trouble threatening a major break-down. German dockyard engineers who examined her estimated ten weeks would be needed for repairs. When her Kapitän, Kurt Hoffmann, reported this news to Grand Admiral Erich Raeder, head of the German Navy in Berlin, the German Admiralty staff were shocked at the extent of the repairs necessary.

Her sister ship *Gneisenau* was also in need of minor repairs. The refit of both battleships went ahead quickly but no French-man was allowed to work on them, for French workmen in the

1

repair depots ashore went as slow as they dared to hold up the work of the German conquerors. Throughout the dockyard and in the town, the inhabitants were not only surly and hostile, but some of them were in touch with French underground agents, who would pass the information about the repairs to Britain.

After the ships' arrival eight depressing days passed with unceasing rain and frequent false air-raid alarms. Then on the evening of 30 March came the real thing. The wail of sirens was followed by the crash of bombs. The flak gun crews poured up a curtain of fire but their shells could not reach high-flying planes.

Ashore, many officers of the German Naval Staff were killed when the hotel where they were accommodated was hit and caught fire. The ships were undamaged but when the fragments of bombs were examined by German experts next day they made an important discovery. The RAF had dropped 500-lb armour-piercing bombs specially made to crash through the armoured decks of the warships. The Germans then knew that this was no routine dock raid. These bombs were direct evidence that the RAF knew they were there. Now the raids would never cease. They were right. The RAF started to come day and night when weather permitted.

At dawn on 6 April a RAF torpedo-bomber suddenly dived out of the clouds. It was a Coastal Command Beaufort from St Eval in Cornwall, piloted by Flying Officer Kenneth Campbell, who made a most courageous and determined attack upon *Gneisenau*. She was tied up to the buoy against a wall at the north end of the harbour, protected by the curving mole. The little hills all around the harbour bristled with clusters of guns and moored near the mole as extra protection were three flak ships.

The battleship's position appeared to be impregnable. Even if an aircraft managed to deliver a low level attack it would not be able to pull out in time and must crash into the high ground surrounding the harbour.

But Kenneth Campbell dived down to deck level and flew steadily past the blazing muzzles of the flak ships' guns. He skimmed over the mole and dropped his torpedo at point-blank range towards *Gneisenau*'s stern. As he did so, the German flak gunners hit him and he crashed in flames into the water.

But he had done his job. Seconds later his torpedo exploded against *Gneisenau* on the starboard side aft. Water rushed in and she began to list heavily. A salvage vessel which came alongside to pump tons of water from her scuppers had difficulty keeping her from sinking.

The bodies of Campbell and his gallant aircrew, Sgts Scott, Mullis and Hillman, were fished out of the harbour and brought on board the battleship. Their bodies were draped in flags and placed on the quarterdeck, where a guard of honour was mounted as a mark of respect.

While this chivalrous ceremony was taking place, the salvage crews managed to pump enough water out to right her, since she, could not remain in danger at the buoy. RAF spotter planes were now informing the British about every move of the battleships. Another attack like Campbell's on *Gneisenau* would probably sink her.

The following morning *Gneisenau* again entered dry dock where inspection confirmed that Campbell's torpedo had wrecked the starboard propeller and shaft tunnel. This would need six months to repair. She would be out of action twice as long as *Scharnhorst*.

When the British heard about Campbell's heroic act he was awarded the highest decoration for gallantry, the Victoria Cross. The citation said: 'Despising heavy odds Flying Officer Kenneth Campbell went cheerfully and resolutely to his task. By pressing home his attack at close quarters in the face of withering fire on a course fraught with extreme peril, he displayed valour of the highest order.'

As a result of Campbell's torpedo both battleships were now due for a long stay so the German Navy decided to put their static fleet to some use. A detachment of a hundred midshipmen were sent from Germany to the Brest battleships to complete their training. They were posted equally to both ships and, as anti-aircraft defence was most vital, this was their main task. It became a brutal battle training for these budding officers. For some it was very short.

On the night of 10 April, the sirens again wailed and the first bomb explosions could be heard above the roar of the flak guns. Suddenly there came a series of tremendous flashes and

3

explosions and a red glow lit up *Gneisenau's* superstructure. She had been hit by three bombs and was on fire. The bombs killed fifty and wounded ninety of her crew, the heaviest casualties being among the flak crews and the young midshipmen. At the time of the raid many of the off-duty midshipmen were in their quarters between decks. Most of them were killed by fragments of other big bombs exploding on the quayside.

As ambulances drew up at the ship's gangway and long rows of stretcher cases were taken to hospital, Captain Hoffmann went across from *Scharnhorst* to offer help. He ordered a working-party to fight the fires on the mess decks, but they had to flood one magazine before the fires were controlled and *Gneisenau* out of danger.

The Germans' main concern was to conceal the extent of the damage from the French, but each battleship could only make ten coffins, and this meant they would have to call in French carpenters to make many more. When the order was given the news of the German dead spread rapidly among the inhabitants of Brest.

After this they arranged for most of the crews to sleep ashore in barracks, leaving only flak gunners and a duty watch in the ship. This raid also decided the authorities in Berlin to step up the A.A. defences of Brest. They increased the number of 4-inch guns to 150 and smaller flak guns to 1,200, to make a murderous concentration of fire. Also the two battleships were moved closer together. The lock gates were closed and protected by nets against torpedoes fired by either intruding submarines or wave-skimming planes.

In *Scharnhorst's* old berth, Hoffmann built a wooden and sheet-iron replica of her on the hull of an old French cruiser, *Jeanne d'Arc*. Nets hung from the battleships' masts to the dockside with paint sprayed over them to make them resemble clumps of trees. On the roofs of the Naval College the surviving midshipmen erected wooden huts to make it look like a village.

A network of artificial smoke-generators which could shroud the port under a thick fog within a few minutes was installed around the harbour. This last precaution aroused protests from the Luftwaffe who maintained that the dense smoke would endanger their fighter operations. This artificial fog also nearly

4

caused a collision between the two battleships when they came to leave harbour.

The flak and the fighters gave them protection during the day but in darkness it was a different story. As the RAF's heavy bombing continued nearly every night it looked as though not only would the ships be damaged but most of their crews endangered. Although many of them were taken at night in lorries to barracks in Brest, many were still being killed ashore so it was decided to move them farther out to avoid the raids.

They were moved at night to La Roche fifteen miles from Brest near the sleepy little Breton town of Landerneau. Both places were on the main line to Paris and the railway was used a lot to move crews about.

Hidden in a small forest of birch trees near Landerneau, barracks were built for the crews of each ship. It was also planned to build extra ones for the crew of another German battleship, *Bismarck*, due in for a refit after her own Atlantic merchant shipping forays. Outside the dockyard at Brest the large buoys swung at their moorings awaiting her arrival.

While the other two German battleships were being repaired in Brest, *Bismarck* was sheltering in the German-occupied Norwegian port of Bergen. But on a moonless night – 20 May 1941 – she slipped out, escorted by the heavy cruiser *Prinz Eugen*. At noon next day, when the news reached the Admiralty in Whitehall, the Home Fleet was ordered to sail from Scapa Flow to intercept the German ships south of the Denmark Straits.

At dawn on 24 May the two German ships were in action with the British fleet, which included the veteran battle-cruiser *Hood* and the battleship *Prince of Wales* on her maiden voyage. The Royal Navy had the worst of the battle. *Hood*, hit by *Bismarck* and *Prinz Eugen*, blew up. *Prince of Wales* was so badly damaged that she took no further part in the action. But smaller Royal Naval ships still shadowed the fast-steaming *Bismarck*.

In the afternoon the new aircraft-carrier *Victorious* was detached from the main force to attack her. When 825 Squadron of Swordfish rose from her flight deck to make a night attack

5

on the German battleship, the leading plane was piloted by Lt-Cdr Eugene Esmonde.

At 11.30 p.m., when they were 120 miles from the carrier, Esmonde's Swordfish squadron sighted *Bismarck*. Flying 100 feet above the waves in the darkness, they let go their torpedoes from less than 1,000 yards. As they banked away there was a roar followed by a flash and a curling plume of flame.

The *Bismarck* had been hit amidships.

The torpedo slowed her down, and after a three-day chase the Home Fleet again brought the *Bismarck* into action. This time she was alone. Four hours before the battle the *Prinz Eugen* had slipped away. The *Bismarck* sank under the guns and torpedoes of the Royal Navy.

It was on the night of 7 May that German naval officers at Brest, surreptitiously listening to the B.B.C. news, heard: 'At 10.37 G.M.T. the German battleship *Bismarck* was sunk.'

The German Navy in Brest took the news of *Bismarck*'s sinking gloomily. Equally depressing was the lack of news of her escorting cruiser, *Prinz Eugen*. Had she too been sunk? Or had she escaped and was preserving radio silence in case her calls were intercepted by the pursuing Royal Navy? For five days there was silence. Then at dawn on 1 June a buzz of excitement went round the battleship crews. *Prinz Eugen* had appeared at the entrance to Brest Harbour.

She brought grim news. When her captain, Helmuth Brinkmann, made a report to Grand Admiral Raeder in Berlin about the fate of the *Bismarck*, he stated that the British battleships now had such good radar equipment that it could not be evaded.

The rest of the situation was also depressing. Despite German precautions, day and night raids on Brest docks became a familiar part of their daily life. Almost every day, the B.B.C.'s nine o'clock news reported that bombers had visited Brest to attack the German warships.

The British realized that this constant bombing might eventually cause the Germans to make a desperate dash home. A series of conferences was held between Admiralty and Air Ministry planners. As a result Coastal Command was ordered to establish three separate dusk-to-dawn radar reconnaissance patrols off Brest and along the Channel. They became known as

'Stopper', which covered from Brest to Ushant, 'Line SE' from Ushant to Brittany and 'Habo' from Le Havre to Boulogne. Fighter Command also organized daylight Channel sweeps known as 'Jim Crow'.

On 29 April 1941 an Air Ministry letter to the three RAF Commands – Fighter, Bomber and Coastal – said: *'Scharnhorst* and *Gneisenau* may attempt to reach a German port up the Channel route during the period April 30th to May 4th inclusive. It is considered probable that the Straits of Dover will be navigated in darkness. It is considered unlikely that the enemy would attempt the passage of the Straits in daylight. But if this should be attempted, a unique opportunity will be offered to both our surface craft and air striking force to engage the enemy ships in force whilst in the Straits of Dover.' Bomber Command was instructed to have strike forces in readiness for the Germans leaving Brest.

At this stage, the RAF were well ahead of the Germans in their tactical appreciation. It was not until 30 May – a month after the Air Ministry had considered the possibility of a Channel break-out – that the German Naval Command West in Paris sent a memorandum to Grand Admiral Raeder in Berlin suggesting a contingency plan: 'The possibility of bringing heavy ships through the English Channel should be carefully examined. The route is shorter than the Iceland passage. There are good escort possibilities, both air and sea. Enemy radar could be jammed. Superior enemy units would not be present and the passage would be in the close proximity of our own harbours to which ships could be taken in the event of breakdowns.'

Raeder reacted strongly against this suggestion. He drew up a formidable list of hazards: '1. The difficulty of navigation in narrow waters. 2. The battleships must be seen by the British. 3. The danger from mines, torpedo boats, torpedo-carrying aircraft and dive-bombers.'

But Raeder's principal objection was that mine-sweepers could not clear a wide enough path for the ships to take avoiding action in the event of torpedo attack. He concluded, 'The naval war staff therefore consider an unobserved and safe escape through the Channel to be impossible.' This view entirely

7

coincided with that of his opposite number in London, First Sea Lord Sir Dudley Pound.

Raeder had good reasons for being cautious. For he had only five battleships – including the 'pocket' battleships – to the Royal Navy's fifteen. He had no aircraft-carriers, although the *Graf Zeppelin* was under construction – but never completed – whilst the British had six operational carriers.

Raeder, one of the ablest and most professional naval officers Germany has ever produced, nursed his ships like a duck with ducklings. During the fourteen years in which he was its Commander-in-Chief no one had guarded the honour of the German Navy more jealously than he.

When Raeder rejected the Channel plan it was generally felt among the admirals in Berlin that this was the end of the matter. For Hitler trusted Raeder's judgement and had promoted him to Grand Admiral, second only to Göring as Hitler's adviser for the prosecution of the war.

It came as a surprise when Admiral Krancke, Raeder's personal representative on Hitler's Supreme Staff, was summoned to the Führer's headquarters and, standing stiffly to attention, listened pale-faced to the tirade of abuse concerning the German capital ships and their officers which Hitler hurled at him.

Hitler, at war with Russia since June, was becoming alarmed at the numerous small British commando raids on the coast of Norway, starting with the Lofotens in March 1941. He considered the Norwegian coastline to be the most vulnerable section of his Western Wall. The news had also reached Hitler that British convoys were bringing tanks, aircraft and guns to the Eastern Front. He decided that Norway, where in any case he had always thought the British intended to open a second front, had now become even more strategically important.

Meanwhile the RAF continued to keep up their non-stop bombing attacks on Brest. A month after Raeder had rejected the Channel plan – on the morning of 1 July – it was *Prinz Eugen's* turn. While she lay alongside the eastern basin of the commercial dock, a RAF bomb smashed the ship's armour-plating and exploded in the most vulnerable compartments – the plotting room and transmitting station. It killed forty-seven men, including her first officer, Cdr Otto Stoos, and wounded thirty-two. It also put *Prinz Eugen* out of action for three months.

On the other hand, *Scharnhorst* was refitted and on the morning of 23 July left for La Pallice, 250 miles to the south, for trials to test her super-heaters and practise firing her guns. Captain Hoffmann chose the shoal-dotted waters around La Pallice because they afforded the best protection against submarines and he needed only a few patrol boats to keep watch.

A tanker took her place in the dock as a decoy and was covered with netting. To disguise the direction of her departure, the Germans put out false oil trails leading north from Brest. In spite of this careful camouflage, the ever-watchful RAF spotted the move and reported that *Scharnhorst* was moving south from her berth. Was she about to break out into the Atlantic? As spotter planes watched her, the opinion grew that this might be the long-awaited escape.

Unaware of the British suspicions, the battleship performed perfectly, reaching a speed of thirty knots without difficulty. She returned to La Pallice that evening, expecting to remain there for several days while minor adjustments were made.

Before dark a group of Stirling heavy bombers attacked her and made one direct hit with a heavy armour-piercing bomb. More heavy bomber attacks during the night damaged La Pallice docks. At dawn a RAF photographic reconnaissance plane was over La Pallice. As it revealed little serious damage it was decided to mount the most massive daylight raid on both battleships.

Ninety-nine RAF bombers took off, arriving over the battleships at 2 p.m. Three Flying Fortresses, sixty-three Wellingtons and eighteen Hampdens attacked the *Gneisenau* in Brest while eight Halifaxes bombed the *Scharnhorst* in La Pallice.

This was the first time Fortresses, fitted with the new Sperry bombsight for high altitude bombing, had taken part in a raid on the Brest battleships. They had arrived in England just three months before and the attack that hot July afternoon on the German battleships was only their third operation.

Because of the height at which they operated they carried special aircrews – none of them over 24 years old. The pilots of the three Fortresses, Wing-Cdr 'Macdougall, Sq. Ldr MacLaren and Flt-Lt Mathieson, were told to concentrate on the *Gneisenau*. At eight minutes past two they started bombing from a height of 30,000 feet, each aircraft dropping four 1100-lb. bombs which burst on the quays and docks. Although accurate flak was seen following them a thousand feet below they were too high for the German defences. After they had released their bombs three Messerschmitts climbed steeply towards them but the Fortresses turned away and lost them.

At the same time Wing-Cdr Maw led the low-level British-built bombers down to 6,000 feet, their bombs bursting among the dockyard buildings. Pilot Officer Payne went down to 3,500 feet and as his bombs straddled the *Gneisenau* both he and his front gunner, Sgt Wilkinson, were wounded by flak.

The Halifaxes attacked the *Scharnhorst* at La Pallice from 12,000 feet. She was easily identified by the high-flying bomber pilots from a cloudless sky, and a row of five bombs hit her. Thick smoke began to pour from her as terrific explosions shook the ship. Two bombs exploded on deck, causing a great rent. Yet she was lucky. The three heavy bombs that penetrated the armoured upper deck and smashed through the hull failed to explode, although they caused her to take in 6,000 tons of water.

The ship began to settle with a heavy list. But the efficient repair-parties quickly righted her and the damage was promptly repaired. A signal went to the port authorities for divers, who found the impact with *Scharnhorst*'s deck had torn the steel off one of the bombs and had helped to prevent it exploding. The holes in *Scharnhorst*'s hull were soon patched up.

Good luck was still with her for, miraculously, there were no casualties. She returned to Brest at twenty-seven knots.

The autumn of 1941 was the beginning of the bad times for the German war machine. Hitler's *blitzkrieg* against the Soviet Union was slowing up at the onset of the savage Russian winter. Hitler was personally conducting the campaign from his headquarters at Rastenburg in East Prussia, known as Wolf's Lair.

Since the start of the Russian campaign Admiral Raeder

had heard nothing from his preoccupied Führer. But on 17 September, as the Admiral was preparing plans for using his battleships in the Atlantic shipping lanes again, he was summoned to a conference with Hitler at Wolf's Lair.

Hitler did not want to hear about the Atlantic plan. He was convinced the British were going to invade Norway and interrupted to say, 'The Atlantic can be left to the U-boats. Your battleships, all your major units, must be stationed along the Norwegian coast. They can be of some use in guarding Norway against invasion. They will be safer there from air attack than in Brest.'

He called Norway the 'zone of destiny'. Hitler, who had referred to himself to Raeder as 'a land animal', said to him, 'Battleships are not good for anything. The big guns would be more useful and less vulnerable in emplacements ashore. I have plans for disarming these steel monsters and using them for the defence of the Norwegian coast.'

There was a second conference in November when Hitler produced a marked map of the Norwegian coast with areas shown from which the two battleships and *Prinz Eugen* could operate against the British. He was impatient with Raeder. What was the major part of German sea power doing bottled up and being bombed in Brest? He ended by inquiring harshly, 'What solution does the Navy have?'

To placate him, Raeder brought out a contingency plan by Naval Group West in Paris which had been pigeon-holed. It suggested that, while awaiting completion of repairs to the battleships, an attempt might be made to send *Prinz Eugen* on a lone dash through the English Channel to a German port. Hitler, who had appeared uninterested, even bored, suddenly looked up and commented, 'Why only the *Prinz Eugen*? Why not all the ships?'

Raeder, who was not expecting even the *Prinz Eugen* plan to be taken seriously, was astonished. He replied, 'A dash through the Channel by a solitary cruiser is a very different matter, *mein Führer*, from a movement by a whole fleet.'

Hitler was the last person on earth to be put off by such a statement. 'The issue of war will be decided in Norway,' he said. 'Unless the British are fools they will attack us there.'

11

As he said this, he looked directly at Raeder and gave the Nazi salute in dismissal. Raeder flew back to Berlin and sent a signal to Admiral Saalwächter, Chief of Naval Group West in Paris, asking how soon the battleships could put to sea. He was not displeased when he received a reply that the two battleships would not be ready until December. It was just as well. By then Hitler, obsessed with the Russian front, might have forgotten this hare-brained idea.

At first Raeder tried to gain time saying he must have discussions with his staff. He explained the position to his Chief of Staff, Admiral Fricke, in Berlin and also to Admiral Wagner, head of the Operations Section directing the war at sea, saying, 'Hitler wants the ships back in home waters, for he believes there might be an attempt at a British invasion in the Norwegian area.'

As the Berlin naval chiefs studied the basic aspects of the plan their first objection was the state of crew training. The better trained the crews were, the more chance they had of pulling off a daring operation like this. Yet through no fault of Captain Hoffmann and his fellow commanders, the crews' training and morale was very much below standard. Brestbound as they were, always under the threatening shadow of the RAF, they were only able to carry out restricted exercises and drills. But the greatest obstacle to the plan would be the need for the strictest secrecy. Except for the most senior officers at Brest, no one could be allowed to know what was to happen. This would mean the crews could not be inspired by their training instructors with a promise of glory.

Yet the more Admiral Wagner studied the Führer's plan the more he found he was not against the operation. This was because the entire world naval situation had changed suddenly on 6 December 1941, when America had come into the war. He considered the days were now over when the Germans could keep the ships in Brest as a constant Atlantic threat.

In his view, to do this indefinitely would be to invite disaster. The situation seemed quite plain; on one side there were the British with the increasingly destructive power of their bombing raids; but on the other side there was the menacing voice of the Führer. 'You will remove the ships where I can employ them in the Norwegian theatre. Otherwise you will give me their guns and I will mount them in shore batteries. Make your choice, *meine Herren.*'

Was there an alternative to a break-out through the Channel? They could bring the ships north of Britain round by the Iceland route. But in their path in Scapa Flow lurked the might of the British battle fleet which was bound to intercept – and send them to join *Bismarck* at the bottom.

However, his intelligence reports revealed that the English appeared to have very little in the Channel.

His chief, Admiral Raeder, still did not like the plan. Like First Sea Lord Dudley Pound in the Admiralty in London he feared for his capital ships. If the ships were put out of action by the RAF or Royal Navy, it would be the virtual end of the German Navy as a force. Feeling that the ships would be too like sitting ducks on the narrow waters of the Channel, he told Wagner, 'I cannot make this proposal to Hitler that we break through the Channel.'

Wagner argued the risk might have to be taken. He said, 'If the ships are dismantled we will present the British with a bloodless victory. The German Navy will never hold up its head again. To concede victory to the enemy without a fight is to sentence the German Navy to death.'

Faced with these views, and the Führer's fanatic insistence, Raeder began to give way a little – but he was still not convinced.

On 29 December, he had a stormy meeting with Hitler when the Führer persisted in his plan. When Raeder said that, after being in port for so long, his ships could hardly be expected to face the powerful British Home Fleet without some preparation, Hitler once again raved about 'the uselessness of the battleships'. He refused even to allow the time for lengthy 'shakedown' sea-going exercises and firing practice which Raeder wanted. For as he pointed out quite reasonably, they might easily be bombed and sunk while on these practices.

Raeder flew back to Berlin and passed the whole matter over to Naval Group West in Paris. Although the operation would be under the immediate command of Vice-Admiral Otto Ciliax who commanded the Brest ships flying his flag in *Scharnhorst,*

Naval Group West in Paris was responsible for all operational directions.

The Commander-in-Chief of Naval Group West was 59-year-old General-Admiral Alfred Saalwächter. Fair-haired and blue-eyed, he had an exceptional mind. Although smallish in height, he was regarded in the German Navy as *riesengross* –'gigantic in stature'.

A Prussian, born at Neusalz on the River Oder, he had been a submarine commander in the First World War, but although he had been awarded the Knight's Cross in 1940, he was no friend of the Führer, with whom, like so many German admirals, he had had differences.

Between wars, Saalwächter had gone round naval ports inspecting establishments and training personnel. He wrote a standard book on naval warfare for the German Navy, *Seekriegsanleitung*, which became the textbook for all officers.

His headquarters – Naval Group West – were in the Avenue Marechal Faijolle, near the Bois de Boulogne. It was a large, four-storied mansion of Napoleon III period. The only indications of its naval importance were two striped sentry boxes at the entrance, each with a German sailor in blouse and gaiters carrying a rifle.

Saalwächter had a staff consisting of about fifteen high-ranking naval officers, with several hundred petty officers and technicians. On the upper floors of the mansion were the 'cabins' where the staff officers lived and took their meals. In the basement was a big garage with a fleet of staff cars. The drivers were civilians, mostly white Russians. Their leader, ironically enough, had been a Russian admiral in the First World War.

As there were few German troops in metropolitan Paris at that time Saalwächter's staff led a strange isolated life. They worked so hard they often did not go out for days at a time but they always had seats at the Paris Opera House because their chief liked opera. The only time Saalwächter appeared relaxed was when he was stealing an evening from his headquarters at the Opera.

At the end of 1941 Admiral Otto Ciliax, commander of the Brest squadron, was away on Christmas leave in Germany. He was not due back until the New Year. Ciliax – a product of the German Naval Academy at Flensburg – was a tall, brusque black-haired man. He was a former captain of the *Scharnhorst* and was not very popular. He was a notorious martinet and nick-named 'The Black Czar'. When a staff officer saluted him and his hand did not travel to his brow with regulation agility, a frown would come on Ciliax's face as he returned his salute. A little bit later he would send a petty officer over to him with a message, 'The Admiral's compliments, *mein kapitän*, but he would like to speak with you.' Ciliax would say angrily, 'I just wanted to tell you I did not like your salute!' As the Germans put it, he was a '*starker Mann!*'

Another reason he was not popular was that he could not delegate authority. In *Scharnhorst*, he and his staff had an admiral's bridge immediately above Captain Hoffmann's navigational bridge, and he was several times snubbed for giving orders on the running of the ship literally over the captain's head.

If Ciliax met an officer whom he did not like the Admiral made him miserable. He suffered from stomach trouble and was frequently in some pain, which may have played a part in his irascibility. But with all his rough mannerisms he had dignity.

His Chief of Staff, the calm 41-year-old, pipe-smoking Captain Hans Jürgen Reinicke, had heard about his reputation before he joined him – so he was prepared. He swallowed what Ciliax said to him in public but later sought him out privately and told him if things continued in this manner he would put in for a transfer. He had no more trouble and Reinicke became one of the few officers who could handle him.

On 30 December just after dinner an urgent signal was brought to Reinicke aboard *Scharnhorst*. It was from Naval Group West in Paris ordering him to report there at 10 a.m. on New Year's Day. As the message said Admiral Ciliax was also being ordered to report in Paris, he realized it was more than a routine matter.

It was too late to catch the evening train to Paris so he took one the next morning. It was evening when he arrived at the Gare Montparnasse and crossed Paris to the Gare de l'Est to meet Admiral Ciliax recalled from home leave in Germany by the same cryptic message from Group West. It was not surprising that Ciliax, never noted for his good temper, came off the train in one of his blacker moods.

'What's this all about, Reinicke?' he growled more than once. But his Chief of Staff could not enlighten him. They would both have to wait for their appointment next morning.

It was New Year's Eve. They had a meal, split a bottle of champagne, and went to bed early.

The next morning they went to Group West headquarters and waited in a conference room for Alfreid Saalwächter. He soon appeared with Admiral Schniewind, the new operational commander of the German Navy. Saalwächter briskly told Ciliax and Reinicke the news – the Führer wanted the three ships to leave Brest, proceed to their German home ports and then to Norway for operations there.

But Admiral Saalwächter revealed he was worried about the fate of his great ships. After he told them of the Führer's demands he asked for their frank opinions. He was trying to organize expert opposition to dissuade the Führer. When Ciliax raised many objections against Hitler's scheme, he told him to go away and put them in writing. After Ciliax had written his detailed objections, Saalwächter forwarded them with his own report to Raeder.

He wrote: 'I submit herewith conclusions for the comprehensive scrutiny that has been ordered into the question of the withdrawal of the Brest Group eastwards through the Channel.

'The hazards applicable to a voyage of battleships through the Channel eastwards are summed up at the end of the outline.

'I view these hazards as being very great. I must for this reason alone give an urgent warning against it being carried out.

'On the 12 November I commented that one single surprise move to the west by one or by several battleships was feasible. But conversely, a move eastwards of the battleships is one combined with *too* great a peril. Subsequent navigation through the Channel would be rendered impossible because the element of surprise would have departed.

'It can be executed only during the period of the longest

nights. It must be accompanied by control of the mine situation and air preponderance in the Channel.

'I do not take the view that the new experiences in the East Asian theatre of war* can be taken as proof of the uselessness of battleships to abandon our warfare in the Atlantic. Our opponent does not think so, as the unchanged characteristics of his heavy forces show.

'I advocate, as I have always done, the conception that the essential tasks of our battleships lie in the Atlantic.

'Our numerical inferiority affords us opportunities for success only by surprise offensive sorties directed at the enemy's weak points which are to be found in his long Atlantic supply routes, and not by continually facing with defensive action a greatly superior enemy.

'At this time the best possibilities of success for the Brest Group lie in surprise action against north to south convoys. The Brest Group's achievements already go to show that the enemy feels and fears this threat and straightaway tries by air attacks to rid himself of it.

'This pressure can only be made permanent if our battleship strength actually goes to sea. Yet even during the long period of repairs the enemy can hardly foretell with exactitude when one or several of the ships are able to pounce. Withdrawal of the Brest Group from the Atlantic means releasing the enemy from this strategic pressure.

'The plan for tying down his heavy naval forces in the Atlantic falls apart. Maintenance of pressure on other theatres of war such as East Asia and the Mediterranean must also stop. A perceptible strengthening of English sea power in East Asia will follow, thereby impeding Japan.

'In addition to actual strategic prizes, there is great prestige for our enemy. On the other hand there would be a great loss of prestige for us which would be made far worse if the ships were lost by the voyage through the Channel. Political consequences very damaging to us and our allies are inevitable.

'If our ships disappear from the Atlantic or from the Atlantic position people would rightly talk about a "lost battle". Naval actions from Norway would not make up for such a move.

* The sinking of the *Repulse* and *Prince of Wales* by Japanese aircraft.

17

'We do not stand there on the Atlantic just for raiding possibilities against the enemy supply routes. We threaten Scotland, Iceland, the North Arctic and Russia.

'In the Norwegian harbours the aerial danger and with it the stresses for the Luftwaffe would hardly be less. The enemy at all times could by choice of place and time have greater superiority. Liaison with any battleships in the Atlantic would be impossible.

'I am convinced that the problem of the Atlantic position as it is at present cannot be gone back upon later. In any case, it is clear that a "bringing back again" of the ships would be enormously difficult.

'Finally, there are indications that if our ships withdrew from the Atlantic after a lost battle, to appear again in home waters and remain there it would be injurious to the psychology of our own ships' companies, of the entire Navy and of the German people.

'I am therefore convinced that it would now be a very serious mistake by us at this time to withdraw the ships from Brest in their Atlantic position.

'I consider their remaining there, even though with heavy damage and lengthy repair times, is the correct course.

'There remains for consideration only the slight relief of the Luftwaffe which would come about in Brest.

'If the withdrawal plan of the Brest Group to the East is adhered to, then examination might be made as to whether *Prinz Eugen* should take part. By the cruiser remaining at Brest, at least a portion of the present strategic operations of the Brest Group would remain in being to confront our enemy.

'I submit with this report extracts from three letters of C-in-C of the ships (Ciliax), corresponding to my point of view, which he sent me after the first conference on the matter in Group West.

'Should the question be put through the Supreme Commander-in-Chief of the Wehrmacht to the Navy: 'Break-out or Disarm?' then I would say with a heavy heart that against the 'Break-out' with its enormous risks, I would prefer temporary disarmament. For when the fortunes of the day change the ordnance could be restored, whilst a loss of these valuable ships and their crews could only bring damage without benefit.'

It was a gloomy and defeatist document and Hitler was to have none of it. He was concerned that the constant RAF bombing was slowly fraying the fabric of crew morale.

Although unaware of Hitler's plan and Saalwächter's strong objections, the RAF bombing of Brest increased in December. And for the first time photographic planes revealed that all three ships seemed to be preparing for sea.

On Christmas Eve the Admiralty ordered seven submarines to form an 'iron ring' around the approaches to Brest.

The navigator of *Scharnhorst*, 42-year-old Helmuth Giessler, was on Christmas leave. When he went off, neither he nor any other naval officers at Brest had any inkling that Hitler was holding a pistol at Raeder's head demanding the ships leave Brest. At that time not even Admiral Ciliax had the faintest suspicion of their fate.

Giessler came back from his leave on the same day as Vice-Admiral Ciliax returned from the New Year's Day conference with Admiral Saalwächter at Naval Group West in Paris. That evening Ciliax summoned him to his cabin. As navigating officer of the flagship he was responsible for the whole squadron so he had to be one of the first to be told about the plan. Ciliax informed him in his usual brusque way about the proposed operation. He added crisply, 'Consider your needs and requirements, Giessler, and what preparations you consider necessary. You have until morning!'

With these words the Admiral dismissed him. That night Giessler climbed into his bunk but did not get a wink of sleep. He tossed about all night with the information racing through his brain.

A voyage of these great battleships through the narrow English Channel had been so improbable that he had hardly looked at the Channel charts – he had never considered them as waters where the *Scharnhorst* might sail. Now the problem was how to obtain these charts without arousing gossip and suspicion.

Next morning he called Chief Petty Officer Wehrlich to his cabin and handed him a list. 'I require these charts of the Mediterranean and these charts of Icelandic waters,' he said.

'Also these of the West African coast.' He also demanded pilot books of the Mediterranean and everywhere else he could think of. Wehrlich kept bringing so much navigational material that towards the end of the day he could hardly enter his cabin for papers and books. Among this pile of material were his charts of the English Channel. In the middle of all his other requests, Giessler had slipped in a casual order for them.

Giessler had an extra problem. He knew Wehrlich was not experienced enough for the magnitude of his task – but Wehrlich's predecessor, Lt Johann Hinrichs was. He was the man he wanted at his side to help plan this vital operation.

He was now the skipper of a fleet of mine-sweeping trawlers, but when Giessler explained the situation to Ciliax, a puzzled Hinrichs received a secret signal posting him back to *Scharnhorst*. When he arrived Giessler let him into the secret. During those January days they sat together in the navigator's cabin. Giessler kept muttering to himself '*Ach so*', and humming tunelessly as they pored over his charts. They worked out the tides, times of darkness, depth of water, and the complete timetable the ships must try and adhere to hour by hour on the voyage from Brest to Wilhelmshaven.

While Giessler was working out his plan, unknown to him something happened which was to help him. On 2 January, the Royal Navy's submarine 'iron ring' faded away. High submarine losses in the Mediterranean and a bottle-neck in the training programme caused the 'subs' to be withdrawn – and surveillance left to the RAF.

Yet, as if to confirm Hitler's attitude, at 8.30 p.m. on 6 January 1942, a RAF bomb burst against the hull of the *Gneisnau* as she was lying in Number Eight Dock. Several yards of her armour were ripped and two compartments were flooded.

On 12 January, Admirals Raeder, Saalwächter and Ciliax were summoned to Wolf's Lair for the final full-scale conference. Raeder brought his Chief of Staff, Admiral Fricke, while Ciliax was accompanied by Captain Reinicke, his own Chief of Staff, and Saalwächter by his mine expert, Commodore Friedrich Ruge. The Luftwaffe was represented by Göring's Chief of Staff, Lt-General Jeschonnek, accompanied by one of Germany's famous fighter aces, Col. Adolf Galland, who had fought in the German Condor Legion in the Spanish Civil War and was a veteran of the Battles of France and Britain.

They arrived in a snowstorm at Wolf's Lair. Lt-General Jodl, Hitler's personal military adviser, who lived and worked there, described the Führer's headquarters as 'a cross between a monastery and a concentration camp'.

Hitler spent his days in a concrete bunker with a 20-foot thick roof. It was a sealed box with no window and no outlet to the open air. Next door was another similar concrete bunker used by Hitler as his map room, where he stood waiting for them. After giving them the Nazi salute he asked them to be seated round the big conference table.

At Hitler's request, Raeder opened the session, saying, 'The question of the passage of the Brest Group through the Channel has been examined by all agencies concerned. In the light of the Führer's opinion, the German Fleet's primary task is to defend the Norwegian coast and ports and, in so doing, it should use its might unsparingly. Since you, *mein Führer*, informed me that you insist upon the return of the heavy units to their home bases, I suggest that Vice-Admiral Ciliax report on the details of how this operation is to be prepared and carried out, and that Commodore Ruge subsequently report on the necessary mine-sweeping measures, to enable you, *mein Führer*, to make the final decision afterwards.'

Hitler replied: 'The Naval Force at Brest has, above all, the welcome effect of tying up enemy air forces and diverting them from making attacks upon the German homeland. But with our ships at Brest, enemy sea forces are tied up to no greater extent than would be the case if the ships were stationed in Norway. If I could see any chance that the ships might remain undamaged for four to five months and, thereafter, be employed in operations in the Atlantic, I might be more inclined to consider leaving them in Brest.

'Since in my opinion such a development is not to be expected, I am determined to withdraw the ships from Brest to avoid exposing them to chance hits day after day. I fear that there will be a large-scale British–Russian offensive in Norway. I think that if a strong task force of battleships and cruisers, practically the entire German Fleet, were stationed along the Norwegian coast, it could, in conjunction with the German Air Force, make a decisive contribution towards the defence of the area.'

Then it was Ciliax's turn. 'I recommend the necessity of leaving Brest under cover of darkness, taking maximum advantage of the element of surprise, and of passing through the Straits of Dover in the daytime. This will make the most effective use of the means of defence at our disposal.'

Hitler agreed, saying, 'I emphasize particularly the surprise to be achieved by having the ships leave after dark.'

Ciliax said, 'I must stress emphatically that a very strong destroyer and fighter protection must be provided on the day of the break-through itself from dawn to dusk.'

'I am aware of the decisive role to be played by the Air Force in this enterprise,' replied Hitler and turned to Luftwaffe Chief of Staff, Lt-General Jeschonnek, who said, 'I do not believe I will be able to provide constant unfailing protection for the ships with the available 250 fighters which cannot possibly be reinforced.'

Even in the presence of the Führer he was exhibiting the Luftwaffe's traditional reluctance to co-operate with the Navy. But with Hitler's cold eyes upon him, Jeschonnek hastily promised to draw on the existing night-fighter formation to provide dawn fighter protection.

Hitler then asked for opinions as to the possibility of using the northern route saying, 'I do not care which route is selected by the Navy, if only it is successful in getting those ships transferred to Norwegian waters.'

The four Admirals explained that the northern route was not suitable for several reasons. Raeder commented, 'The present disposition of enemy forces is against such a move; there are two or three battleships and two aircraft-carriers in the Home Fleet. Moreover, the German air forces would not be able to provide the necessary air cover.'

Commodore Ruge, commanding the seaward defences of the occupied French coast, including the mine-sweeping and mine-laying forces, was asked to report. Ruge was able to assure Hitler that the menace from mines, always regarded as the main danger to forcing a passage through the Channel, was not as bad as imagined.

Raeder, still unsure of the Luftwaffe's full support, repeated his demands to the Air Force for a very strong fighter cover. He also asked for attacks on enemy torpedo plane bases in the early morning of the day of the break-through, and possibly a few days earlier.

Lt-General Jeschonnek replied stiffly, 'The constant air cover demanded will leave insufficient aircraft for the heavy air battles that are sure to develop on the day of the break-through. We may expect our fighter force to become very inferior in strength – at least during the afternoon. Also our own anti-aircraft personnel are susceptible to fatigue in the afternoon as experience has shown.'

Col. Galland, who was to command the Luftwaffe fighter cover, also offered his opinion, 'The strong Spitfire forces at the disposal of the British will render things difficult for the long-range fighters which we are going to employ.'

Raeder remarked that tide and daylight would determine the timing of the operation. That was the reason the date could not be changed. When he asked what should be done in case one or several ships were unable to move on the date set, Hitler decided, 'If two battleships are in a position to move, they are to undertake the operation, if necessary without the cruiser. If only one battleship and the cruiser can move, they must do likewise. But in no case should the *Prinz Eugen* do so alone.'

Then Hitler, cutting through both air and naval objections, said briskly, 'The ships must not leave port in the daytime as we are dependent on the element of surprise. This means that they will have to pass through the Dover Straits in the daytime. In view of past experience I do not believe the British capable of making and carrying out lightning decisions.

'This is why I do not think they will be as swift as is assumed by the Naval Staff and the Admiral Commanding Battleships in shifting their bomber and pursuit forces to the south-eastern part of England for an attack on our ships in the Dover Straits.

'Picture what would happen if the situation were reversed – if a surprise report came in that British battleships have appeared in the Thames estuary and are heading for the Straits

23

of Dover. In my opinion, even we would hardly be able to bring up air pursuit forces and bomber forces swiftly and methodically.'

He added dramatically, 'The situation of the Brest Group is comparable with that of a cancer patient, who is doomed unless he submits to an operation. An operation, even though it might be a drastic one, will offer at least some hope that the patient's life may yet be saved. The passage of our ships through the Channel would be such an operation. It must therefore be attempted.'

Finally Hitler said, 'Nothing can be gained by leaving the ships at Brest. Should the Brest Group manage to escape through the Channel, however, there is a chance that it might be employed to good advantage at a later date. If the ships remain at Brest their ability to tie up enemy air forces may not continue for long. As long as they are in battle-worthy condition they will constitute worthwhile targets, which the enemy will feel obliged to attack. But the moment they are seriously damaged – and this may happen any day – the enemy will discontinue his attacks. In view of all this and in accordance with the suggestion of the C-in-C Navy I decide that the operation is to be prepared as proposed.'

That was it. After the conference Hitler entertained his admirals and generals to dinner in the concrete shelter where he lived. He ate frugally as usual but was more genial than anyone had seen him for a long time. He said, almost jovially, 'You will find that this operation will turn out to be our most spectacular naval success of the war.'

He revealed his only doubt – would the Luftwaffe manage it ? He realized that Galland with his fighters was the key figure in the operation. Saying good-bye to him he asked quietly, 'Do you think they will bring it off ?' When Galland assured him he thought they would he dismissed him with a rare smile.

The decision was made. Far from dismantling the great ships the Germans were to fight them through the English Channel in daylight. An attempt like this had not been made by an enemy of England for over three centuries – since the Spanish Armada of 1588.

2

Invitations to a Masked Ball

When Hitler made his decision on 12 January in Wolf's Lair there remained only a month to go before the operation, which was now code-named Cerberus.

The time most suitable for the break-out had already been worked out. Ideally it would be a night with low cloud cover, no moon, and worsening visibility and weather conditions. From the beginning of February darkness prevailed from 7.30 p.m. until 7.30 a.m. G.M.T. The new moon was on 15 February. The most favourable tides and currents were between 7 and 15 February. Therefore the operation must be carried out during this period. But the date depended upon the weather.

An exact forecast was extremely difficult as German meteorologists had only the scantiest weather data. Their sole information came from long-range reconnaissance planes over the Atlantic. So three U-boats were diverted from the Atlantic to Iceland – the area that determines the weather – for meteorological observation. Their reports enabled the Germans to make an accurate weather forecast. The meteorologists predicted favourable weather for 11 February, so it was decided the ships would sail from Brest that night.

Zero hour was fixed for 7.30 p.m. on 11 February. But a more critical zero hour was due at noon next day. This would be the time when the battleships would begin steaming through the Dover Straits.

The time schedule for the operation was: put to sea from Brest in the evening, pass the narrows of Dover–Calais by noon of the following day; navigate along the Dutch coast in the afternoon; enter the North Sea in the evening. A twenty-eight-knot cruising speed was planned.

The Germans now overwhelmingly agreed that a daylight passage was the only answer. Every officer in the secret appreciated that to force the Dover Straits in daylight was a practical if perilous plan. A night dash past Dover when the ships almost certainly had been detected in daylight seemed frighteningly difficult. For then the British defences would be alert and waiting for them. During a night voyage along the French coast there was just a possibility they might take the British by surprise.

But the first and greatest danger lay in the heavily mined narrow waters. The main burden of trying to ensure a mine-free lane fell to Commodore Friedrich Ruge, in command of all the mine-sweeping flotillas along the Channel coast.

Group West ordered him to throw every available minesweeper into clearing a channel for the battleships. A meeting at Group West attended by Giessler and the three captains showed the provisional route running through the series of numbered squares into which the Channel was divided. This route avoided mines laid by the RAF and Royal Navy leaving, if possible, only German mine-fields to be dealt with.

Ruge's headquarters was in the Bois de Boulogne – a hundred yards away from Group West in Paris. Only his Chief of Staff, Captain Hagen, and his first operations officer, Cdr Hugo Heydel, knew what was happening. Obviously Heydel could not continue to work in the general operations room in case the secret leaked out. But how could he leave it without starting gossip ? Ruge devised a little plot. He told Heydel to complain that the clamour in the busy operations room made it impossible for him to concentrate. Then Ruge took up his complaint and arranged for him to exchange with an officer who had a private room. No one suspected anything and Heydel could get on with his planning in secret.

But Ruge faced a much greater problem of secrecy. This was that he could not hold an overall briefing conference with his captains nor order his mine-sweeping flotillas to sweep an obvious course. Instead he divided the route up into a jigsaw and directed his mine-sweepers to sweep individual sections. These individual pieces of the mine-sweeping jigsaw were plotted day by day by Heydel on a secret chart in his private room.

26

Ruge's other problem was finding suitable excuses for issuing his orders, in case his crews began to wonder why all this intensive mine clearing had started. Many pretexts had to be devised to enable him to make a complete sweep of the proposed route. False reports were concocted about British mine-fields as an excuse for sweeping German mines. These reports were given to the mine-sweeping officers and men as genuine operational information.

The orders given by Commodore Ruge to his flotillas were crystal-clear. He laid down that the Channel was only to be swept at night and time limits for each stage were to be punctually adhered to. But to the officers carrying them out in ignorance of the over-all picture the whole operation seemed bewildering and purposeless.

Although Ruge could not rouse his crews to enthusiasm for the task which they were doing, they carried it out with the utmost efficiency. During January, under cover of darkness, German mine-sweepers groped their way along the heavily mined route. Continual bad weather made their task more difficult.

On 25 January the destroyer *Bruno Heinemann*, sailing to Brest to form part of the escort for the battleships on their break-out, struck a mine off Ruytingen and sank. This was the first indication that a new British mine-field had been laid on the intended course of the German battleships. Despite worsening weather the mine-sweepers exploded over thirty magnetic mines in this area. In the first days of February they worked in the Straits of Dover only a few miles off the English coast. All the route was continually swept until the last moment. Ruge was at last able to report to Group West that the many tasks imposed upon the small number of mine-sweepers available were carried out punctually and with the loss of only two boats.

At the same time, destroyers and torpedo-boats needed to screen the battleships began sailing westward down the Channel. Their movements were made an excuse for some of the mine-sweeping operations required.

The next big question was how to mark the swept channel. Not only were buoys only possible for a short inshore part of the course but there were also dangers in placing more buoys outside Brest. In the first place they might be spotted by British reconnaissance. Also the tendency in those mid-war days was to remove buoys – and to anchor new ones might puzzle French port officials and cause suspicion.

To avoid this, Ruge arranged for some of his small mine-sweeping craft to anchor as 'mark-boats' along the most important points of the route, while the operation was in progress. When the captains of the mine-sweeping craft came to open their secret orders they were mystified. For each contained instructions to sail to a certain position in the Channel at a time laid down, and anchor there to act as a 'living buoy'. They had to endure the hazards of air attack with no idea of the vital importance attaching to their role. But no explanation was possible.

Meanwhile, based on Ruge's information, Admiral Saalwächter's staff officers in Paris prepared the navigation charts. They were delivered to the ships in Brest by 'safe hand' officer messengers with the rank of naval captain. Yet in spite of the most careful planning, several of the mark-boats were off position on the day. But no operation, however well planned, can be perfect.

Next to mines, the greatest danger to the ships was the unseen eyes of radar stations strung along the English Channel coast. The Germans already knew from the reports of Captain Brinkmann of the *Prinz Eugen* that the British were ahead in radar. But they were still not certain how far ahead.

Even before the outbreak of the war they were curious about British radar. When in the spring of 1939 350-feet aerial masts were erected from the Isle of Wight to the Orkneys, German Intelligence marked them down as radio transmitters. But General Wolfgang Martini, the Head of the Luftwaffe Signals Service, was not satisfied that they were.

He was suspicious of the fact that these latticed aerials were on different wavelengths from the crude German Freya and Wurzburg radars, which German firms were developing. Was this possibly more advanced radar than his own country had? At a meeting with German Air Force chiefs, Göring and Milch, Martini came forward with a startling suggestion. He suggested a Zeppelin reconnaissance. When Göring asked, 'Why not use an aeroplane?' Martini explained that only an airship could remain stationary in the air to record a series of signals. Göring ordered one of Germany's two remaining Zeppelins to be converted into an airborne radar spy.

One night in May 1939 the 776-feet long Zeppelin LZ 127 left Frankfurt and headed over the North Sea with aerials rigged underneath her gondola. She flew towards the Bawdsey Research Station at Orfordness, Suffolk, where tall masts could be seen. Aboard her was General Martini. While the Zeppelin cruised along the Suffolk coast technicians in her gondola manned special radio detectors. All they picked up was a loud crackling.

At Bawdsey, the radar operations staff gazed in astonishment at the largest 'blip' they had ever seen travelling slowly across the radar screen. They guessed correctly that it was a German airship carrying out radar investigation. As she flew along the east coast the Zeppelin picked up only more crackling in her receivers. General Martini landed in Frankfurt still as ignorant of the development of British radar.

A month before the outbreak of war – on 2 August 1939 – the Zeppelin made a second trip. Her instructions were to keep fifteen miles off the east coast of Britain and note the wavelengths, strength and position of all high-frequency signals. Martini was not aboard this time but sent his senior officer, Lt-Col. Gosewisch. Once again no transmissions were detected – and British radar did not pick up the airship.

But she was seen. Coastguards in Aberdeenshire reported her and two RAF fighters took off from Dyce and identified the airship. But she was well outside territorial limits as Martini had ordered.

She cruised near the British naval base at Scapa Flow, catching glimpses of British warships through the clouds before setting course back to Germany, again without detecting any high-frequency signals.

A month later, when war broke out, such Zeppelin cruises off the coast of Britain were impossible. In spite of the two abortive Zeppelin flights, General Martini was convinced that Britain was ahead in radar. He persevered in trying to find out more about their sets.

The fall of France in 1940 gave him his opportunity. Special teams of Luftwaffe and Navy signal experts were sent to the Channel coast to find out whether instruments similar to their radar had been established on the English south coast. Until then the Germans had no definite proof that the British were ahead. When these radar intelligence receivers recorded a number of English radar sets on meter and decimeter wavelengths, reconnaissance planes helped to pinpoint their locations for an exact map of all existing radar. From these precise observations, the Germans were able to deduce a good deal about the development of the British radar devices. Martini decided to jam them.

During the next year jamming stations were established in Ostend, Boulogne, Dieppe and Cherbourg. They were equipped with very efficient directional beam antennae, synchronized with the search impulses of the British equipment. They could achieve effective jamming from Cherbourg to the Isle of Wight. Several aeroplanes also had jamming equipment.

When told of Operation Cerberus, General Martini personally directed his 'interference' operations. At dawn each day during January English radar stations had a few minutes of jamming, deliberately made to appear like atmospherics. Every day the length of the jamming increased slightly. By February British radar operators were wearily accustomed to this interference. They reported it as 'caused by atmospheric conditions'.

This brilliant, painstaking radar plan was to play a decisive part in delaying the British defences.

The day after the New Year conference a staff car appeared on the quai Lannion. Ships' officers recognized the visitor it contained as the famous Battle of Britain fighter ace Col. Adolf Galland.

Galland was a popular figure with the Navy, which was unusual because the Luftwaffe – and especially its chief Hermann Göring – was not. Not only did the Navy feel that the Luftwaffe was the younger, more favoured child but it resented the fact that Göring had used his influence with Hitler to resist any attempt to give the Navy its own Fleet Air Arm, as the Royal Navy had.

Although *Scharnhorst* carried three reconnaissance aircraft in her hangar, they would be useless in this operation, which needed a vast Luftwaffe force. Col. Galland came aboard *Scharnhorst* to discuss this air cover with Admiral Ciliax and his Chief of Staff Reinicke. With them he worked out an elaborate air defence plan of fighter forces under his command.

Galland's headquarters were to be at Le Touquet, geographically in the centre of the operation. He set up one command post at Caen for the early part of the break-out, and another at Schiphol in Holland for the last leg.

The problem was to have the greatest possible number of aeroplanes at all times because, as Hitler had predicted, the success of the break-out depended on how soon the British could mobilize the full force of the RAF against the surprise appearance of the German ships.

Owing to the great demands in Russia the Luftwaffe was short of aircraft. But three fighter groups were available with 250 fighters and 30 night-fighters. To cover the battle squadron, all the 280 fighters stationed along the Channel coast would be brought into action. Night-fighters would give protection before dawn and as soon as dawn broke 16 day fighters would be constantly overhead. Each flight would last thirty-five minutes. Ten minutes before they left another wave would arrive. This meant that for twenty minutes of every hour there would be 32 fighters overhead.

Planes were to remain over the ships as long as their fuel reserves permitted, then fly to the next airfield where they would quickly be refuelled and supplied with new ammunition ready to fly off again. The first planes were to meet the ships somewhere in the Seine Bay before dawn and accompany them to the North Sea.

At 2 p.m. the control centre was to move from Le Touquet to Schiphol, and the air-bases in the area of the mouths of the Rhine and Scheldt had to be ready. By evening the planes were to join bases in the Wilhelmshaven area.

Galland arranged to put Luftwaffe officers in each of the three big ships to help German fighters to deal with the RAF during the break-out. On the *Scharnhorst* was their commander Col. Max Ibel who was in charge of the Fighter Control Board.

There were also to be fighter controllers on *Gneisenau* and *Prinz Eugen*.

After the Hitler conference, Luftwaffe Col. Ibel received orders to co-ordinate and take charge of the air umbrella. On 20 January he arrived with Lt-Col. Hentschel and Lt-Col. Elle with a staff to be posted among the ships. Captain Rutsch was attached to *Gneisenau* and Lt Rothenberg to *Prinz Eugen*. To avoid RAF bombing interfering with their preparations, they lived outside Brest in the ironically named château 'Beau Repos'.

The Luftwaffe installed additional radio equipment in the ships to direct the fighter pilots. The radio contact between the flagship *Scharnhorst* and the command centres along the German-occupied coast was achieved by very-high-frequency – VHF – radio telephone or by means of long-wave coded messages. Radio telephone communications were established between the fighter command centres and the airfields. Particularly important and difficult to install was a line from the crow's nest to the *Scharnhorst*'s bridge, to give the earliest possible warnings of RAF attacks.

Their next problem was to ensure the faultless adjustment of the ships' equipment, so that it would accurately guide the fighters from the ship, pick up the exchanges of conversation of the low-level cover – above all in the morning and evening twilight – and receive the beamed air warnings from the Luftwaffe command post.

The Luftwaffe officers were aboard when the ships went out to the 'Dalbenplatz' – Dolphin Place – in the Bay of Brest for calibration of direction finders. The Dalbenplatz was more than a mooring at which a ship swings with the tides. It was an elaborate iron grill permanently made fast in deepish water. Ships could be 'strapped' motionless fore and aft to the Dalbenplatz while the necessary delicate adjustments were made with the ship afloat but completely rigid. *Prinz Eugen, Gneisenau* and *Scharnhorst* were calibrated on 22, 23 and 28 January respectively. Afterwards, the three Luftwaffe colonels had a conference with Admiral Ciliax to finalize details of arrangements for protecting the ships from constant air attack.

Galland faced the same problem of keeping the secret as

Commodore Ruge and the battleship senior officers, since the plan had to be concealed from the German aircrews as well. He had to invent fanciful excuses for the trial runs while this extensive communication apparatus was tried and co-ordinated. Nearer the time, the Luftwaffe pilots were told that a convoy with a very important cargo was to pass the Channel from east to west and they were to protect it.

The excuse given to the ships' crews for the Luftwaffe preparations was that plans were being made for joint exercises with the Luftwaffe south of Brest. The story was that the ships were to leave Brest after sunset on 11 February, carry out exercises between La Pallice and St Nazaire during the 12th, and return to Brest on the following night. To allay suspicions, the usual small percentage of men were sent on leave.

Targets were ordered for gunnery practice off St Nazaire and concentrated patrols were scheduled against British submarines in the same area. These German anti-submarine patrols were unnecessary, as the nearest British submarines were fifty miles out in the Atlantic guarding against a break-out there – not through the Channel.

Setting up such an air protection network required many rehearsals. During the first week of February the Luftwaffe flew 450 sorties simulating actual conditions as near as possible. With wry humour, the Luftwaffe code named these rehearsals 'the beginning of Spring'. British radar picked them up but no one was alarmed.

Admiral Ciliax was also having his problems. For *Scharnhorst*, *Gneisenau* and *Prinz Eugen* were no longer the fine fighting ships they had been. Nor did they look it. The once smart, well-painted ships were showing signs of rust and were stained at the water-line by the scum of oil which covered Brest harbour.

Although normally the German sailor is a stolid, level-headed chap, the ships' companies were not living under the conditions that enhances morale. Sailors were virtually only day lodgers aboard their ships.

Also, while the ships remained immobilized in Brest, there had been a drawing off from the regular ship's company, especially naval technicians for urgent requirements elsewhere.

Unobtrusively, the crews were strengthened by the return of experts and technicians with extensive combat experience who had been posted away. But it was still difficult to train the inexperienced crews when there was no opportunity for 'shake-down' cruises.

When Hitler gave his order it left only a month to go. Would they in fact ever get the crews ready in time? Due to the urgent time factor and the deep secrecy, opportunities for training the new recruits were limited. It was not possible to let the officers responsible for trying to bring the crews up to fighting efficiency into the secret of the great enterprise that lay ahead. There could only be talk of exercises which inspired no one.

Yet in spite of continual heavy air attacks, the repairs to the three ships were far advanced, although there was still work to be done in the dockyard. But this could not be hastened in case it aroused suspicions. For the same reason, the ships only dared to make one, or at the most two, short runs out of Brest to the Dalbenplatz for ranging practice on air and sea targets. As these short practice trips were not enough preparation to get the ships into fighting trim, firing practice had to be done at their normal berths on the quai Lannion. This firing practice was so urgent that *Scharnhorst*'s gun crews even carried it out while she was still in dry-dock.

While this was going on, there could be no feeling of urgency reflected upon the faces of the half-dozen senior officers who knew about the coming break-out. Yet all these officers agreed it would be miraculous if no leakage took place.

For the perils were many. Not only did RAF reconnaissance aircraft fly regularly over Brest, but the port was working normally with French labour. Coastal traffic and fishing were being carried out as usual, and the Germans used French tugs manned by French crews. Any one of these could have their suspicions aroused and pass on information to the unseen army of French resistance agents lurking in the town.

There was one comforting factor for the Germans. There had been no sabotage at Brest. Although there was sullen hostility among the locals, the Germans went ashore freely. Officers often indulged their favourite recreation – riding – galloping alone for miles along the coast.

While the ships lay at the quai Lannion secretly preparing for the break-out the major task was to make the French believe they would not be leaving for a long time, and to mislead them about their destination. So tropical helmets were brought aboard to give the impression the ships might be off to Africa or the South Atlantic. Barrels of lubricating oil marked: 'For use in the tropics', were conspicuously loaded into the ships by French dock workers. Gossips discreetly spread rumours around the cafés that the battleships were leaving for a southern destination.

A further ruse to put them off the scent was the organizing of a fancy dress party at a hall ashore. It was getting round to the traditional German masked carnival before Lent – Fasching. Not only were members of the German women's services in Brest all organizing their Fasching costumes, but a number of French officials and their families were invited to this party.

Captain Hoffmann went out of his way to tell the German women at Brest that he hoped they would make this 'Fasching' a success. Women always have new frocks for Fasching and Hoffmann urged them, 'Go ahead. Buy the material!' Later he was to add with a chuckle, 'But we had our *Kostüm Ball* at sea.'

Further to confuse the enemy, names of officers invited to dine with Admiral Saalwächter in Paris on 11 February and attend a shooting party to be given by him the next day at Rambouillet were collected in the wardrooms of the three ships. The hunting party was to be an elaborate affair. With all the formality of peacetime, Admiral Saalwächter sent out printed invitations to thirty selected officers in Brest, and they accepted the invitations to dine with him in Paris at 8 p.m. on Wednesday, 11 February. To lend even more authenticity, sporting rifles were obtained and ostentatiously brought on board. Many of the French people ashore were aware that this party was to be held.

Another stratagem was the boarding of a detachment of the Naval Coastal Guns with their 20-mm quadruple mounted guns. Each detachment wore grey army uniform, but instead of the usual army buttons they had gold buttons with anchors on them. As these were shore-defence gun crews, which did not go to sea, it was hoped enemy agents would take their presence on board as a sign that the battleships would remain permanently in port. They were in fact extra flak guns intended to be used against the RAF in the break-out.

Although the final plan became known as Operation Cerberus, six code names were also applied to it at various stages to confuse British agents.

While these secret preparations went on, the RAF were still very active. On 1 February, an air attack destroyed 300 German seamen's billets in Brest, but there were no casualties.

Next day, Admiral Saalwächter issued a six-page Operation instruction from Paris. They were sent to Ciliax, Ruge, Captain Bey, commander of destroyers, and Luftwaffe Col. Galland.

The instruction was headed: 'Task: Break-through the Channel by the Brest Group – *Scharnhorst, Gneisenau* and *Prinz Eugen* under the command of the C-in-C Vice-Admiral Ciliax. Homewards in the new moon period. The task is to be executed, even if on the day of the issue of the code-word only one battleship is operational.

'Forces Participating:

'Ships: *Scharnhorst, Gneisenau, Prinz Eugen* – in Brest.

'Destroyers: *Beitzen, Jacobi, Ihn, Schoemann, Z.25, Z.29* – in Brest.

'Torpedo Boats: 2nd Torpedo Flotilla with *T.2, T.4, T.5, T.11, T.12* – in Le Havre.

3rd Torpedo Flotilla with *T.13, T.14, T.15, T.16, T.17* – in Dunkirk.

5th Torpedo Flotilla with *Kondor, Falke, Seeadler, Iltis, Jaguar* – in Flushing.

E-Boats: 2nd, 4th, 6th Flotillas.

'With respect of navigation, the most favourable period for executing the task extends from the 10th to the 15th of February. Earliest period for setting-off is the 10th of February.

'Commanders of Torpedo boats, E-boat-Flotillas, Channel Coast and Commandant of the Sea Defence Pas de Calais are receiving sealed orders which are to be opened at the last moment.

'Should proceeding to sea be delayed for a short time by air attack, the Task is to be put into operation. If the delay is more than two hours do not proceed. Report immediately to Group West. Proceed again after new issue of code-word.

'Should the Squadron leaving Brest on a correct west course, or in the direction of Ushant on a north-westerly course be recognized by enemy aircraft alter course. Then fresh start of the under-taking on the basis of new code-word issue.

'Should the Squadron be discovered by the enemy after passing Ushant on a north-east or easterly course, hold on.

'The decision rests with the C-in-C or with Group West. It will be based on messages picked up by the Interception of Enemy Messages Air Warning Service (B-Dienst). Group West is to be speedily advised about any move to return by the Squadron so that all other ports involved can be instructed accordingly and the secrecy of the project securely maintained.

'C-in-C of Western Security Forces: The Commander-in-Chief of Western Security [Ruge] proposes distribution of security vessels. Assistance in case of breakdown included. Running in to ports of refuge is to be allowed for. The Commander-in-Chief [Ciliax] and the air fleet will be instructed by Group West about the distribution.

'The Destroyer Flotilla Leader has to provide according to the weather situation: On the deadline night a feint undertaken by an E-boat group in the vicinity of Dungeness–Beachy Head.

'Coastal Batteries: The long-range batteries in the Pas de Calais Sea Commandant's sector are receiving orders to hold down by their own fire, as much as possible, any enemy batteries which open fire on the Squadron. The coast will be informed about the undertaking as far as is necessary under sealed orders.

'Harbours of Refuge: The ports of Cherbourg and Le Havre are provided as ports of refuge in the Group West sector. Moorings and berth descriptions were handed out to the C-in-C. No special preparations for receiving the ships are being made. The Channel coast will not receive instructions for freeing the mooring berths until X-night.

'Holding back through Breakdown: If a ship, destroyer or boat, drops out or reduces speed in consequence of the effects of enemy action, or of technical trouble, the Squadron is to continue to go ahead without stopping. The C-in-C will dispatch vessels suitable to the position that has arisen, in support.

'Vessels will be brought up as quickly as possible by the C-in-C of Western Security according to the position.

'As a general principle, the ships should strive to continue the progress eastwards, so long as their speed is not hopelessly reduced.

'Any ships damaged that are capable of movement, are to try by all means to reach the nearest harbour of refuge.'

By the first week in February Paris had detailed all the forces necessary to cover the three battleships. The destroyers and torpedo boats were all lying in their allotted ports.

Ciliax had to carry out the operation as Group West had decided in their secret instructions. He had his share of the detailed planning and was responsible for carrying it out – and if anything went wrong he was the man who would be blamed.

But in spite of the busy, cleverly disguised preparations, one nagging thought persisted in Ciliax's head. Was noon the most favourable time for them to sail through the maximum danger zone, the Straits of Dover?

English coastal radar stations were thought to have a range of less than thirty-five miles and as they steamed up the Western Channel they might be out of range. But radar detection would not matter as they sailed through the narrow Straits off the French coast for, if the weather was fine, they would be clearly visible to watchers with telescopes on the Kent cliffs.

The Royal Navy and RAF were certain to launch a mass attack in the Straits of Dover. Group West planners summed up the Dover position like this: 'At first glance it appears tempting to pass this point at night under the cover of darkness. Yet this would have the disadvantage that the ships would have to leave Brest in the forenoon and steam through the Channel in broad daylight. It would give the British air reconnaissance warning in good time. They will not only get ready their torpedo and bomber aircraft and MTB flotillas in the Straits, but might also bring their large units from Scapa Flow. Our presence at night is certain to become known so we must go through there in daylight when we can best defend ourselves.'

The German admirals were only too conscious of the ever-present menace of the British Grand Fleet. Although the distance from Brest to Terschelling was 575 miles it was only 450 miles from Scapa to Terschelling – 125 miles shorter. If the Royal Navy received warning as soon as the battleships sailed they would have plenty of time to mass an annihilating battle fleet.

But would the British commit them ? Two months before, as Saalwächter had pointed out in his report, they had lost two battleships by risking them too close inshore off the coast of Malaya. The lesson of the sinking of these two battleships on 10 December 1941, 400 miles from the nearest Japanese air- field, was not lost upon the Germans. They did not regard it as a happy omen for their three heavy ships which would be sailing along the English Channel for eleven hours. Yet they decided to risk their ships through the Straits in daylight, even though at the narrowest point they would be less than 100 miles from London.

It was a carefully calculated decision. One particular advant- age was that during a night passage of the Straits the Germans would be without effective fighter cover and the anti-aircraft defences would be much less effective. They feared the night attacks of British MTBs or torpedo bombers such as had crip- pled the *Bismarck*. In daylight Galland's Luftwaffe umbrella might be able to fight off the RAF. Also the battle squadron's heavy fire power would be helped by the massed escort vessels to put up a savage curtain of fire against torpedo and bomber attacks. The most daunting factor was that as they sailed in daylight along the Western Channel towards Dover they would be in an area criss-crossed by British air patrols. Their presence would quickly be revealed.

While the Germans went about their preparations with meti- culous thoroughness and secrecy, the British, not really believ- ing the Germans would attempt it, made some efforts to counter a channel break-out.

During January, a stream of RAF Fighter and Coastal Command reports told of destroyer and E-boat flotillas passing through the Channel in the direction of Brest and a great deal of mine-sweeping along the French coast. They had spotted Ruge's flotillas. One report said, 'The *Scharnhorst* and *Prinz*

Eugen can be expected to sail from Brest any time after 24 January. *Gneisenau* is not fully seaworthy and cannot sail until about the end of January.' In other words, they not only had ample warning but even calculated the possible time of a break-out.

As a result of these reports, what precautions did the Royal Navy take to see that the *Scharnhorst* and *Gneisenau*'s hiding-place was turned into a trap? Their 'iron ring' of submarines, on watch outside Brest waiting for a chance to torpedo the ships if they ventured from the harbour, had already been withdrawn. It was replaced on 29 January by two 440-ton old-type submarines, *H.50* and *H.34*, which were ordered to patrol thirty–fifty miles away from the port along what was considered the most likely escape route – into the Atlantic. Two days later *H.34* broke down and returned to Falmouth. On 1 February her place was taken by *H.43*. Twenty-four hours after the two H-Class submarines had taken up their patrol positions, RAF spotter planes reported great activity among the German ships.

On 2 February the RAF estimate was remarkably accurate when it said: 'There are possibly five large and five small destroyers at Brest. The short cut for the German ships is via the English Channel. It is 240 miles from Brest to Cherbourg and another 120 miles from Cherbourg to the Dover Straits. Ships can make the passage from Brest to Cherbourg, or from Cherbourg to the Dover Straits in the same dark period, but cannot make the complete passage from Brest to the Dover Straits in one dark period.

'This passage up the Channel seems hazardous for the Germans. However, as their heavy ships are not fully efficient, they might prefer such a passage, relying for their security on the destroyers and aircraft, which are efficient, and knowing full well that we have no heavy ships to oppose them in the Channel.

'We might therefore find the two battle-cruisers and the heavy 8-inch cruiser with five large and five small destroyers, also say, twenty fighters constantly overhead proceeding up the Channel. To meet this sortie we have about six MTBs at Dover, but no destroyers with torpedo armament.

'Our bombers have shown that we cannot place much reliance on them to damage the enemy, whilst our Coastal Command torpedo-bomber aircraft will not muster more than nine.

'Taking all factors into consideration, it appears that the German ships can pass east up the Channel with much less risk than anticipated.'

Although Hitler did not know how ill-prepared the British were, this RAF report coincided with his view.

Exactly as the British High Command predicted, the battle squadron would consist of *Scharnhorst*, *Gneisenau* and *Prinz Eugen*, escorted by six large destroyers. After passing Cherbourg and entering the narrow Channel, two E-boat flotillas of ten boats would join them. Off Cap Gris Nez at the entrance to the Straits of Dover, twenty-four more E-boats, with gunboats and mine-sweepers of the Western and Northern naval commands, would bring the total up to sixty-three ships.

The six German destroyers in this formidable fleet were heavily armed modern ships compared with the six small, slow British destroyers available to intercept them. The German E-boats were also faster and more manœuvrable boats than British MTBs – and they outnumbered them three to one. And the German fighter umbrella of 250 planes was ready to deal with the RAF.

Yet the German Navy was not optimistic. They accepted the risk of losing one battleship and possible serious damage to another.

It could easily have happened. As a result of the RAF report on 2 February, Admiral Sir Max Horton, Flag Officer commanding submarines, sent a top secret message to the two submarine commanders saying: 'Most secret source indicates enemy ships in Brest are ready to sail.' The Admiralty also signalled: 'Admiralty now appreciates most probable course of action of enemy ships at Brest will be to break eastwards up the Channel and so to home waters.'

In the first week in February, Rear-Admiral Power, Assistant Chief of Naval Staff (Home Operations), who maintained liaison between naval and air planners, talked to Sir Philip Joubert, Chief of Coastal Command. They were both convinced the Germans would come up the Channel, entering the Dover

Straits during darkness. Admiral Power drove to give these views to Vice-Admiral Bertram Ramsay, C-in-C Dover. Admiral Ramsay shared the view that the Germans would reach the Straits of Dover in darkness – probably about two hours before dawn. Admiral Power reported this to First Sea Lord, Sir Dudley Pound.

Then came more reports by Hudson reconnaissance aircraft crews of further large-scale mine-sweeping operations by Ruge's flotillas along the Channel. This decided Sir Philip Joubert to give warning. On 8 February in a Coastal Command appreciation, he wrote: 'There are four large destroyers and a number of small motor torpedo boats and mine-sweepers in Brest. There are indications that the number of destroyers may be increased. During the past few days all three big ships have been carrying out exercises in open waters and should be reasonably ready for sea.

'As from the 10th the weather conditions in the Channel would be reasonable for an attempted break-through in darkness. On 15 February there will be no moon and the tidal conditions at Dover would favour a passage between 04.00 and 06.00 hours.

'Finally, the large number of destroyers and small torpedo boats that have been concentrated at Brest would seem to indicate an attempt to force a way up the Channel – any time after Tuesday, 10 February.'

This was remarkably accurate. Yet Sir Philip hesitated to act upon his own document. Beaufort torpedo bombers under his command, which were possibly the greatest danger to the German ships, were left where they were. None were moved towards Dover. This decision was to bear heavily on the outcome of the battle. Also Joubert's RAF staff officers, impressed by the top secrecy of the operation, locked the battle-plans carefully away in safes. They considered their contents too secret to be revealed to the aircrews. No pilots were told what to look for before they took off.

Admiral Power and his planning staff were convinced if the Germans broke out into the Channel it would be 'a simple battle'. When they fully realized the possibility of a break-out by the *Scharnhorst* and *Gneisenau*, the Home Fleet, apart

42

from ships patrolling the Denmark Straits, was anchored in Scapa Flow keeping a watchful eye on the German battleship *Tirpitz* hidden in a fiord near Trondheim.

What had they ready to meet the break-out? Very little. The mine-layer *Welshman*, steaming at 39 knots, laid 1,000 magnetic and contact mines between Ushant and Boulogne. In the first week in February Bomber Command also laid 98 magnetic mines off the East Friesian Islands.

The Admiralty also made three small defensive gestures. It moved six Swordfish torpedo-carrying planes from their base at Lee-on-Solent to the fighter field at Manston on the tip of the Kent coast, and alerted six MTBs stationed at Dover and three at Ramsgate. They also ordered six old destroyers to Harwich in readiness to intercept the German battleships.

Yet the behaviour of the Admiralty is not entirely to be dismissed by hindsight as ineffectual and puzzling. It was the blackest period of the war for Britain. In the defence of Singapore – due to fall to the Japanese forty-eight hours after the *Scharnhorst* and *Gneisenau* break-through – the two British capital ships, the *Repulse* and the *Prince of Wales*, had been sunk by land-based Japanese aircraft. The *Prince of Wales*, sister ship of *King George V*, was one of Britain's newest battleships. When she went down with her commander, Admiral Sir Tom Phillips, it was a numbing blow to the Royal Navy. It weighed very heavily with the First Sea Lord Sir Dudley Pound.

That is why he hesitated. His naval power was stretched to the limit from Singapore to Scapa Flow. If he operated his great ships near the occupied coast of Europe they might also be sunk by determined attacks by German aircraft. It was a chilling thought. Like Jellicoe, Royal Naval Chief in the First World War, 'He was the man who could lose the war in an afternoon.' If several of his battleships were sunk or put out of action, needing months of repairs, it could change the whole picture of naval warfare in European waters.

This was why Dudley Pound stated, 'On no account will heavy ships be brought south where they will be exposed to enemy air attack, torpedo-boat attack and risk being damaged by our own and enemy mine-fields.'

His staff queried this point of view asking, 'But surely the light forces available will be totally inadequate to deal with the German battle fleet?' The curt answer was, 'We have scraped together all that is at present available.'

The real reason was that he never really believed that the Germans would be foolhardy enough to try and bring their ships through Dover Straits in daylight. Dudley Pound was an orthodox career admiral of the old school. The *Dictionary of National Biography* called his personality 'reserved and unbending'. Appointed in 1939, he was at 65 already over retiring age. He was also overworked, tired and ill. Although too old to cope with his job unaided, he did not even have a deputy.* Also, he greatly under-estimated the resolution of the former Austrian corporal, the 'land animal' Adolf Hitler, who had ordered the daring plan.

Pound made one other move. A third submarine, H.M.S. *Sealion*, commanded by Lt-Cdr G. R. 'Joe' Colvin, hastily sailed from Portsmouth for Brest. *Sealion* was a fast 768-ton S-Class boat built in 1934 with a speed of fourteen knots. Colvin's orders were: 'Your operational area is designed to intercept the main enemy units should they break out into the Atlantic or proceed south-eastwards to another Biscayan port.' As the Admiralty were still undecided about the battleships' possible route, Colvin decided to keep patrolling as near to Brest as he dared.

Why were only his new submarine and two old ones sent to watch for such an important target? The reason was that seventeen British submarines had been lost in the Mediterranean alone since Italy had declared war in June 1940, and others had been sent to the Far East for the war against Japan.

Although *Sealion* was considered to have a good chance of encountering the battleships either by night or day, Joe Colvin had an extremely difficult task for many reasons. The tides along the Normandy and Britanny coast were running between

* A few months after the break-out, in the summer of 1942, a deputy was appointed – but too late to give Pound the relief he needed. His health was already failing. He kept the job until his last illness, dying in harness, aged 66, on Trafalgar Day, 21 October 1943 – eighteen months after the break-out. On 27 October a cruiser sailed from Portsmouth and scattered his ashes at sea.

three and four knots, and large waves breaking over the rocks made it very difficult to keep accurate station.

Colvin had a bigger problem. *Sealion* had just returned from three months' service with the Russian Navy, and at the end of this tour of duty most of the crew of reservists had been relieved. He had taken aboard twelve replacements. These included the torpedo-gunner's mate, one of the key men in a submarine. Even his First Lieutenant, E. P. Young, a wartime sailor, had only joined with two other new officers just before sailing.

On the morning he sailed from Portsmouth, Colvin had no doubts about his scratch crew's courage, but they needed time to master the intricate system of dials and levers in their modern submarine. His main worry was whether his crew would be able to man the torpedo tubes efficiently, for there could be no fumbling when the moment came. There was also a problem with the torpedoes themselves. He had sailed so hurriedly that he had a mixed cargo of torpedoes consisting of four modern ones and four old, not very effective, Mark Four type.

With this inexperienced crew aboard, Colvin nosed *Sealion* towards Iroise Bay, which surrounds Brest. His intention was to sneak among the German battleships while they were exercising, fire his torpedoes and escape submerged out to sea. For three days he cruised at periscope-depth watching and waiting for the battleships, but they remained in harbour.

On 7 February, a signal from Sir Max Horton said the German ships could be observed exercising in the approaches to Brest. For another forty-eight hours Colvin patrolled between 14–20 miles from Brest harbour – and still saw nothing.

On 9 February, he decided the moment for encountering the German ships was near. He fired off his four Mk-Four torpedoes in one salvo at sea and replaced them with the later type ready for immediate action. Then he sailed submerged into the northern part of the bay towards the boom guarding Brest Harbour. Shortly after midday Colvin raised his periscope in a choppy sea with good visibility and sighted Whistle Buoy, marking the end of the swept channel into Brest. As this was where the battleships must come out, he dived near the buoy and lay there until darkness came. At 8 p.m. he surfaced to wait for the Germans to come out for night exercise. While he lay in the dark on the surface, another signal from Sir Max Horton reported the German ships still lying at their berths inside the harbour. But Colvin still kept up his vigil.

An hour after receiving the signal a Dornier bomber, with its searchlights switched on, came swooping down to 200 feet. As the beams lit a pathway through the water ahead of *Sealion*, Colvin and his crew scrambled down the conning-tower hatchway and the submarine dived. But he had been spotted. An hour later, as he lay underwater near Whistle Buoy, depth-charges made *Sealion* rock and shudder, but they were not near enough to damage her. When the propellers died away Colin sailed submerged farther out to sea.

What other preparations did the British make, apart from Colvin's solitary submarine, to prevent the Germans steaming up the Channel? First they gave the possible break-out the code name 'Fuller'. On receipt of this code-word, all available forces would be alerted.

But what forces? Since the First Sea Lord Sir Dudley Pound had decided not to engage with capital ships, his preparations were barely adequate. If they came, he believed the RAF would bomb them to the bottom as the Japanese planes had done to the *Repulse* and *Prince of Wales*. It seemed to be overlooked that heavy bomber crews, used to attacking targets at night from a great height, were not trained for accurate bombing of ships steaming at thirty knots and taking evasive action. It was the most formidable bomber force the world had yet seen. But it still could hardly hope to hit fast-moving ships at sea.

The main fighter opposition to the Luftwaffe was Number 11 Group, consisting of Kenley, Hornchurch, Debden, Biggin Hill and Tangmere wings. Their job was to protect the bombers against the escorting Luftwaffe umbrella.

The only planes which had much chance of damaging the big ships were torpedo carriers. The British had two types of these – the Fleet Air Arm's Swordfish and the RAF's Beauforts.

The most experienced squadron of Swordfish was 825 which had helped to sink the *Bismarck*. After the *Bismarck* operation, 825 Squadron reformed at Lee-on-Solent in December 1941. They had only six Swordfish, seven pilots, six observers and six air-gunners. Only two of the pilots and four of the observers had had operational experience. The air-gunners alone were fully trained and operational. One of them, Leading Airman A. L. 'Ginger' Johnson, had won the Distinguished Service Medal for the *Bismarck* attack.

The leader of the half-squadron of six Swordfish was Eugene Esmonde, a 32-year-old Irishman from Drominagh, Tipperary. Before the war he had been a pilot with Imperial Airways, a forerunner of BOAC. In April 1939 he joined the Fleet Air Arm with the rank of Lieutenant-Commander and was posted to Lee-on-Solent, the Fleet Air Arm's base near Portsmouth, to take command of a Swordfish training squadron.

He was a short man – only five feet six – who was one of the Navy's most experienced and successful pilots. He also had the quality of firm leadership. He never barked brusque words of command, keeping his orders to a minimum and giving them in a quiet voice. If his aircrews were not actually on duty, he did not care what they did – they could creep up to London for a few hours if they wished when they were not wanted. This made the aircrews – most of them at least ten years younger than he was – feel that, however hazardous the operation he asked them to do, they could not let Esmonde down.

He was, of course, a much more experienced pilot than any of them. One of the troubles was keeping up with him. He could fly flat out in a Swordfish loaded with a torpedo, whereas none of them would dare in case they overturned it.

These single-engined biplanes – the Royal Navy's only torpedo bombers – were designed like First World War aircraft. They had a fabric fuselage stretched across light metal struts and open cockpits. They carried a crew of three – a pilot, and observer, and a rear-gunner manning a Vickers machine-gun on a swivel mounting.

Yet these old planes could absorb tremendous punishment. Anti-aircraft shells passed through the fabric instead of exploding against it, as they did with more modern metal fuselages. But the 'Stringbags' – as the Navy affectionately called them – had a top speed of only ninety knots, which made them sitting ducks in daylight.

During January, Esmonde was trying to bring his new

aircrews up to operational standards, carrying a rigorous training programme in mock torpedo attacks at Lee-on-Solent. It seemed inconceivable that the Admiralty would allow 825 Squadron to remain at half-strength. He waited daily to hear news of another six Swordfish and more aircrew arriving. None came.

In the first week in February, as part of Operation Fuller, the six aircraft were transferred to Manston in Kent to lead the attack on the Brest ships if they tried to force the Straits of Dover at night.

The six Swordfish flew from Lee-on-Solent to Manston in a blizzard, and landed on an airfield covered with frozen snow. When he arrived Esmonde told Wing-Cdr Tom Gleave, the station commander at Manston, 'I shall need a month to get my chaps trained.' Next morning the maintenance crews, commanded by Observer Edgar Lee, arrived in lorries from Lee-on-Solent.

Then Esmonde, with RAF squadron commanders, was ordered to a special briefing given by senior officers from the Admiralty and Air Staff. They were told, 'We believe that an enemy dash up the Channel is imminent. We believe also that he will attempt to run through the Straits of Dover under cover of darkness about two hours before dawn when tides and high-water levels will be most favourable. There is only one way we can prevent this and destroy him – by throwing in the greatest available torpedo fire-power by combined air and sea attacks. It is intended, therefore, that the Swordfish of the Fleet Air Arm and Coastal Command Beaufort torpedo bombers should stand by to support light naval forces for this purpose.

'It will be pretty fierce when it starts. But with the protection of darkness the Swordfish should have a chance of delivering their attacks and getting away. We want the big chaps crippled so that heavier forces can sink them at will.'

Later a signal arrived for Esmonde saying, 'The squadron commander to operate only those crews which he considers would contribute to the achievement of the object.' He received this message with a wry grin, for he had barely enough fully trained aircrew to fly his planes, and half of them had never seen action.

As the Admiralty never considered the German battleships would ever try to pass the Straits in daylight, Esmonde continued to prepare for a night attack. In conjunction with Wing-Cdr Tom Gleave, he worked out a tough training programme for low-level torpedo attacks. His inexperienced aircrews needed as much practice as they could get.

Apart from the six Swordfish, the only effective air weapon which could sink or cripple the battleships were Beaufort torpedo bombers. They were a much more formidable aircraft, being able to fly twice as fast as the Swordfish.

Three squadrons were available under the command of Sir Philip Joubert, Chief of Coastal Command. One of them was No. 43 Squadron of fourteen Beauforts, stationed at Leuchars in Scotland, whose main task was to help the naval operation against the German battleship *Tirpitz* in the Norwegian fiord.

Following the Coastal Command appreciation, Joubert ordered these Beauforts from Leuchars south to Coltishall near Norwich. The decision was correct but bad luck intervened. For three days heavy snowfalls prevented them flying. There were also the usual 'administrative delays' – in other words, ground inefficiency. Although Joubert ordered the Leuchars squadron south to meet the urgent threat, he made no effort to plan for his torpedo bombers to attack together.

Twelve aircraft of No. 86 Beaufort squadron, reinforced by three Beauforts of 217 Squadron, were at St Eval in Cornwall. Their role was to deal with a break-out from Brest into the Atlantic. The seven remaining aircraft of 217 Squadron were at Thorney Island, near Portsmouth, ready for action in the Channel.

They were much nearer the Germans' course, and could have attacked before the Swordfish at Manston. But the main burden of the immediate attack was left to the six Swordfish, because senior officers were convinced the dash through the Straits would be made at night – and the Swordfish were certainly the ideal planes for such an attack. Under these conditions they had destroyed the Italian fleet in Taranto harbour in 1940.

The Admiralty made one other disposition. They alerted six 20-year-old destroyers, drawn from the 21st Flotilla, based on Sheerness, and the 16th Flotilla at Harwich. With these six old destroyers were four smaller Hunt Class destroyers, which were not armed with torpedoes. The Admiralty decided that if the Germans were to sail through the Channel, these destroyers would attack.

The combined flotilla was commanded by 42-year-old Captain Mark Pizey aboard HMS *Campbell*. He was ordered to sail for Harwich in *Campbell*, accompanied by *Vivacious*, to join Captain Wright commanding the 16th Destroyer Flotilla in *Mackay*, with *Worcester*, *Whitshed* and *Walpole*. Both these flotillas were normally out day and night escorting convoys along the east coast, to protect them against German E-boats.

Late in the afternoon of 4 February, Captain Pizey sailed into Harwich and went straight to the Commodore's office, where he talked on the green scrambler telephone with Dover. They gave him the Admiralty's view of the possible *Scharnhorst* and *Gneisenau* break-out, saying if they came through the Channel his six torpedo-carrying destroyers must attack them. To be ready for the attack, they were to remain in Harwich harbour at short notice for eight days, the period that favourable tides lasted.

Captain Pizey was also handed a teleprinter signal from the Admiralty, timed 20.09 February 3, which read: 'To Captain D 21 flotilla from Vice-Admiral Dover. If signal "Proceed in execution of previous orders" is made, destroyers are to proceed forthwith at best speed to North-West Hinder Buoy, latitude 051 degrees 33 minutes North, longitude 002 degrees 36 minutes East, via 53 buoy. You will be kept informed of movement of enemy ships through Dover Straits and you should endeavour to intercept them in the approximate latitude 051 degrees 30 minutes North. MTBs will not operate north of latitude 051 degrees 23 minutes North. Acknowledge.'

He acknowledged the signal by teleprinter and went back aboard *Campbell*. A lamp signal ordered all the five destroyer Captains whose ships were secured to buoys in Harwich harbour, to come aboard his flagship for instructions. These were to be at five minutes' notice for steam from dusk to daylight, which meant that the Chief Engineer must be able to report 'Engine room ready to obey telegraph' within a maximum of five minutes. They were to be moored with cables through the ring of the mooring buoys, ready to be instantly slipped and hauled aboard. Everyone slept in their clothes and the signal office was on twenty-four hours duty ready to receive Admiralty radio orders. Each evening at five o'clock, Pizey invited the five Captains aboard *Campbell* to discuss battle-plans and any new tactics – 'tatticks' as the Navy calls them. Everyone scanned the charts thinking of every conceivable situation – but no action signal came.

As all night leave was stopped, the ratings assumed that something big might happen. Ted Tong, 41-year-old P.O. steward aboard *Whitshed*, told his wife Violet, who was living near Harwich, that something big was brewing. He confided to her that Lt-Cdr W. A. Juniper, captain of *Whitshed*, kept walking up and down the wardroom twisting a match-box in his hand, as he always did when he was thinking over a problem.

The only other forces ready when the attack came were six motor-torpedo boats in Dover and three in Ramsgate. The Dover boats were commanded by Lt-Cdr Nigel Pumphrey, the Ramsgate boats by Lt D. J. Long.

So, to contest the passage of the battleships through the Dover Straits the Royal Navy had six Fleet Air Arm Swordfish at Manston, nine MTBs at Dover and Ramsgate, and six 20-year-old destroyers at Harwich. It was a pathetic force to put against the might of the German battle squadron, steaming at thirty knots under the shadow of the greatest air umbrella any ships had ever had.

On 11 February reconnaissance reports showed *Scharnhorst*, *Gneisenau* and *Prinz Eugen* out of the repair yards and lying against fuelling wharves. Six destroyers were also in harbour. But the boom defences were still in place.

Admiral Ramsay at Dover made his preparations. His plan was to slow down and cripple the battleships with combined torpedo attacks by the MTBs and Swordfish, while they were in the range of the Dover heavy guns. If the Germans sailed through in moonlight, the Swordfish were to attack as a squadron. If the night was moonless they were to attack singly. They were to be directed by Flt-Lt Gerald Kidd, the RAF Controller at Swingate, while Hurricane fighter bombers were to drop flares over the German ships. If they managed to scrape through the Straits they would be attacked by the whole might of the RAF. Captain Mark Pizey's six destroyers were then to attack off the Dutch coast, in an area where they could fight unhampered by the British minefields.

It was not much of a plan even for a night dash.

3

'You will Kiss your Wife Tonight'

On 11 February a German supply petty officer went ashore as usual to collect the officers' laundry and the mail. The officers had to wait a long time for their clean shirts and the crew for their mail, as he received an additional order to stay ashore and await further instructions. Not until the ships had sailed did he receive his orders – to deliver the bags to Wilhelmshaven and Kiel. Eventually he brought the ships' laundry and the mail by a regular German train running across France direct from Brest to Wilhelmshaven. It was known as the Submarine Train, as it mostly carried U-boat supplies.

Among the officers who had to wait a long time for his shirts was Chief of Staff Reinicke. Although he spent most of his time aboard *Scharnhorst* he had rooms ashore where he kept personal belongings. When he boarded *Scharnhorst* that morning he left all his clothes behind. He did not dare pack anything in case French dock workers on the quai Lannion might notice his taking a suitcase on board – and wonder why.

As a result of this precaution he had to borrow shirts and collars for seven weeks. But not everyone was deceived by these elaborate subterfuges. Small oversights occurred. Thirty-six-year-old Lieutenant Wilhelm Wolf was one junior officer who did not fully believe in this 'exercise' of the ships. A car was used for ferrying officers to and from the camp outside the town, where the ship's company sheltered from the nightly RAF air attacks. When he saw this car being taken on board it seemed to him a strange cargo for a short exercise.

And in the German naval bases of Kiel and Wilhelmshaven the coming break-out was an open secret, particularly among the wives of the destroyer crews. As they left one by one to steam westwards down the Channel the women gossiped over their coffee, 'They are going to escort the battleships home through the Kanal.' In spite of these indiscretions, since these were German naval bases, not French ports surrounded by hostile inhabitants, the secret remained safe.

Everything stood ready for the break-out. Ruge's mine-sweepers reported they had cleared a safe passage. Captain Bey's destroyers and torpedo boats were concentrated in Brest.

Colonel Galland had brought up 280 aircraft for the air umbrella. Fuel reserves were held ready at French coastal airfields and new temporary air strips had been laid out. The liaison between Ibel's Luftwaffe officers aboard the ships and the fighter cover had been fully and finally tested. General Martini's powerful radar installations strung along the English Channel coast were ready to paralyse the British radar by jamming.

It looked as if they were to have the best conditions – a strong tidal current running with the ships. The meteorologist also predicted low cloud and haze along the Channel.

With everything prepared and the weather forecast proving ideal, Ciliax decided to go ahead. At noon he called Captains Helmuth Brinkmann of *Prinz Eugen* and Otto Fein of *Gneisenau* to join Captain Kurt Hoffmann and himself in the Admiral's cabin aboard *Scharnhorst*.

Once again he reiterated to them the importance of following Group West's instructions to the letter. There was little chance any of them would not do so as these secret orders appealed to their temperament. They were a model of meticulous planning with little scope for personal initiative. Ciliax said, 'It is a bold and unheard of operation for the German Navy. It will succeed if these orders are strictly obeyed. There is no margin for interpretation. They must be adhered to at all times. Ships will sail in the following order –*Scharnhorst, Gneisenau* and *Prinz Eugen* – with escort forces taking station outside harbour in accordance with their instructions.

'Do not seek combat, but only engage the enemy if the operation cannot otherwise be carried out. The task of proceeding eastwards quickly is paramount.'

Then he ordered champagne and they drank to the success of 'Operation Cerberus'. After the toast he said farewell to his commanders and wished them good luck before they returned to their ships.

Despite his champagne toasts to the operation's success, Ciliax remained privately pessimistic. He had not changed the view he expressed in his memoranda to Admiral Saalwächter. He did not mind the fact that Group West's orders left him no room for manœuvre, but he privately thought the operation had at best only a chance of partial success.

So that afternoon after the Captains had left, he sat down and wrote the following entry in his log: 'I want to take this opportunity to make the following observations to give my point of view upon the completion of preparations so long planned. I no longer regard the withdrawal from Brest as absolutely necessary. The danger from the air is not so great now we have flak fighters, camouflage, barrage balloons and artificial fog.

'It also appears that the enemy has come to the same opinion. Although his air-force still comes over by day and night, the flak defence in its full strength, supported by the fog apparatus, considerably reduces the effectiveness of attack.

'Random hits are of course possible and must be taken into account, but this is really only a matter of chance. Therefore Brest must be regarded as a usable base in its present state of defence, especially taking into consideration that the shipyards are able to meet all possible requirements. Long-term missions such as were undertaken in the spring of 1941 cannot be mounted again, but local sorties can be carried out in co-operation with the Luftwaffe or with U-boat reconnaissance. These can lead to noticeable successes against north–south convoys and in the sea area west of Gibraltar.

'Against this, we must reckon all the imponderables inherent in sailing through the Channel. If the break-out in the Channel does succeed we must reckon with damage which the ships concerned will suffer. This may mean they will only be operational again after a considerable time.

'I do not venture an opinion as to the strong strategic threat to the Norwegian zone. Accordingly, I cannot give a judgement as to the necessity of the defensive operational role of the ships on the Norwegian coast and in the North Sea.

'In this situation the decision of the Führer is clear and

unequivocable. We now have to be employed in a new role. But it must be stated that operating from a base without repair yards, such as Trondheim or Narvik, will bring with it very great dangers. Transfer of the battleships to be repaired in German ports brings the possibility of danger, and in air defence none of the Norwegian ports equal Brest. Aircraft-carriers could approach and long-distance bombers attack, since the local Luftwaffe forces in Norway have not got the same defensive capacity.

'Heavy enemy forces now being held down will be reduced particularly in the North Atlantic and on the main convoy routes to Gibraltar. The move from the Atlantic port of Brest will have an unfavourable effect on the strategic position, freeing enemy forces for redeployment in the Mediterranean and the Far East. Against this, the occasional operations in the Norwegian zone will produce different defensive problems hard to solve. If the enemy really attacks Norway with heavy forces we can no longer reckon with our own superiority. On the extended coastline, it will be impossible to give a decisive warning of the approach of an invasion fleet or to intervene effectively against landings.

'Even small raids cannot always be hindered and the pressure of the British to attack our heavy ships will not let up. From the beginning the employment of our surface forces has always been offensive. In spite of the numerical inferiority of our ships, they gave us success because the unexpected led us to our objective. This principal is now being given up and the battleships employed in a defensive task, which means that the initiative will remain with the enemy.

'In conclusion I would like to express the hope that the decision to evacuate our heavy ships with great difficulty from the Atlantic position will find justification in the future development of the war situation.'

A few hours after writing this dissenting report he put to sea as ordered by the Führer.

As darkness fell on the evening of X-day, 11 February 1942, the warships' boiler-room fans roared as steam pressure was raised. At 6 p.m. the usual rush before leaving port prevailed on all ships. The order was given: 'Prepare to proceed on exercise.' The orders were to carry out exercises between La Pallice and St Nazaire during the 12th, and return to Brest the following night.

This was the 'secret' order given to the ships, the destroyers, and the port authorities, as tugs with their red, green and white navigation lights fussed across the harbour ready to tow the big ships from their berths. Boats were lowered and handed to the yard. Telephone, steam lines and other connections with the shore were disconnected. Everyone except a few senior officers believed they were preparing for a night exercise due to start at 7.30 p.m.

At 7.25 p.m. the German ships had doubled their mooring ropes in readiness for slipping, and hauled in the hawsers from the tugs. The weather was fine with a fresh northerly breeze.

The binnacle light glowed in the darkness revealing shadowy figures moving on *Scharnhorst*'s bridge. They were Captain Hoffmann with his navigating officer Helmuth Giessler.

'Sir, it's seven-thirty p.m.', a signalman reported to the Captain who gave an order for the mooring ropes to be slipped. Tugs began to churn the water.

Signals from *Scharnhorst* were about to blink sailing orders when the Brest sirens howled. The RAF had arrived. Within seconds, the alarm bells – *Glöcken* – were ringing in the ships. It was a nerve-racking situation. The battleships were lying with steam up and tugs alongside. Worse still, in order not to interfere with fire control and gunnery practice on the pretended 'exercise', the elaborate camouflage netting had been removed and rolled up on the jetty. This left the ships at the mercy of flashlight bombs from RAF planes. To avert this dangerous situation, artificial fog was hastily churned out by dockside apparatus. Everyone began choking as they breathed in the filthy stuff. Captain Brinkmann on the bridge of *Prinz Eugen* took a mouthful of the fog and had a paroxysm of coughing.

As anti-aircraft guns opened up, aircraft could be heard droning in the sky, obscured by the artificial fog. Only the pale flickering flashes of the massed A.A. guns could be seen through the thickening mist. When a slight puff of the wind tore a hole in the fog blanket over the port area, the crews could see the white beams of the searchlights fingering the starry sky. Amidst the roar of the A.A. fire they could make out the hissing sound of falling bombs, followed by the crash of their explosions.

When the news of the break-out reached Brest, wild rumours swept the town that the 'raid' had been arranged by the Germans as part of a ruse to clear the streets while the ships slid away. The raid was, of course, genuine. Between 7.45 and 8.30 p.m. sixteen Wellingtons dropped bombs. Although some fell on the town, none hit the ships. But photographic planes took pictures in the glare of the flashlight bombs exploding overhead.

This was to prove the first piece of extraordinary good luck for the Germans. For when the reconnaissance pictures were developed that night in Britain, some showed through gaps in the fog the ships still in harbour. This lulled the British into thinking nothing was going to happen.

At 9 p.m., although the Wellingtons had left for home half an hour before, there was still no 'all clear'. Admiral Ciliax checked the time. If the battleships did not sail by 9.30 p.m. they would never make up for lost time, and the elaborately dovetailed plan would fail. He would have to postpone the operation, as Group West had ordered, if there was a two-hour delay.

Ciliax was just about to cancel the sailing when at 9.14 p.m. the 'all clear' sounded. He immediately gave orders to get under way. The crew thought this late departure only meant a delayed practice firing as had happened before.

When the fog lifted sufficiently for the tugs to begin towing the battleships out, they were nearly two hours late on Group West's schedule. Clearing Brest harbour under ordinary night conditions was not easy and now, because of the artificial fog, the two pierheads could only be made out dimly.

With *Scharnhorst* leading in the smoky darkness they groped their way out. The gap they had to sail through was only 200 yards wide. Suddenly one of the big floating buoys loomed up 300 yards dead ahead of *Scharnhorst*. But the other buoy marking the channel could not be seen. If they did not spot her the chances were even that they would pass on the wrong side. They did. When this buoy came abreast on the wrong side, Captain Hoffmann suddenly realized he was on top of the harbour nets. Any moment he expected his propellers to catch in the steel net barrage which would put an end to his part in the break-out. There was nothing he could do except to let her drift clear. He ordered: 'Stop engines!' With propellers idle, he tensely watched *Scharnhorst* glide slowly clear of the nets.

At last the 32,000-ton battleship was free of the heavy wires of the net defences without her propellers being fouled. Only when they were well clear did the officers on the bridge breathe again and Hoffmann ordered: 'Slow ahead.'

Prinz Eugen ran into worse trouble. The first tug's hawser became entangled with the cruiser's starboard propeller. When the second tug eased her tow rope it also fouled the stern of the ship. It looked like deliberate sabotage, but it was probably only the habitual deliberate carelessness of the French tugmen working for the Germans. Anyway there was nothing they could do about it. The first priority was to get the ships clear.

When divers went down to clear *Prinz Eugen's* propeller, thick artificial smoke was still drifting over the harbour. Orders had been given for the machines to keep churning out fog as a further safeguard for the break-out. As a result marker buoys could not be identified and squadron navigator Giessler aboard *Scharnhorst* used his compass to edge the ships out. He dared not flicker a searchlight to check his position. Even if he had done so it would have only reflected on the fog.

Soon *Scharnhorst* was able to cast off, leaving her two tugs to port. As a precaution the French tugs were ordered to steam a course off Brest until midday next day. This was ostensibly to await the Squadron's return from the 'exercise' but in fact this ensured extra security. They would not return to port until it was certain the battleships had been detected by the British.

As *Gneisenau* and *Prinz Eugen* inched their way out of harbour in *Scharnhorst's* wake, the escorting destroyers moved to their planned position in Brest Roads to protect them.

There was a Morse-flash from a night signal lamp as they came out of harbour. It was the only communication between the ships. The strict order was no radio messages to be transmitted between them until the British were sighted, rendering such precautions unnecessary. The signal was: 'Flagship leading. *Gneisenau* and *Prinz Eugen* following in line ahead.'

A few minutes later the crews could see by the rising of the slightly phosphorescent bow waves and feel by the vibrations

59

of the ships that they were slowly working up towards thirty knots. With long white wakes behind them, the destroyers raced alongside the big ships.

It was a dark night but the stars were visible. Although the break-out had started it was still not definite. If they should be spotted by a chance RAF patrol or by Colvin's submarine a swift return to Brest was planned. Course was due west and there was still time to revert to the fiction of 'an exercise' if they were spotted.

Where was Colvin's submarine? On 10 February he received another code signal reporting the German ships still in harbour. As this meant they had not exercised for four days, Colvin was certain they must come out soon. Next day, 11 February, he crept in once again towards Whistle Buoy and the shoals at the mouth of Brest Harbour.

His submarine was lying only six miles away from the German battleships but his batteries were running dangerously low. Although he knew he must soon go out to sea to surface and re-charge them he decided to hang on as long as possible. By 2 p.m. he had sighted nothing so he went out to sea on the ebb-tide.

When the German battleships sailed out of harbour, Colvin was thirty miles away cruising on the surface to recharge his batteries. He was nearly as far away as the two H-Class sub-marines. This was the first piece of bad luck for the British.

As the ships steamed through the starlit night away from Brest, Wilhelm Wolf, officer of the watch aboard *Scharnhorst*, turned to the navigator, Giessler, and asked, 'What course now, sir?' When Giessler replied, 'Alter course to starboard. New course three-four-zero,' he looked at him in amazement. For this would take them right through the Channel. Giessler grinned in the dim light. 'Course correct,' he said. 'Tomorrow you will be kissing your wife in Germany!'

Sailing at twenty-seven knots and protected by a screen of destroyers, the battleships made their way towards the English Channel. At 10.20 p.m., *Scharnhorst* sighted the first mark-boat and signalled to the other two ships to reduce speed and follow her across the danger area.

All sounds seemed to be suppressed. Only the constant slap-ping of the bow waves and the distant noise of the boiler-room fans could be heard. The sky over them was like soft black velvet but the brilliant stars indicated a change of weather. There was hardly any wind and the sea was smooth with only a light swell. This could be detected aboard the battleships from the constantly changing height and shape of the luminous bow waves of the destroyers sailing on both sides. A thin haze rose from the sea and made the night still darker. Then the dark shadow of the high coastline of Ushant could be seen with powerful binoculars from the bridge.

By midnight the ships sailed past Ushant – only seventy-two minutes behind schedule. They were at the point of no return. The breakout had begun. Yet still none of their crews aboard knew where they were bound.

Just after midnight all the ships' loudspeaker systems called for attention. It was an announcement from Admiral Ciliax saying:

'Warriors of the Brest Forces! The Führer has summoned us to new tasks in other waters. After great success in the Atlantic, the ships of the Brest Group – despite all the enemy's efforts to put them out of action and free himself from this threat to his sea communications – became ready for combat again with the vigorous help of everyone and with the prompt aid of the dockyard personnel.

'Our next task, to the execution of which we were called upon last night, lies ahead of us. It is: 'Sail through the Channel eastwards into the German Bight.'

'This task imposes on men, weapons and machines the highest demands. We are all aware of the difficulties of the task.

'The Führer expects from each of us unwavering duty. It is our duty as warriors and seamen to fulfil these expectations.

'What tasks await us after sailing into the German Bight need not concern us at the present time.

'I lead the Squadron conscious that every man at his post will do his duty to the utmost.'

Jubilant cheers rang out. For the Admiral's announcement meant that at last every man in the Squadron knew what he was facing. The audacity of the enterprise excited the sailors. At last they were leaving hateful bomb-torn Brest – even if they did have to pass through the narrow Straits of Dover. This news operated like an electric shock to everyone. In a moment all hands were fully awake and whispered discussions of the broadcast could be heard everywhere. Unusual guests – the ship's doctor and the paymaster – appeared on *Scharnhorst*'s bridge to talk about the situation.

What would be the outcome of it all? After the excited cheering and whispering came second thoughts. Men gazed stonily at the dark phosphorescent seas frothing by. When daylight came and they neared the Straits their presence was bound to be detected. Would they succeed in passing through them as Hitler had demanded? Or would they go to the bottom?

The Germans became even more jumpy when just after the announcement they picked up what they thought was an English radar frequency. Were they already detected? Although *Gneisenau* reported that nothing was on her monitors, *Scharnhorst*'s monitoring was certain it was a British aircraft detection radar. Then Admiral Ciliax realized the bearing was not moving. He thought that the destroyer *Richard Beitzen* was causing it.

A Morse message requested her to make a check-up. Twenty minutes afterwards the emissions ceased. An electrical installation mounted on a gun was not switched off and this had caused the so-called radar emission.

As they raced through the night, steaming to the north-east still undetected by the British, most of their special navigational aids failed them. The only one of real value was the tidal-stream and current atlas, freshly compiled by the Wilhelmshaven Marine Observatory.

They were using radar range-finding for the first time. Radar navigation in 1942 was in its infancy and German systems were markedly less efficient than the British. Yet the more advanced British radar did not score any success either on that vital night.

Range-finding equipment, situated along the French coast to locate the battleships' direction and measure their distance away, was supposed to signal information to the Navy and Luftwaffe staffs about the progress of the break-out.

The range-finding transmitters on the ships were not switched on. That was too dangerous, as they could be monitored by the

British. However, the receivers could pick up the shore beacon signals to check their position. But the bearings either came too late – or the information was wrong. Some of them did not transmit. Human error was not the monopoly of the British that day.

Gradually the navigators realized the system had failed. This was partly the result of too much secrecy. Security had ruled out any question of advance exercises by the radar operators, who were mostly untrained and some of whom were French. And no one had been able to tell them that they must exercise the greatest vigilance on that night.

This meant a nightmare for the Squadron navigator Giessler. Without the radio bearings, he had to navigate by dead reckoning while sailing at twenty-seven knots through the channel swept by Commodore Ruge's forces. It was only a mile wide and had been swept to a depth of twelve fathoms. By the calculations of the Wilhelmshaven tide tables, he reckoned this would just about give adequate margin to escaped moored mines.

As they steamed through the narrow swept channel, still the overriding anxiety was – had the British detected them? No radio signals were intercepted from them. All remained quiet as they sailed steadily towards dawn and Dover.

Occasionally dimmed red or green lights were seen and flash signals with darkened blinker tubes could be read, as some mine-sweepers, which had cleared the way, returned to ports on the ragged northern coast of France. Then the shore lights of the Casquets hove in sight and Giessler was able to check their position. The strong tidal current was helping them to make as much progress eastward as possible during darkness, and they were catching up with their schedule.

Although Group West kept sending out coded radio messages for guidance following the hold-up leaving Brest they were based on a two-hours' delay. The ships had already made up over an hour, but radio messages picked up made Ciliax realize that the command posts on land were still reckoning the ships to be behind schedule. At dawn swarms of fighters were due and they must not miss the battleships. So he decided to send a message to give the Luftwaffe an exact 'fix'.

He ordered a destroyer to sail towards shore and transmit

radio signals giving the Battle Squadron's correct position. The location of the destroyer when it sent its coded radio message would baffle British direction-finding apparatus. It was not picked up. The British radio still remained quiet.

One of the German radio monitors listening in on British wavelengths reported shortwave telephone conversations between patrol boats in Portland Bay and the Isle of Wight – nothing to worry about.

At 4 a.m. a disturbing signal came from one of the mine-sweeping flotilla, reporting a new mine barrier twenty miles south-west of Boulogne exactly across their course. There was no chance of dodging it as the areas on both sides of the swept channel were known to be filled with new and old mine-fields which had not been surveyed in recent months.

Commodore Ruge was sitting in an armchair in his Paris headquarters reading a Dorothy Sayers crime novel in English, which he had picked up in a local bookshop, when this information was signalled to him. He ordered that even if it risked his boats, the mine-sweeper commander must sweep a gap through the mine barrier in time for the battleships' arrival there just before dawn. It was the only order Ruge gave during the night.

Apart from the new mine scare nothing out of the ordinary happened from departure until sunrise – all went according to plan. As the night drew towards dawn German radio-intelligence monitors still reported no unusual radio communications from the British. This meant they had slipped through most of the Channel unobserved by the enemy. On board the morale of the crews was high.

At 6.13 a.m. the ships began transmitting course signals by the infra-red lamp which the British could not pick up. At 7.00 a.m. they passed Cherbourg. Daybreak was about forty minutes away.

At 7.11, as they were passing German-occupied Guernsey, they began picking up radio position signals which again proved completely useless; they were as wrong as those from the French coast.

At 7.16 in the darkness before dawn the loudspeakers shouted: *'Klarschiffzustand!'* – 'Clear for action.' *'Alle Mann auf Gefechtsstationen!'* – 'All hands to battle stations.'

The stars began to fade and the faint grey of dawn appeared.

In what the Germans call 'musket light' – the first glow of dawn – four German night-fighters were heard coming from a westerly direction astern of the ships. After firing off their recognition signals they took over protecting duties.

Watchful in the dawn twilight, Colonel Ibel, Luftwaffe liaison leader, was on the Admiral's bridge with Ciliax. Colonel Hentschel, controller of the fighters, was in the crow's nest. Colonel Elle was in the Air Communication Centre in constant touch with Ibel and Hentschel.

The shapes of the ships became clearer as the first of Galland's fighter planes roared overhead to begin their vigilant defence, which would not end until nightfall. Then the crews standing at battle-stations could distinguish the dark-painted German night-fighters with yellow belly rings circling overhead beneath the clouds.

A hazy sun rose and the sky began to show a high, thin cover of clouds travelling fast to the north-east. The Germans noted with satisfaction that this was the first indication of an approaching storm.

The question, *'Hat der Tommy Kenntnis von unserer Absicht?'* – 'Does Tommy know what we're up to?' – was on everyone's lips. They had been steaming unmolested up the English Channel for nearly eleven hours. Surely 'Tommy' knew they were there? Every man stood to his post tense and expectant waiting for the British dawn attack.

4

Three RAF Patrols

The Germans had sailed so far undetected because the RAF
night patrols had all missed them.

Coastal Command, which had the task of watching the
Channel for the German ships, kept a dusk-to-dawn watch using
relays of Hudsons fitted with rudimentary radar called ASV
Mark II. The Channel patrol Hudsons had forward-looking
antennae capable of detecting the presence of large ships up to
thirty miles away. By the end of 1941, 94 per cent of all night
sightings came from this radar. But it was still not more than 50
per cent efficient.

Equipped with this radar, three overlapping dusk-to-dawn
air patrols flew every night between Brest and the Straits of
Dover. The most vital of these was the westerly one, called
'Stopper', which covered the coastline from Brest to Ushant.
The second, known as 'Line SE', patrolled from Ushant to the
north-east corner of Brittany. The third, 'Habo', extended from
Le Havre to Boulogne.

Their interlinked patrols over the Channel formed one continuous search pattern, which meant in theory that if one plane
failed to detect the German ships there was a very good chance
another patrol would spot them. To make these patrols effective,
intensive crew training was needed and this had not reached as
high a standard as it should have.

At 6.27 p.m. on 11 February, a Hudson commanded by Flt-Lt
C. L. Wilson of 224 Squadron took off from the darkened RAF
station at St Eval, Cornwall, as patrol 'Stopper'. It was such a
black night that Wilson could hardly see his wing-tips. On such
a night, visual reconnaissance was impossible, and he had to

rely entirely on radar for his patrol over Brest and the tip of the Breton peninsular.

At 7.17 p.m., while flying at 1,000 feet near Ushant, a German JU-88 flew near, almost colliding with Wilson's Hudson. As he dodged away from the German night-fighter, his crew hastily switched off the radar. But when they turned it on again it was dead. The crew, Sergeants George Thomas, G. Cornfield and R. Cooke, tried to make it work but they could not. At 7.40 p.m., as his radar was still out of action, Wilson decided to return to base.

When he landed at St Eval, technicians tried for forty minutes to repair the radar breakdown. They looked for some obscure fault, but it was eventually found to be a blown fuse. As the ground crews did not find it quickly, Wilson was ordered to take over another Hudson to resume his patrol. This aircraft refused to start. Another fifty minutes passed before they found the cause of this trouble – a damp plug. By the time it was discovered, a third Hudson commanded by Sq.-Ldr G. Bartlett had taken off to resume 'Stopper' patrol.

While they were wrestling with a blown fuse and a damp plug at St Eval, Brest remained unwatched for three hours. Wilson went off patrol at 7.40 p.m. It was 10.38 p.m. before Bartlett arrived over Brest. The German ships had sailed over an hour before.

At 2 a.m., Bartlett saw an orange light astern which he thought was probably a German night-fighter and dived away from it towards the sea. By this time the German battleships were over 100 miles eastwards along the English Channel.

Twenty-one minutes after 'Stopper' took off – at 6.48 p.m. – another Hudson commanded by Flt-Lt G. S. Bennett took off on 'Line SE' patrol. He arrived over his patrol area between Brest and Le Havre at 7.40 p.m., the same moment as Wilson in 'Stopper' decided to return.

Bennett also found his radar equipment had broken down. He remained on patrol for ninety minutes while the crew tried to repair the radar, but it was so dark there was no effective reconnaissance over this period. At 9.13 p.m., Bennett decided it could not be repaired so he broke radio silence to report and the aircraft was ordered to return. When he landed the fault turned out to be an obscure one, which three weeks later was still under investigation.

Bennett's plane was not replaced. This was a vital mistake. It was a quarter of an hour after midnight when the battleships steamed past Ushant into the 'Line SE' patrol area. They continued to steam through 'Line SE' patrol area for most of the night, and if a relief aircraft had been sent it might have flown right over them. If it had not been for this double failure of radar, one of the Hudsons would almost certainly have spotted the battleships.

The third patrol, *Habo*, which covered the Le Havre–Boulogne area until dawn, was a responsibility of 223 Squadron based on Thorney Island. Sergeant Smith and Sergeant Watt, who went on patrol between 12.32 a.m. and 5.54 a.m. only reported 'White light seen off Barfleur'. From 3.55 a.m. to 7.15 a.m., the second 'Habo' plane with Flying Officer Alexander and Sergeant Austen was on patrol.

The mist was very heavy over this part of the Channel, and the Station Controller feared it might turn into fog and they would be unable to land. So he ordered Alexander to make only two circuits and return. This brought the patrol to an end an hour earlier than usual.

Once again a gap was left in the British air-guard. Had the patrol been maintained until dawn its radar might have picked up the German battleships steaming off Le Havre. As it was, when the battleships reached the 'Habo' line, the aircraft had left an hour before. When Alexander returned, he reported, 'Duty performed. Nothing sighted.'

The British defence line, which included a submarine and three air patrols stretching from Brest along the Channel to Boulogne, had been pierced repeatedly by the Germans. This was not due to their own skill. It happened because of an awesome mixture of bad weather, bad luck, and inefficiency on the part of RAF Coastal Command.

The German ships, as they steamed towards the Straits of Dover, were approaching weapons which might prove formidable or even decisive – the big coastal guns.

When the British Expeditionary Force departed amid civilian

cheers for France, no one envisaged the day would come when heavy guns would fire across the English Channel. Then came 1940 – and Dunkirk.

After the fall of France, the Germans lost no time in bringing heavy guns into the Pas de Calais. These German guns were not taken from the Maginot Line as was rumoured. They were 8-inch and 11-inch mobile railway guns. Old-fashioned and not very accurate, they did little damage – but they dominated the narrow straits. They had three main objectives – to defend the French coast, fire on British shipping and harass the coast of Kent with shell-fire. Their secondary function was to prepare for the invasion of Britain.

Churchill had strong views about meeting the challenge of these German heavy guns. While the last details of Operation Sealion – the invasion of Britain – were being studied by Nazi generals, Churchill ordered heavy guns to be mounted on the Dover cliffs as soon as possible.

On 10 June 1940, a week after Dunkirk, at a meeting between Fourth Sea Lord Vice-Admiral Sir Bruce Fraser and Vickers-Armstrong executives, it was decided to proceed immediately to mount two 14-inch guns at Dover. They were naval guns destined for the new-type battleships, the *King George V* class. As they fired 1,590-lb shells and had a range of 48–50,000 yards, they could easily control the Calais–Boulogne area.

Two days later, a thousand 14-inch shells were delivered to the Navy. At the same time, the Director of Operations, Captain J. Leach, who later went down commanding the *Prince of Wales*, chose a site for the first gun. It was a mile inland from St Margaret's Bay at Cliffe. Two 50-ton and one 45-ton railway cranes, the largest in Britain, were used to mount the gun.

Churchill insisted upon the elaborate camouflage of a tubular steel network with string netting and interlaced coloured steel wool to protect the gun. The Germans were not deceived. From their side of the Channel they interestedly watched the gun being mounted. At this time, the invasion of Britain was a serious intention and one of the first German objectives must be to knock out the Channel guns. They did not know, however, that on 3 August 1940, Churchill visited the first 14-inch naval gun position, manned by Royal Marines, which was promptly dubbed 'Winnie'.

On 15 August Junkers dive-bombed 'Winnie's' gun site. They did little damage, but it was a curtain-raiser for the Battle of Britain. At that time 'Winnie' was not quite operational, but a week later Lt-Col. H. D. Fellowes fired 'Winnie's' first round. It was the first shell ever to be fired across the English Channel from a gun located in Britain. It burst within 300 yards of a German battery at Cap Gris Nez. Two more followed, but then the artillery spotter plane was attacked by 50 Nazi fighters, and it was ordered back to base.

While the two 14-inch guns were being made ready, Churchill rightly insisted that they were not enough, saying, 'We must control the Dover Straits.' But where were other big guns to be found?

In July, Colonel Stewart Montague Cleave, an expert on super-heavy railway guns from World War 1, gave the answer. He discovered four 13·5-inch World War 1 guns in an ordnance depot near Nottingham. They came from the old *Iron Duke* class battleships and their gun-barrels, weighing 97 tons, were covered in cobwebs. Their 1,400-lb shell was too heavy to reach targets in Calais, but if they fired a lighter 1,250-lb shell it would give them a range of 40,000 yards – nearly as far as a 14-inch. Colonel Cleave recommended using these 13·5s on railway mountings. In the case of invasion, these guns could be rapidly moved by railway track from one place to another, and retire into a tunnel when not in use.

Impressed by their mobility and range, Churchill ordered them cleared of cobwebs and rushed to the Channel coast. One 13·5 was placed at Lydden Spout, another in a cutting outside Guston tunnel.

On 20 September 1940, only five weeks after 'Winnie' first fired at the Germans in the Pas de Calais, the first mobile gun, nicknamed 'Scene Shifter', was ready for action. Another one, 'Peacemaker' was ready on 27 November 1940.

On 8 February 1941, the second 14-inch naval gun, sited behind St Margaret's village and inevitably nicknamed 'Pooh', was operational. The other two 13·5 railway guns, 'Gladiator' and 'Bochebuster', were ready on 8 May 1941.

70

By the spring of 1941, these six clumsy, slow-firing guns were the only heavy armament on the English side of the Dover Straits. They were fairly useless. The four railway guns were difficult to load and bring to bear – and 'Winnie' and 'Pooh' could only fire at five-minute intervals against fixed targets in France. All six guns could only reach the German batteries in the Pas de Calais by firing super-charged naval ammunition. This meant that after eighty rounds a new barrel was needed, and the three largest cranes in England had once again to be called in to lift it into position. As this complicated, lengthy operation could easily be observed by the Germans on the French coast, it needed a Cabinet decision before it was carried out.

These difficulties meant the guns were not fired much. In addition, to shell France indiscriminately was considered a futile and unfriendly gesture to a defeated ally. The Germans, of course, had no such inhibitions. Without provocation, their heavy batteries used systematically to shell Folkestone, Dover, Ramsgate and occasionally Deal. Whenever the British guns did shell across the Straits, they always replied at once. That is why the town clerks of those four towns were always warned before the British opened fire to give out a double-siren warning of German shells, which would soon arrive.

The situation was unsatisfactory and perilous. Obviously, faster-firing, longer-ranging, more modern guns were urgently needed. In September 1940, it was decided to construct three new batteries in the Dover area. They included batteries of 6-inch anti-convoy guns at Fan Bay with a range of 25,000 yards. When they were ready in February 1941, the 540 Coast Regiment, commanded by Lt-Col. J. H. Richards, was formed to man the new guns.

Then South Foreland battery with four 9·2s was formed. The guns had a range of 31,000 yards and their rate of fire was one round per minute, compared with the five minutes of the old-fashioned 14-inch guns. When the South Foreland heavy guns were ready at the end of October 1941, it was planned to place a third and heavier battery of 15-inch guns at Wanstone Farm.

The Germans also replaced their guns on the other side of the

Channel. In June 1941, when the Russian war started, the German mobile guns were withdrawn to be replaced by heavy guns of Coast Artillery regiments in concrete emplacements. There was the *Batterie Lindemann*, with three 16-inch guns taken from the captured French battleship *Jean Bart*. They fired armour-piercing shells, which could penetrate 50 feet before exploding. The other two batteries were *Batterie Todt* with three 15-inch guns, and the *Batterie Grossekurfurst*, with four 11-inch guns.

All the German batteries were active and most troublesome. Whenever a British battery fired at German shipping trying to scuttle through the Straits, German shells began to land in Kent less than five minutes afterwards. They seemed to have their guns permanently loaded.

There was no secrecy about the positions of the German guns. The British knew where all of them were. On fine days, gunners like Albert Mister, attached to a British 6-inch gun anti-convoy battery at Fan Bay, watched through their field-glasses while the Germans built gun emplacements across the Channel.

From their daily reconnaissance flights, German Intelligence also knew the exact position of all the British batteries. To deceive the German pilots, dummy guns made of lathe and plaster were placed near the new guns. They failed in their purpose. One day a German plane came over and derisively dropped a wooden bomb on them.

The 15-inch Wanstone battery was not ready* and the six old-fashioned heavy guns were far too slow against moving targets – except for a thousand-to-one lucky shot. If the ships hugged the French coast, the fast-firing six-inch British guns could not reach them.

The only dangerous guns were the 9·2s at South Foreland. As with everything else in this operation, this peril depended on whether the British had sufficient warning. With good advance information, their four 9·2 guns in the narrow Straits might be able to lay down an arc of fire to damage or disable

* It was not until May 1942 that the third battery, the 15-inch guns called after Wanstone Farm, which were capable of reaching the French coast, were ready. And it was not until August 1942 that there was a combined action with the 9·2s and 15-inch guns firing together.

the ships enough for them to be finished off by the Navy or the RAF.

As they approached the Straits the German Captains had one great fear – was there any possibility that their reconnaissance might be proved wrong? Did the British have extra heavy long-range batteries hidden, which could turn the Dover passage into a cauldron of fire?

5

A Group Captain Obeys Orders

Just after eight o'clock it was raining in the English Channel, but the wind was moderate and the sea fairly calm. The German warships, at sea for more than ten hours, had covered 250 miles and were only fifteen minutes behind their planned timetable. Speeding at nearly thirty knots, which they had maintained most of the night, the battleships were almost exactly where they should be, in spite of the failure of their radar aids to navigation.

No one had detected them yet. So far the bluff had succeeded. The Admiralty in London remained blissfully convinced that the battleships were still in Brest.

Just after dawn, the German ships were off Barfleur and had almost caught up on their timetable. It was colder up-Channel than it had been at Brest but there was some February sunshine. The morning wore on with little incident. The official camera-man filmed shipboard scenes in the intervals of bright sun-light. The gun crews had a meal of lentil soup and sausage and coffee.

They knew it would be their last hot meal for a long time. One problem to which the planning staff had paid great attention was victualling for the lengthy period at battle-stations. As the two cooks detailed for service during action could not prepare warm meals, concentrated rations were deposited at each combat station, to be opened only on orders. For the German planners knew that combat excitement, with its physical over-exertion, can be best removed by small repeated amounts of food. The ships' doctors went round distributing slabs of chocolate and vitamin tablets.

Everyone remained tense. For the crews of all the big ships now understood why Luftwaffe staff officers and additional A.A.

crews had embarked before sailing. The decks and even the coverings of the gun turrets bristled with flak guns.

The state of tension was revealed when *Scharnhorst* repeatedly made short smoke screens and shot off ranging shots in different directions. As no RAF aircraft of any kind was in sight, the reason for this was not perceptible to the other ships. When Captain Fein of *Gneisenau* made a semaphore signal to the *Scharnhorst* inquiring why, Ciliax replied: 'We are doing it for the protection of the Squadron.' But there was still no sign of the RAF or the Royal Navy.

When the task force was off the mouth of the Somme – about forty miles from Dover – the night-fighters were replaced. They flew to Holland for refuelling, ready to guard the ships again in the evening. The fighter escort was taken over by Messerschmitt 109s.

The fact that the German ships were still steaming undetected in full daylight up the Channel was due to the failure of the RAF Coastal Command night patrols. This combination of bad luck and inefficiency was beginning to emerge as the pattern for the operation from the British side.

Now it was the turn of the day patrols. At dawn and dusk every day one Spitfire patrolled from Cap Gris Nez to Flushing, another from Cap Gris Nez to Le Havre. If they sighted anything important their orders were to maintain radio silence, return to base and report. The German battleships were nearing Dieppe when the Spitfires known as the 'Jim Crow' patrol took off.

Commanding 'Jim Crow', from 91 Squadron stationed at Hawkinge near Manston, was Sq. Ldr. Bobby Oxspring. His squadron's task was to cover the coastal ports and try to discover any overnight movements of ships. It was called the 'Milk Run'.

There was no liaison between Oxspring's squadron and the Coastal Command 'Habo' patrol, which came off patrol as dawn broke, to be relieved within minutes by 'Jim Crow' Spitfires. Neither was aware of each other's existence. But this lack of liaison had an even more serious aspect. Oxspring and his pilots had no knowledge of the code-word 'Fuller'. The RAF had become so security-minded that no one had told the 'Jim Crow' squadron that this was the warning code-message for the possible emergency of a German battleship dash through the Channel. It had been unofficially passed, often on the 'old boy net', to RAF controllers like Bill Igoe at Biggin Hill, Southern England's most important fighter base, but it appeared to be unknown to the duty officers at No. 11 Group at Uxbridge, which controlled the hundreds of fighter aircraft over southern England.

When the two 'Jim Crow' Spitfires went out as usual that morning, the Cap Gris Nez–Le Havre Spitfire spotted some fast-moving light craft leaving Boulogne. These were the German E-boats congregating to escort the battleships through the Straits of Dover. As he flew on towards Dieppe, clouds came right down on to the sea and as he could see nothing he returned to base. He did not know that the German battleships were steaming just behind the weather screen. Fifteen minutes later they appeared exactly where he had been patrolling.

The second Spitfire on the Flushing run only sighted seventeen small vessels off Zeebrugge, which looked like fishing smacks. Obeying orders to maintain radio silence during flight, both planes returned to base to report what they had seen.

This blanket radio silence appears inexplicable after the event. Yet there was a good reason for it. At that time big RAF fighter sweeps were being carried out daily over France. Hundreds of aircraft piloted by brave but young crews took part. If someone started talking over the radio, the German direction finders would soon pinpoint them at whatever height they were flying – whether at ground level or 15,000 feet – and attack. To avoid this, orders were given that everyone must be silent unless an emergency occurred.

It was upon the interpretation of what was an 'emergency' that much depended. Later that morning two RAF officers flying in Spitfires over the Channel were to put entirely different meanings on it.

When the two 'Jim Crow' Spitfires landed, British coastal radar stations were already registering numerous 'blips' which seemed to come from German aircraft constantly changing course.

But how many early radar warnings were ignored? David Jackson, a 23-year-old lance-bombardier, was in charge of a radar detachment in a wooden cabin perched on the tip of Beachy Head. For weeks their old M-set with bedstead aerials suffered from continual interference, which they called 'running rabbits and railings'. They were certain this persistent jamming was caused by the Germans. They switched off their old-fashioned M-sets and used the K-set, which they had had for only three months. It was a newer, more efficient short-wave radar, which the Germans did not know existed and therefore could not jam.

Just before dawn Jackson's detachment plotted something moving too fast for shipping, and assumed it to be a heavy movement of German aircraft over the Channel. After fifteen minutes the plot faded. Although being gunners their job was to look for ships only, they decided to advise the RAF about this unusual plot. They also reported it to Naval H.Q. at Newhaven. But as their report did not concern shipping, the Wren who answered the phone was not very interested. Neither was the RAF. This sort of situation occurred on many airfields and radar stations during the morning.

Aboard the German ships everything was peaceful. The weather was still fine and there was no sign of the British. The only problem was exact navigation. One of the officers said jokingly to Giessler, 'This could well be an instruction trip for quartermasters.' It was so quiet that the crews began to worry. Why were the British apparently doing nothing? Was it all a dreadful trap?

They did not know that all morning General Martini's electronic interference had almost completely deceived the British. Two specially equipped Heinkel-III aircraft had left Evreux, north of Paris, in complete darkness in advance of the fighters. Each had jamming equipment which could simulate twenty-five aeroplanes. Over the Channel, the recognizable search pulses of the British equipment were soon received on their cathode-ray tubes. When they switched on their jammers, British radar impulses wavered, altered their synchronized position and their amplitude, or changed occasionally to another frequency. The planes could follow these changes without difficulty.

Both jamming planes flew parallel to the English coast to give the British radar direction finders (RDFs) the impression that German planes were circling there. This was to distract attention from the night-fighters circling over the battleships. As the German warships passed the mouth of the Seine the British radar stations, holding on to the deceptive impulses, did not detect them.

Martini ordered his land-jamming installations strung along the French coast not to be switched on until 9 a.m. All known British RDF transmitters were each monitored by German groups, to which they were tuned in exactly. These stations knew precisely the behaviour of 'their' British transmitters.

They soon observed that several British transmitters began to alter their frequency in an attempt to avoid the jamming. Two switched off completely. Then suddenly a new station between Eastbourne and Dover, which had not been observed for several months, was tuned in. This was also jammed.

This was the first engagement in pure high-frequency war. Martini's plan was succeeding – but not completely. Although the British radar operators were confused by these counter-measures, at the same time the German computing centre at Boulogne picked up transmitters with seven to eight centimetre wavelengths. These were the new K-sets for which the Germans had no jammers.

British radar station K-set, located at Swingate, was beginning to report that several aeroplanes were circling over a group of ships sailing at a speed of about twenty-five knots. As a result of this report, and the accumulation of evidence about radar-jamming, the British began at last to suspect that there might be something special going on in the Channel. It remained a suspicion. They still had no confirmation.

At 8.25 a.m., when Wing-Cdr M. Jarvis, Senior Controller of the radar filter room at Fighter Command headquarters at Stanmore, West of London, came on duty, a number of plots of German aircraft were coming in from the British south coast radar network. The operations table at Fighter Command seemed to show them circling in a small area. Between 8.25 a.m. and 9.59 a.m., four plots appeared intermittently. Three seemed to indicate the presence of a single German aircraft – the fourth possibly two German aircraft.

No one took much notice. Plots like these were common over the Channel. They usually indicated aircraft circling over

78

coastal shipping, aircraft testing their guns or air-sea rescue planes.

At 8.24 a.m., Swingate RAF radar station located several small groups of German aircraft, flying at 3,000 feet, twenty-five miles to the north of Le Havre. They plotted them until 9.20 a.m., then again from 9.47 a.m. to 9.59 a.m. The plotters diagnosed the 'blips' as aircraft circling over ships steaming at about twenty-five knots.

They were Colonel Galland's early duty fighters, which had joined the ships at 7.50 a.m. If the pilots had obeyed orders Beachy Head would not have picked up their plots. Their orders called for very low flying to avoid radar detection. But it was not dawn until just after 8 a.m. on that foggy winter's morning, so the German fighters did not risk much wave-hopping – and Beachy Head detected them.

At 8.45 a.m. – twenty minutes after the first 'blips' were reported – Fighter Command talked to 11 Group about them. Jarvis was particularly interested in the Swingate plot, which showed a number of aircraft circling somewhere off Le Havre. He informed 11 Group, whose job was the protection of London and the south coast, that this was probably German aircraft escorting coastal shipping. There were also reports of interference, but as this had been experienced frequently recently he paid little attention to it.

When he discussed the radar reports with the duty controller of 11 Group at Hornchurch, they both agreed that there was 'Some sort of air-sea rescue operation going on out there'.

At 8.35 a.m. Vice-Admiral Bertram Ramsay, commanding the Channel from Dover Castle, 'stood down' his coastal forces from the critical before-dawn alert.

At 9.00 a.m. fourteen Coastal Command Beaufort torpedo bombers of 42 Squadron took off from Leuchars, heading for Coltishall in East Anglia. It was a precautionary flight, based on Coastal Command's estimate of a possible Channel break-out. They had first received the order to fly south four days before, but their flight had been delayed by blizzards and 'administrative difficulties'.

No one was seriously alarmed. There was no jamming yet. This was because Doctor Von Scholz, in charge of General

79

Martini's operation, was obeying the most stringent orders against any jamming until after 9.00 a.m., in case it gave the British a clue too early. This order was rigidly observed.

While the filter room at RAF Fighter Command Stanmore analysed these 'blips', a number of radar stations began to report intense jamming. This was Martini's plan coming into action. It continued intermittently for fifty minutes. Even when it became continuous English Channel radar stations still reported it as 'interference'.

The filter room at Fighter Command started receiving their reports from 9.25 onwards. During the next half-hour they discussed them with 11 Group. At 10.00 a.m., Jarvis, who had been receiving more continual plots of circling aircraft, decided that surface vessels were making their way up the Channel. Once more 11 Group dismissed the radar plot as 'possibly German aircraft exercising'.

Yet Biggin Hill, one of the fighter stations heavily involved in the battle, was not deceived. When Sq. Ldr Bill Igoe, the Controller, came on duty he noticed a series of circular radar plots moving out from the Cherbourg peninsula. It was Galland's fighters moving into position. The speed check he took showed the bigger 'blips' were moving at twenty-five knots. This meant that the aircraft were covering some shipping. As a convoy could not move at twenty-five knots, he concluded that they must be the *Scharnhorst* and *Gneisenau*.

This was the first evidence to suggest that the battleships were out. As the plots continued up the Channel, he rang 11 Group shortly after 8 a.m. and passed the alarm saying, 'I think it's "Fuller!"' He had the impression no one at the other end knew what the code-word meant. Uncertain of 11 Group's reaction, Igoe, on his own initiative, asked Oxspring at Hawkinge to take off to make a check. For even if it turned out to be a false alarm, it would be a good tactical exercise.

Shortly after 10 o'clock, just as the German night-fighters above the ships were handing over to the ME.109s, Igoe phoned Sq. Ldr Oxspring at Hawkinge and said, 'Look, Bobby, radar is showing a lot of German fighters in the Somme estuary. They seem to be going round in circles. At first we thought they were forming up for a sweep, but they still keep circling round.

I don't understand it. It looks as if they are protecting some shipping. Go and have a look. But be damned careful as there are a lot of Huns about.'

Whenever 91 Squadron expected trouble of this sort they flew in pairs. Sq Ldr. Oxspring took Sergeant Beaumont with him in a second Spitfire.

At 10.16 a.m., the RAF radar station at Swingate began to plot three big 'blips', indicating ships fifty-six miles away in the direction of Boulogne. The size of the 'blips' and the estimated distance indicated they were much bigger than anything ever before seen. But the only German ships of any size were locked up in Brest. Or were they?

The radar station commander, 31-year-old Flt-Lt Gerald Kidd, a solicitor in civilian life, suddenly asked, 'Are these the *Scharnhorst* and the *Gneisenau*?'

At the same time, other radar stations began picking up constant circular plots, which they identified as patrolling German E-boats. But they were in fact Galland's fighter umbrella circling over the German battleships.

It was 10.20 a.m. The German ships had been at sea for eleven hours undetected. Now at last Kidd had deduced the truth. When he carefully examined the reports, the size of the 'blips' absolutely convinced him that the German warships were approaching the Straits of Dover in daylight.

When Kidd tried to telephone a warning to Dover Castle, the GPO line was defective. Further attempts to call on the scrambler proved equally frustrating. Later investigation of the defective telephone revealed that both the GPO and the secret scrambler were plugged into the same line, so anyone in the area could eavesdrop on Swingate and Dover discussing top secret radar reports.

Just before Gerald Kidd saw the 'blips' on his radar near Dover, Group Captain Victor Beamish, one of the more dashing aces of the RAF, was looking at the weather report at Kenley fighter aerodrome. As it was too cloudy and misty for his new and inexperienced pilots to fly operationally, he thought it was going to be 'one of the quiet days of the war'. So he decided to take Wing-Cdr Finlay Boyd with him to do a two-man sweep 'just to keep things moving'.

At 10.10 a.m. they climbed into their Spitfires. Flying over the Channel twenty minutes later, they saw two Messerschmitts and climbed up to attack them. They had stumbled into the outer guard of Galland's air umbrella protecting the German battleships.

The Spitfires had discovered the ships at their most vulnerable moment. They were nearing the square on the chart in which there had been the new mine alarm during the night. The First Mine-Sweeping Flotilla under Lt-Cdr Bergelt, with only four boats, was still trying to clear them. As the big ships hove into view, they had just managed to produce a very narrow channel free of mines. Between 10.26 a.m. and 10.47 a.m., Bergelt's mine-sweepers with their gear out went ahead, while the ships followed them through the channel at only ten knots. During these twenty-one terrifying minutes they saw the Spitfires overhead.

At 10.30 a.m., Jarvis at Fighter Command became seriously worried about the heavy jamming, which he now decided might be deliberate. Were the Germans doing it to hide something coming up the Channel? When he suggested to Number 11 Group that they send off a special reconnaissance plane, they pointed out that twenty minutes before the 'Jim Crow' flight consisting of two Spitfires had taken off from Hawkinge. They did not know about Victor Beamish's trip over the Channel.

As the German ships were sailing slowly through the narrow swept channel, Oxspring and Beaumont flew between 1,200 and 1,800 feet in rain showers just below the heavy clouds, ready to nip into them if they encountered German fighters. Visibility was so poor it was hard to distinguish between cloud and sea.

At 10.40 a.m., Kidd from Swingate finally succeeded in telephoning his first warning to Dover by routing his call through Portsmouth. He was ordered to come to Dover Castle at once.

At the same moment, Oxspring and Beaumont dived through the clouds fifteen miles west of Le Touquet. They quickly nipped back into cloud as flak shells began to burst round them, and a dozen Messerschmitts raced towards them. They had arrived

82

over the E-boat screen. As they dodged the fighters, they sighted three big ships sailing close together. Oxspring and Beaumont thought they were British vessels, even though the ships kept firing at them as they seemed to be pointing straight at Dover. In the RAF view, the Royal Navy was notoriously trigger-happy after Dunkirk.

As Oxspring and Beaumont swung over the German convoy, with rain beating at their cockpit perspex and dimming their vision, they suddenly sighted two fighters beneath the clouds. They turned to attack them but as they closed to 500 yards on their tails, Oxspring saw to his astonishment red, white and blue roundels on their wings. He hastily called over the intercom to Beaumont, 'Don't fire, they're Spitfires!'

It was Group Captain Victor Beamish and Wing-Cdr Finlay Boyd. They had also seen three large warships steaming towards Dover. As they went down to have a better look, neither Beamish nor Boyd noticed the two other Spitfires above them, because flak began to burst around them as well and German fighters roared on to their tails. Oxspring and Beaumont watched their two Spitfires turn and dive down on the ships.

E-boats and destroyers threw up a tremendous screen of flak and more German fighters plummeted down towards Beamish and Boyd. To escape the pursuing Messerschmitts, they dived straight through the flak, and the German pilots did not try to follow them.

As they came lower, they saw two large ships with trident masts. Flying down to sea level to get a better look, they could see the bow waves curling over the foredecks of the battleships and their long lines of escorts.

On the bridge of the *Scharnhorst*, Admiral Ciliax watched the wave-hopping planes and said to Captain Hoffmann, 'This is the start of it. We are now discovered. The attack will come at any minute.'

As they were now out of the narrow mine-free lane, he ordered the battleships to increase speed to thirty knots. Mist and low cloud came drifting down over the Channel. It was bitterly cold and driving rain began to fall as the German gunners waited for the British attack. Why did it not come?

It should have, for this was the first piece of luck for the

British. By coincidence, four Spitfires had arrived together over the ships. Three of the pilots were experienced, high-ranking RAF officers and if they all identified them there could be no doubt.

Yet nothing happened. The main reason was that Beamish never thought to disobey the radio silence order. This was the supreme moment, when he should have ignored all the regulations and warned the British forces that the German ships were just about to begin their dash through the Straits of Dover. All he had to do was to switch on his radio and repeat the word 'Fuller' – and the whole of the British defences would have been alerted. But regulations said that radio silence should be observed on all operational flights. So with a wave to Boyd to follow him, he led the way back to Kenley preserving radio silence on the way.

His junior officer, Sq. Ldr Oxspring, was much more enterprising. Watching the other two Spitfires courageously dive into the thick flak, Oxspring instantly realized that such a large number of ships sailing so close to England must be protecting German battleships. As his job was reconnaissance, not fighting, he decided this was the moment to disobey orders, and break radio silence to warn the Biggin Hill controller. It was one of the most sensible decisions made that day. He did not know the code-word, as his senior officer Beamish did, but he flicked over his switch and gave his recognition phrase, 'Barman Blue Leader. Three large German ships, probably battle-cruisers, escorted by twenty-plus craft sailing off Le Touquet heading towards Dover.'

He then called to Beaumont, 'Get back to base,' and both planes headed for Hawkinge. The time was 10.35 a.m.

The Germans heard him. The German B-Dienst listening service picked up his message, and informed Col. Adolf Galland at Le Touquet, that 'A British radio message reports a large German naval formation consisting of three capital ships and about twenty warships is steaming towards the Straits of Dover.'

At last the secret was out. The decision for giving the order to drop all attempts at disguising the operation lay with Galland. But he refused to be driven to rash measures by this alarming message. He continued to observe radio silence to keep the operation hidden from the British.

For he suspected that the RAF would not believe one lone message. The wisdom of his decision was proved by the fact that the first counter-measures were not taken by the British command for another hour. Galland says, 'It appears the British gave no credence to the reports. They simply sent up another reconnaissance plane and ordered a full alert. An hour later, the second aircraft brought confirmation of the feat which had been regarded as impossible.'

Meanwhile Oxspring and Beaumont were racing back to base. It only took them eight minutes to return to Hawkinge from over the German fleet. When Beaumont climbed out of his cockpit, he said thoughtfully to Oxspring, 'You know, before I became a pilot I used to be in the RAF marine craft section on the Solent. I am certain one of those ships is the *Scharnhorst*. I saw her at a pre-war review. I recognize her superstructure.'

Oxspring was immediately called to the phone in the briefing hut, where Controller Bill Igoe asked, 'What's all this, Bobby?' He told him the story – not the least puzzling feature being the presence of two other unknown Spitfires, which no one could account for.

Igoe, who had been convinced for hours the German battleships were coming up the Channel, but no one had taken any notice, suggested Oxspring get on the phone to tell 11 Group at once. He said he would listen-in so as not to waste time repeating his information. While Oxspring was telephoning 11 Group, the Intelligence Officer sent for a book of silhouettes of German ships. The man sent on his bicycle to bring the silhouette book stopped at the NAAFI for a cup of tea on his way back, wasting another precious fifteen minutes. When he did arrive Beaumont leafed through the recognition book until he came to *Scharnhorst*.

'That's the ship I saw,' he said emphatically. He was certain that his memory of the tripod mast and superstructure of the *Scharnhorst* was correct. The only doubt was that as visibility had been obscured by rain, he did not have a very clear view. In spite of the fact his identification was almost certain most people, except Igoe, tended to discount Beaumont's theory.

When Oxspring and Igoe tried to speak personally to the Air officer commanding 11 Group, Air Vice-Marshal Trafford Leigh-Mallory, they discovered he was at Northolt reviewing Belgian air force units, and his staff officers would not interrupt him. The attitude of 11 Group was, 'We are not going to bother the AOC. You saw some fishing boats. Send out another recce.'

More and more convinced that it was the *Scharnhorst*, both Igoe and Oxspring asked for a message to be passed at once to Leigh-Mallory. When he was told that he was on parade and not available, Oxspring said, 'I suggest you tell him. He'll be livid if he's not told.' But no one did.

While they were frantically trying to pass a message to Leigh-Mallory, Beamish and Boyd were flying back to Kenley – much farther away than Hawkinge. As they preserved radio silence, another thirty-five minutes passed before they could confirm Oxspring's sighting.

Beamish landed at Kenley at 11.10 a.m., and also immediately tried to get on the telephone to Leigh-Mallory to tell him the news. He too was unsuccessful, but he told Biggin Hill. A few minutes later Igoe came back on the phone to Oxspring and said, 'Group Captain Beamish with Wing-Cdr Boyd were in the other two Spitfires. They confirm what you say. It *is* the *Scharnhorst*.' At the same time, other evidence was building up. Five minutes after Flt-Lt Kidd had managed to phone Dover via Portsmouth, the radar at Fairlight just east of Hastings picked up two big ships at 67,000 yards in the vicinity of Boulogne. This was a record for that type of set – and it confirmed Kidd's plot.

When this report reached Wing-Cdr Bobby Constable-Roberts, Air Liaison officer on Admiral Ramsay's staff, whose job was to keep in constant touch with Fighter Command's Number 11 Group and Coastal Command's 16 Group, he picked up the telephone and asked 11 Group for a special reconnaissance over the Boulogne area. Number 11 again refused, saying it was unnecessary. Constable-Roberts then telephoned to warn 16 Group at Thorney Island saying, 'It might be our friends out in the Channel.'

He suggested that the Beaufort Squadron at St Eval, and 42 Squadron on its way from Leuchars to Coltishall, should be alerted and ordered to fly directly to Manston. But he had no authority to order it.

At 11.05 a.m., although the RAF and the Navy were still unconvinced these were the German battleships, Constable-Roberts telephoned Manston and told Lt-Cdr Eugene Esmonde to put his six Swordfish on readiness. This was the first decisive step taken by the British armed forces to intercept the *Scharnhorst* and *Gneisenau*'s daring dash. It was made by a junior Wing Commander.

At 11.30 a.m., when the coast-watching radar set at Lydden Spout between Dover and Folkestone, picked up a plot at a range of 46,000 yards, Beamish was trying again to reach Leigh-Mallory, who was still unavailable. Three times a staff officer came to the phone, and each time Beamish refused to talk to him. It was nearly another half-hour before Leigh-Mallory eventually came to the phone. He was in a very bad temper at being pestered personally on the phone by a mere Group Captain – he was a very rank-conscious officer – but he began to listen carefully when Beamish confirmed Sergeant Beaumont's identification. Only then was Leigh-Mallory convinced and the RAF issued a signal: 'Group-Captain Beamish was with "Jim Crow" so there is no doubt.' It was 11.35 a.m. An hour had passed since Oxspring had radioed his first urgent warning from over the German ships in the Channel.

At the same time, Dover Command was officially informed of the break-out by telephone from the Admiralty War Room. Immediately, Constable-Roberts asked Number 11 Group for fighters to protect the Swordfish. Then he rang Esmonde at Manston and told him what he had done. Victor Beamish also telephoned from Kenley to the Manston commander, Tom Gleave, saying, 'It's "Fuller", Tom!'

Although the day had started out with some sunshine, it turned progressively to cloud and rain as the German ships raced up the mine-free lane in the Channel. They were approaching the Straits of Dover and still the British had taken no measures to stop them. Navigator Giessler aboard *Scharnhorst* looked at his synchronized watch. It showed 11.45 a.m. Galland was still maintaining wireless silence. So messages could not be sent between the ships and the Luftwaffe pilots. A flag that now began to fly constantly on the ships was the yellow square flag of the aircraft alarm signal, billowing against a grey sky alive with patrolling Luftwaffe fighters.

By noon they were off Cap Gris Nez, and tracked constantly by British radar, they were entering the narrowest part of the Straits. Up to now they had only had a glimpse of the RAF and there was still no sign of the Royal Navy. On the bridge of *Scharnhorst* the unspoken question was: What about the British heavy guns guarding the Straits? Although it was difficult to hit a battleship sailing at thirty knots, it was not impossible. Shore batteries firing armour-piercing shells could cripple the biggest ship if they had enough warning – but Martini's German jamming and bad RAF reconnaissance had made sure the British did not receive it.

The German squadron was now a most formidable armada. The protecting destroyers *Richard Bietzen, Jacobi, Friedrich Ihn, Hermann Schoemann* of flotilla 229, and six destroyers of 225 flotilla, sailed ahead of the main force. As the German battle-squadron arrived off Cap Gris Nez, a force of little ships joined them. The Second and Third and Eighth Torpedo Boat flotillas steamed up with five boats each. With them came the Second, Fourth and Sixth E-boat flotillas.

At 12.15 p.m., exactly according to their timetable, they arrived at the narrowest part of the Channel between Dover and Cap Gris Nez, where the British should be waiting to sink them with massive air-sea attacks and coastal gun barrages. Through gaps in the mist, they saw the English coast and began to catch an occasional glimpse of barrage balloons. Then the white cliffs of Dover came into view and they could plainly see the framework of the radar antennae.

The first officer, Cdr Ernst Dominik, who had been on board the *Scharnhorst* ever since she was commissioned, waited for reports from every department of the ship. All the crews stood to, manning guns, waiting by boilers and engines. Others stood ready for damage and fire control. Every man of the 1,900 aboard *Scharnhorst*, the leading battleship, was expecting action.

Admiral Ciliax stood on the bridge gazing into the mist, with the collar of his heavy sheepskin coat turned up and his big Zeiss glasses hanging on their leather slings around his neck.

Broad-shouldered Captain Kurt Hoffmann sat on the little emergency seat next to him, also wrapped in a sheepskin coat with a thick scarf wound several times round his neck.

Acting Chief Petty Officer Willi Goode stood at his director column at the side of the bridge with his night optical lenses which were also useful for day look-out. His telephone apparatus was slung around his neck ready for instant communication with all the ships' commanders.

Little was to be heard above the slap of the waves as *Scharnhorst* bounced through the narrow Straits at top speed. There was the occasional slam of a water-tight door, or the clatter of heavy boots down companionways. The faint regular hum of the electric generators spread through the stillness of the control positions and gun turrets. Everyone was conscious that at any minute the alarm might sound, and the silent ship would be suddenly transformed into a fire-belching monster.

To ease the tension, Admiral Ciliax pulled a packet of cigarettes from his sheepskin coat pocket and gave one to Captain Hoffmann. Tall, blond Chief Quartermaster Jurgens stepped forward to offer them a light. Inhaling deeply, the Admiral thanked him and offered him a cigarette.

Another officer remarked to Giessler, 'It's still like a practice cruise.' Giessler nodded, as he checked their position on the chart. He indicated with his pencil, '*Hier, Herr Kapitän.*' Hoffmann checked it and showed it to Ciliax adding, '*Jawoh!, Herr Admiral.*'

They were nearly past the cliffs of Dover. Quietness still reigned. Why were the British so silent? They had almost come to believe they were to force the Straits unmolested, when there came a flash and a bang from the haze and a single shell fell harmlessly into the grey-green Channel behind them, a mile to port of the last ship, *Prinz Eugen.*

Although their intelligence reported the British guns were not so formidable, naturally Admiral Ciliax and his captains remained doubtful. They based their fears on their own batteries of 15-inch and 16-inch guns emplaced in the Calais area. So when the first shell splashed into the sea astern of *Prinz Eugen,* the Germans braced themselves for a ferocious bombardment from the heaviest British coastal guns.

6

The Channel Guns Open Up

Just before midday 22-year-old Auxiliary Territorial Service private Nora Smith was sitting in a café in Dover's Market Square eating egg and chips. She was one of the eight ATS girls who for the past three weeks had been in the process of taking over the Dover Castle plotting room operation from the men.

Channel operations were directed from Dover Castle. A rabbit-warren of a place, standing high over the harbour, it was the command post and nerve-centre of the Channel war. It was commanded by Vice-Admiral Bertram Ramsay, who had Bobby Constable-Roberts as his RAF liaison officer and Captain Day as Navy liaison officer. Also under his command was Brigadier Raw, who was in charge of the coastal artillery.

Nora Smith and the other girls slept and ate underground and sometimes a week went past without their seeing daylight. Due on the afternoon shift in Dover Castle starting at 1 p.m., she was enjoying a much-needed morning off when the double-siren went off giving warning of imminent shelling.

At this period of the war shell warnings were almost a daily occurrence in Dover. Six times in succession she had tried to see *Gone With the Wind* at the local cinema and each time there had been a shell warning. During them everyone was supposed to stay put. As they often lasted a long time Nora Smith's one idea was to get back to report for duty.

As Ciliax's battleships began steaming through the narrowest part of the Channel, Nora Smith left her meal unfinished and started running up the hill towards the Castle. Normally it took nearly half an hour to walk that mile-long steep slope. This time she did it in ten minutes.

She found the morning-shift ATS girls at the plotting table

busily marking the position of the German battleships on the grid maps with chinagraph pencils. Although different plots came in from radar every three minutes the girls working at the large table were not sure what they were plotting. All they knew was that something very big was coming through the Channel. Some of them thought it might be the start of the invasion. Although the morning-shift girls were shortly due for relief they kept on plotting and could not be interrupted. So Nora Smith decided to make herself useful and went off to bring them cups of tea.

The place was in an uproar. The ten-line switchboard was completely jammed and everyone was shouting at once. Six or seven doors were flung open – a thing no one had ever seen before as most of them led to secret rooms. High-ranking officers darted in and out. Others rushed to the windows to look out to sea. All anyone could see was a swirling mist.

Admiral Ramsay kept dashing from his own room to the plotting room where the girls were working. Often hurrying people fell over the Admiral's two bulldogs.

Much of this confusion was caused by the primitive communication arrangements at Dover Castle. The Army plotting room, which directed the coastal guns, was five minutes' walk on the other side of the Castle from the Naval operations room. There was no direct telephone line and everything had to be channelled through signals. If signals were busy, this led to a delay. If a secret message came over the teleprinter in code, messengers had to walk with it as fast as they could through the tunnels to Naval H.Q., which caused further hold-ups.

Also there was very little co-operation between the three services. For instance, although Flt-Lt Kidd's RAF radar at Swingate was better equipped than the coastal gunners, it could not transmit any information direct to them. Some of the girls even had maps with the grids wrongly placed. One officer complained of this but no one took any notice of him.

In the middle of this confusion at Dover Castle sat Brigadier Cecil Whitfield Raw, studying the first radar reports. A former accountant who had risen as a Territorial to the highest rank normally available to a non-regular, he was the Commander of 12 Corps Coastal Artillery.

In spite of General Martini's attempt to jam the British radar sets totally, they were now plotting the battleships' course accurately. These were the K-sets which had displaced the M-sets, and their longer wavelengths – since the shorter the wavelength the greater the accuracy.

The South Foreland battery had a K-type radar set which had just been installed. As its 'blips' continued to track the battleships, Admiral Ramsay told Raw to 'Engage when ready'. Raw gave a 'Take post' order to South Foreland's four 9·2s – the only guns capable of engaging the battleships. They were all he had. The much-needed 15-inch battery at Wanstone was not yet completed and the 14-inch guns were useless for this type of target. Although they could reach the ships, they were not tied to the control system and with their slow rate of traverse they could not keep up with a speeding battleship. At their rate of fire, there would only be time for each 14-inch gun to fire one round on a predetermined position – and it was a million-to-one chance that they would hit anything.

Nor was Raw too optimistic about the 9·2 guns' contribution to the action. For they had not completed their first firing practices. Also it was the first time they – or any other guns – had ever been fired by radar control. As he waited for the moment to open fire, Brigadier Raw also thought that the 9·2s firing at their extreme range of 34,000 yards – twenty-two miles – might not have much effect against the heavy armour of the great ships.

On this misty, cold morning the 9·2 Battery was doing practice drills. The plotting officer, Second Lt Dennis Hagger, a wholesale grocer in civilian life, was in his operations post on the cliffs by the South Foreland lighthouse. For two weeks, he and his fellow gunner officers had been hearing rumours that the German battleships were going to try and force a passage through the Channel. The rumours were so persistent that officers, not wishing to miss their first chance of firing their heavy guns in anger, cancelled their leave. But it had begun to look very like the cry of 'Wolf'. So when a klaxon sounded giving Brigadier Raw's signal for action stations, Hagger thought it was a false alarm. Telling his gunners to continue their practice drill session, he picked up the telephone and queried the order with his battery commander, Major Guy Huddlestone, who barked, 'This is the real thing. Take post!'

It was three minutes after noon. The *Scharnhorst* and her sister ships were 32,000 yards away from the South Foreland battery when the gunners' fire control post reported, 'Ready for Action'.

At 12.10 p.m. their K-type radar showed the battleships 27,000 yards away coming up towards Cap Gris Nez. The clear 'blips' on the battery's radar showed their course and estimated speed as twenty-two knots – eight knots below their real speed. As the battery radar was now clearly following the ships, Brigadier Raw gave the order to fire.

At 12.19 p.m. Huddlestone fired two shells. The flight of these heavy armour-piercing projectiles took fifty-five seconds. When they burst with a splash and a plume of yellowish-black smoke behind the third ship, *Prinz Eugen*, the battle of Dover had begun.

Everyone aboard the German ships waited tensely for the heavier attacks which they felt must come. Luckily for the Germans, the mist which had cleared for a brief interval, revealing a glimpse of the white cliffs of Dover, now closed again.

The German crews saw flashes from the cliffs and several splashes to port. Then came the crunch of more heavy shells bursting. Although their shots fell unevenly and short of the ships, it meant to the German commanders that there was no doubt at last they had been detected. As they steamed on through the narrowest part of the Channel, they began to swing violently on their course to baffle the British.

Brigadier Raw, looking through captured Italian binoculars, tried unavailingly to watch where their shells were landing. The weather was too thick to see anything from the cliffs but after a minute came the rumbling echo of the shells exploding. Like his Brigadier, Major Huddlestone, officer commanding the 9·2s, also tried to catch a glimpse of the battleships from his observation post. He too saw nothing but mist. As maximum visibility was less than five miles, Raw realized that the firing would have to be all done by radar. The problem that faced him was that there could be no observation of the 'fall of shot' by either sight or radar. For their radar could not indicate where their shells were landing.

Without seeing where they were falling, they could not make any accurate corrections. Were they on target? No one had fired heavy guns by radar before so it was difficult to know.

Martini's jamming, however, was not interfering with the K-sets and the echo of the battleships' course came in loud and clear. The K-sets began to track the German ships as they snaked to and fro. This looked as though the shells were landing near them.

Following the radar tracks, Huddlestone fired two more shots at 12.23 p.m. At 12.28 p.m., after another two shells had been fired and their explosions unobserved, Raw ordered Major Huddlestone to start firing full-battery four-gun salvoes without waiting for fall-of-shot reports.

A minute later came the crash of the first four shells fired together. A second salvo was fired at 12.30 p.m. Out of the mist came the rumble of heavy shells landing, but they were not followed by louder explosions indicating a hit. As it looked as though they were still missing the battleships, Raw ordered, 'Add 1,000 yards to the range.'

At 12.31 p.m., just as they were about to fire at this new range for the first time, extra 'blips' showed faintly on the screen. Radar had managed to pick up the second salvo landing. These 'blips' clearly showed their shells were still falling short of the ships, so Raw shouted down the phone to Huddlestone, 'Add another 1,000 yards.'

When this fourth salvo was fired, one of the new faint radar echoes showed a stronger 'blip' which seemed to indicate a shell hitting one of the ships. The gunners looked at each other questioningly. They knew if they had hit a ship in these difficult conditions it was a very lucky shot. Yet even if it had missed it must have landed very near, because clear 'blips' on the radar plot showed the German ships drastically altering course. The guns were now on target – but they only had about five minutes left before they were out of range.

Around midday, Corporal Ernest Griggs and his comrades of

'D' Company, the Royal Sussex Regiment, who had been on anti-invasion alert for three weeks, marched along the snow-covered cliffs carrying their tommy-guns to the Green Blinds café at St Margaret's Bay not far from the 14-inch naval guns, 'Winnie' and 'Pooh'.

Just as they sat down and ordered cups of tea, there came a nerve-shaking crash as two 9·2 guns opened fire. Peering through the wide sun-trap windows of the café they saw their shells spinning through the air like balls of fire. When the four guns of the 9·2 battery began firing at once, making the air tremble and deafening the troops with the noise, someone shouted above the din, 'The guns are practising again!' Griggs replied, 'No, they are not! They are firing full charge.' Neither he nor the rest of 'D' Company had any idea of what was happening – except they knew it could not be an invasion, because as first-line infantry they would have been alerted.

Then came a different noise as shells whined over the café to land on the farmland behind St Margaret's Bay. The German cross-Channel batteries had joined in the gun battle, aiming at the South Foreland batteries. Their shooting was as inaccurate as the British coastal guns. Six German shells fell 200–300 yards apart in a straight line near the 9·2s, plopping into soft chalk. Others churned up mud on the snowy ground, but they did not make much of a crater. No one at the South Foreland battery was hurt nor any gun damaged.

At 12.35 p.m., half a dozen more German shells exploded on the farmland near the 9·2s. They were answered a minute later by four shells from South Foreland.

As the battleships were now moving out of the extreme limit of the guns' range of 34,000 yards and radar had not echoed the fall of the last three salvoes, Raw ordered the guns to cease fire.

He and his gunners thought they had been aiming at the leading battleship, *Scharnhorst*, so Raw ordered them to try and pick up the second and third ships in the convoy. Although their radar set succeeded in following the ship they had been firing at to a range of 65,000 yards, they failed to find any new targets within range. This was because their shells had been landing near the last ship *Prinz Eugen* – not the first.

The radar could not locate any further targets so the 9·2s did not fire again. The salvo fired at 12.36 p.m. was their last.

The Germans kept up their bombardment. They fired two more salvoes at 12.50 and 12.52 p.m., which burst harmlessly in the snow-covered fields of Kent. Then they also ceased fire.

At the end of the gun duel Brigadier Raw reported, 'This was the first action against German vessels forcing their way through the Straits. The ships, protected by their heavy armour, sailing at thirty knots, were neither sunk nor halted.'

Neither Brigadier Raw nor his officers caught a glimpse of the battleships they were firing at. It was the first action in which long-range guns were directed to their target by radar. As a result, they had to make up their own procedure as they went along – and a lot of it was guesswork.

Brigadier Raw said, 'The action was the first to be fought by new radar equipment, directed by an untried method of fire control still in the experimental stage. In seventeen minutes thirty-three rounds were fired, three of which were possible near-misses and an RAF pilot reported that one ship had been hit. The only matter for regret was that the 15-inch guns of Wanstone Battery were not ready to fire.'

Although the 9·2 battery had failed to halt the German ships, their performance had been satisfactory. If they had had a little more warning, they might have been much more effective.

The rest of the British coastal guns remained silent. The task of 6-inch batteries was to fire on German convoys coming through the Channel or prevent an attack on Dover Harbour. They were 'tight' guns, which meant they could not fire without special orders from Admiral Ramsay, in case they interfered with the operations of the RAF and the Navy.

Major Bill Corris, duty officer on a 6-inch gun battery at the top of Lydden Spout, spent a typically frustrating morning. Looking down from the top of the cliffs 400 feet up, all he saw below was a cotton-wool eiderdown of cloud. Although visibility was less than 100 yards, he watched all kinds of planes coming towards the Channel and diving into the clouds. Then came the distant firing of guns and excited talk over the telephone told him and his fellow officers there was 'a flap on' and 'a convoy coming through the Channel'. They stood ready to fire – but no orders came. The ships were too far away for them to waste ammunition.

7

The MTBs Attack

Had the German battleships obligingly come through at night as the Admiralty predicted, there was a sophisticated plan for co-operation between thirty-two motor torpedo boats and Esmonde's six Swordfish torpedo bombers. There was to be a joint converging attack on both sides of the ships' bows, lit by flares from aircraft.

They had been practising this since the beginning of February. Then two days before the break-out, the Admiralty decided the emergency was nearly over. They ordered Pizey's destroyers to 'stand down' on the morning of 12 February. The day before, they removed most of the MTBs leaving only six boats in Dover commanded by Lt-Cdr Nigel Pumphrey. His boats were also ordered to 'stand down' from fifteen minutes readiness to four hours. The crews welcomed this, because they had been living in their boats for nearly two weeks with no leave and no chance to do maintenance.

Pumphrey's boats, with a captain and eight crew, had power-operated gun turrets, two torpedoes and depth-charges. That morning they left Dover between 7 and 8 a.m. to practise torpedo runs. Instead of a warhead, they fired torpedoes with smoke-emitting heads attached which could be picked up again after their run. If the German ships had arrived earlier the MTBs might have been caught with practice torpedoes. When they came back to Dover later in the morning, the crews immediately began to put in the warheads – known as 'action fish'. This took roughly twenty minutes to half an hour for each torpedo.

At 11.30 a.m., the crews were resting with the six Dover MTBs tied up in the train ferry dock, where in peacetime the car-carrying cross-Channel steamers docked. Lt-Cdr Nigel Pumphrey was in his office making out reports on the morning's practice and waiting for a call from one of his officers, Lt Paul Gibson, a Frenchman who had escaped from occupied France and taken an English name to serve with the Royal Navy. Gibson was on his way to the naval stores to see about clothing.

While Pumphrey was waiting, the telephone rang. It was Captain Day, the naval Chief of Staff to Admiral Ramsay at Dover Castle, who said briskly, 'How soon can you get cracking? The German battle-cruisers are off Boulogne.'

Pumphrey slammed down the phone and dashed into the operations room shouting, 'Man all the boats – the *Scharnhorst* and *Gneisenau* are in the Straits!' Lts Hilary Gamble and Cornish, whose boats were tied up in dock, thought he was playing a joke. Was this a case of 'Wolf' again? The German battleships had become such a myth to the Dover MTBs that the idea of setting off after them in broad daylight did not seem possible. When they realized he was serious they all rushed down to the quay. Even then, most of the crews still believed it was another false alarm, although a messenger came running from the operations room shouting, 'Get going at once! They're out!' Not all the MTBs were in running order. Pumphrey's own boat, *38*, was in dry-dock for a change of petrol tanks. As Gibson was still missing Pumphrey took over his boat *221* and his crew.

Nor were the two smaller fast 43-knot gun-boats ready. Their commanders, Stewart Gould and Roger King – another Frenchman with an assumed English name – were in Dover. Pumphrey told the duty officer to get hold of them at once. If they were to intercept the battleships sailing at near thirty knots there was not a second to be wasted.

As each boat let go the ropes, the crews pulled on their steel helmets and made the 'V' sign. Pumphrey's boat was the last to leave the ferry dock, so the others waited for him in the harbour until he could lead the flotilla out.

The five boats left harbour steaming at twenty-four knots – ten knots slower than the German E-boats. Behind Pumphrey's *221* came young RNR Sub-Lt Mark Arnold Forster in *219*. Then came Hilary Gamble in *45*, Australian Sub-Lt Dick Saunders in *44* and Tony Law in *48*. As Pumphrey led them through the breakwater, it was 11.55 a.m. – only twenty minutes after he had received the telephone call from Captain Day.

There was a stiff breeze across the narrow harbour entrance, making it difficult to get out. As they set course for Number Two Buoy it was wet and rough with a strong westerly wind. Almost as soon as they left harbour they saw smudges of smoke made by the German E-boat screen.

At 12.10 p.m. a Focke-Wolfe 190 squadron came out of the mist. They had never seen FW 190s before, and at first they thought they were American Curtiss fighters as they had the same radial engines. They identified them from recognition charts before opening fire. The planes were cruising a few feet above the surface with their flaps and wheels down to slow them up, looking for British torpedo bombers. As they were flying too low to dive on the MTBs they left them alone.

Yet they came close enough for the MTB crews to see the goggles of the German pilots. They fired at them, but the Germans did not fire back. They were saving their ammunition for the massed RAF bombers which they were expecting. Even when Hilary Gamble shot pieces off the wing of one of the German fighters, it still did not fire.

Going flat out at their top speed of twenty-seven knots, the MTBs had difficulty in keeping station and were already a straggling force. As they raced towards the black smoke, it suddenly cleared and Pumphrey and Arnold Forster in the two leading boats had a clear view of the great grey ships streaking through the Straits in patches of sunshine. The Germans were about five miles away with half a dozen destroyers astern of them and two dozen aircraft circling overhead.

When he clearly saw the German battle-fleet Pumphrey sent a momentous signal. His boat tapped out in Morse: 'O break U.' It was the first time an enemy battle-fleet had been sighted in the Straits of Dover since the Spanish Armada.

Pumphrey added: 'Three battleships bearing 130 degrees, five nautical miles distance, course 70 degrees.'

He was to be criticized for this signal later by Captain Day. The Royal Navy, sticklers for detail, deplored the colloquial phrase 'battleships' – it should have been 'Two battle-cruisers and one cruiser'.

In spite of the incorrect wording the Navy acted upon Pumphrey's signal instantly. A silence descended on all wavelengths, broken every few minutes by the Admiralty in London and Dover Castle repeating the dramatic 'O break U' signal.

At 12.23 p.m., when Pumphrey's signalman tapped out the incredible news, it was the first definite confirmation that the German battleships were in the Straits.

The German B-Dienst also picked up Pumphrey's message and translated it within a few minutes. When a German signalman handed it to Admiral Ciliax aboard *Scharnhorst* Raw's shells were already crashing into the waves near his ships. He learnt that at long last his battleships had been sighted by the Royal Navy after steaming for fifteen hours in inexplicable uncanny silence, and it was almost a relief.

Mark Arnold Forster, in the second British MTB, waited for Nigel Pumphrey's sighting signal but as he did not receive it he also ordered his signalman, Leading Telegraphist Pitchforth, to tap out in Morse: 'O break U.' He added: 'Two battleships, one battle-cruiser with 20 destroyers and E-boats.'

Hilary Gamble's signalman in the third boat was still ignorant of the situation. When he picked up Arnold Forster's signal it only confirmed his views that it was all a false alarm. He said, '*219* says he's seen a ruddy battle-fleet. It must be an exercise.'

The Germans were going at their top speed of thirty knots and the English boats had difficulty in catching them. They had left in such a hurry that the engines had no time to warm up. The MTBs could only make twenty-seven knots and their problem was how to intercept the battle-fleet. The battleships were travelling three knots faster and the E-boats with a speed of thirty-five knots could outsail them easily. Although the MTBs best torpedo firing range was 800 yards, they realized they would be lucky to get as close as 5–6,000 yards. As they came up towards this range, the E-boats made more smoke to protect the battleships. But they were not keeping station very well, and there was a gap between them which Pumphrey aimed to crash through.

The cold oil made the MTB engines sound rough but they kept going at full speed as no one could afford to ease down –

except Dick Saunders, who was having engine trouble. He fell miles astern with one engine out.

Two more FW 190s came down to fifty feet but once again did not attack. The MTBs, cramming on every knot of speed, were still getting back over the radio from Dover and the Admiralty their 'battle-fleet sighted' reports. Dover Castle was sending out radar reports every few minutes, which meant Pumphrey was able to fix the battleships' speed exactly. Even without this his crews could see their superstructures towering above the smoke.

When the FW 190s flew away, they saw ten E-boats steaming half a mile apart. The faster-sailing E-boats kept their positions to protect the battleships, and started firing at two MTBs from 1,000 yards. The British only had machine-guns, but the E-boats had 20-mm. cannons and their shells began smashing into Pumphrey's hull. Then his engines cut out so suddenly that the bows went down into the water. While Pumphrey fought with the controls, the remaining four boats astern slowed up to maintain formation. Then Pumphrey's engines came to life again and he turned to drive his flotilla through the E-boat screen. As he plunged forward through the rough sea, the E-boats kept up a heavy fire. With their shells throwing spray round his boat, Pumphrey suddenly saw a great ship with destroyers surrounding her looming out of the smoke made by the E-boats. He thought it was *Prinz Eugen*, but it was in fact the leading ship *Scharnhorst* steaming at thirty knots. She was only 4,000 yards away from his MTB.

Wilhelm Wolf and the other officers on the bridge of *Scharnhorst* watched the approaching MTBs as if in a theatre. They commented on the wonderful sight of the MTBs and E-boats firing as they raced over the waves, with spray tossing everywhere. Then the escort destroyers also received the order to make artificial smoke, and as Wolf remarked, 'Soon the pretty picture was veiled from our vision.'

Pumphrey's boats shuddered and groaned as they pressed on every ounce of speed to try and draw ahead of the ten E-boats barring their path to the battleships. It was useless. The E-boats screwed on a few more knots and easily continued to maintain their protective patrol. The temptation for the

E-boats, who outnumbered the British MTBs two-to-one, to turn towards them and shoot them out of the water was almost irresistible. But like the FW 190s, they obeyed orders and remained in station.

Out-steamed by the E-boats and even by the battleships, Pumphrey had to make up his mind quickly. His boats were on an ideal bearing – 45 degrees to the bow of the leading battleship – but the range was too far. He decided the only course was to continue to try and fight his way through a gap in the E-boats to narrow the range to 2,000 yards.

It was a dangerous decision which might mean all his boats would be lost. But as he turned to charge through the E-boat screen it was taken out of his hands. His starboard engine failed and his speed fell to sixteen knots.

There was only one thing to do – wait as long as he dared, until the E-boat fire became too heavy, then fire at 4,000 yards. Pumphrey chugged along at a dangerously low speed but fortunately the sea was too rough for accurate shooting. The E-boats fired frantically at his boat but missed. When machine-gunning German fighters dived low over the MTB he ordered the others to split up and make individual attacks.

Although his damaged boat was being attacked from air and sea, he still held his fire. If he could keep afloat and wait until the battleships came abreast of him, he could fire at a range of two miles.

While machine-gun bullets and cannon shells whistled past his boat, exploding on the waves, a battleship came into his sights. He was pointing *221*'s nose at her ready to launch his torpedoes, when warning shouts came from his gunners. Two E-boats had raced up to within 800 yards and begun firing. His gunners fired back at the E-boats, as he pulled the release lever and his two torpedoes splashed into the sea. A great crash split the air, and he thought it was one of his torpedoes registering a hit. Then he saw a shell splash mushrooming from the sea. It was one of the 9·2 shells from South Foreland landing near the battleships. Pumphrey realized his torpedoes had missed. There was nothing more he could do. He swung his boat away from the battle.

Meanwhile the other MTBs were trying desperately to

approach nearer to the battleships. Arnold Forster of *219* and Tony Law of *48* twisted their boats furiously as they were attacked by the E-boats and increasing swarms of fighters. They steamed to within 400 yards of the E-boat screen to launch their torpedoes from a range of 3,500 yards.

When they approached their nearest to the German battleships, Able-Seaman McDonald suddenly rushed on deck carrying an old Ross rifle. Arnold Forster says, 'It was a World War I rifle which was used for sentry-go while we were tied up ashore. He started firing at the *Prinz Eugen* with this old rifle. He fired twenty-five rounds in all. I don't think he did any damage but it made him feel better.'

German fire now became so heavy that they sheered off and watched their torpedoes running. The Germans then switched their fire to Gamble, who followed in *45* ready to launch his torpedoes.

The torpedoes from the three MTBs began to run, but *Gneisenau* and *Prinz Eugen* turned 90 degrees to port and their last hope of a lucky hit vanished. *Scharnhorst* also turned towards the MTBs. This presented Australian Dick Saunders who had caught up, his engine working again, with a distant target. After firing his torpedoes he saw a plume of smoke spout up, but he too had missed. It was another shell landing. As the E-boat commanders, realizing the British boats had fired all their torpedoes, broke off the action and resumed station, suddenly out of the smoke-screen came the German destroyer, *Friedrich Ihn*, steaming at high speed towards Pumphrey's MTBs. Without torpedoes, they were helpless against the destroyer so they too immediately made smoke and scattered.

Friedrich Ihn chased them but her gunnery was inaccurate and all her shells missed. Yet she was overhauling them fast and any minute it looked as if they would be hit, so Arnold Forster and Law practised a little crude psychological warfare on the German destroyer. While she fired her 4·7 inch guns at them, they turned across her bows giving the impression that they were going to drop a depth-charge in her path. This confused the German gunners and caused her captain, Lt-Cdr Wachsmuth, to change course rapidly.

The chase lasted for five minutes. Arnold Forster's boat was bracketed by German shells, and he expected one to hit him at any moment. The two MTBs, dodging frantically, made for the Kellett Gut, a passage through the Goodwins too shallow for the destroyer to follow them. They hoped to put Wachsmuth's ship aground but a wreck on the sandbank marked the beginning of the passage, and when the destroyer spotted it she sheered off.

While Arnold Forster and Law were being chased by the *Friedrich Ihn*, British gun-boats *43* and *41* suddenly appeared. They had no torpedoes – only an Oerlikon 20-mm gun and two half-inch machine-guns. Stewart Gould and Roger King, hopping mad at having nearly missed the battle, made straight for the *Friedrich Ihn* at forty-three knots in their 63-foot boats, blazing away with their single Oerlikon guns.

Senior Officer Stewart Gould said, 'When we got within 1,000 yards of the destroyer, her fire was unpleasantly accurate. She had a small turning circle and her manœuvring made us very uncomfortable.' They intended to try and sink the destroyer with their depth-charges but Wachsmuth, taking them for MTBs armed with torpedoes, veered away and steered *Friedrich Ihn* back towards the battleships. The Luftwaffe also suddenly turned away from the retreating MTBs and circled once again over the battle-fleet.

At Dover Admiral Ramsay was waiting for the MTBs to return and report. They were to tell him bad news. The first battle of the Straits had been lost.

Pumphrey in his report said: 'I feel a certain uneasiness in the fact that the MTBs engaged at such long range as to avoid danger and casualties. There were undoubtedly two courses open to me when I realized there was no prospect of crossing ahead of the E-boats. My first intention was to attempt to fight through the screen.

'This plan was abandoned as far as my own boat was concerned when the engines failed. The second alternative was to fire at the range dictated by the E-boat escort and this was what was done.

'When I signalled "Out of action – continue", to the MTBs I expected them to try and pierce the screen.

'I wish to emphasize that no order was given to them to do so – and in my opinion they acted correctly. For the choice lay between a slight chance of hitting at long range, coupled with the possibility of avoiding heavy damage to the MTBs, and an almost complete certainty of all boats being destroyed or so damaged as to be unable to fire torpedoes before the range had been appreciably reduced.'

In conclusion, Pumphrey complained about the lack of fighters and the late arrival of the gun-boats saying: 'With either, or preferably both, the MTB attack might have been a different story. The only fighters present were Germans, who attacked the MTBs intermittently and in a half-hearted manner.'

8

'Poor Fellows . . . It is nothing but Suicide'

On Wednesday 11 February, while Admiral Ciliax and his Captains in Brest worked on last-minute details of their break-out plan, Lt-Cdr Esmonde, leader of the Swordfish squadron at Manston, had an important function to attend. He drove to Margate, caught a train to London and went to Buckingham Palace to receive from King George VI the Distinguished Service Order awarded for his part in the *Bismarck* operation.

That evening when he returned to Manston, a small party to celebrate his 'gong' was held by the RAF and his own Fleet Air Arm flying crews. The party ended early and soberly for the crews had to be by their aircraft at four o'clock in the morning ready for take-off. This was a routine alert ordered for the pre-dawn danger period, when the Admiralty believed the Germans might force the Straits.

They were 'stood down' at dawn on a cold crisp morning with freezing snow swirling over the runways at Manston. In the corner of the field by the Margate Road their six fragile, old-fashioned biplanes shook as their canvas-covered fuselages flapped.

After breakfast, the most experienced crew was down to lead the first practice torpedo flight. The pilot, Sub-Lt Brian Rose, had been on the carrier *Ark Royal*, and his observer, Edgar Lee and his gunner, Leading Airman Ginger Johnson, were both *Bismarck* veterans.

As they climbed into their aircraft standing high on the cliffs along the south coast, Britain's radar sets were already picking up circling 'blips' of Galland's fighters over three big ships coming along the Channel. When the first reports came to Dover Castle and Wing-Cdr Bobby Constable-Roberts, air-liaison officer, reported to Vice-Admiral Bertram Ramsay that these 'blips' must mean the *Scharnhorst*, *Gneisenau* and *Prinz Eugen*, both he and the Admiral realized that the only aircraft immediately available to attack them were the six old biplanes at Manston preparing for a night attack. But how could they send these slow-moving planes in daylight against the ferocious flak and heavy fighter escorts of the German battleships? It was certain death.

Admiral Ramsay thoughtfully picked up the telephone and asked for the First Sea Lord, Sir Dudley Pound, in Whitehall. He pleaded with him not to be asked to send these eighteen flyers on such a suicidal mission. Sir Dudley replied, 'The Navy will attack the enemy whenever and wherever he is to be found.'

Ramsay put down the phone and nodded to Constable–Roberts. He telephoned Wing-Cdr Tom Gleave at Manston to say, 'The *Scharnhorst* and *Gneisenau* are out and approaching the Straits of Dover. Tell Esmonde.'

Esmonde was on the airfield supervising training practice when a battered Morris Minor came tearing down the runway with a messenger shouting, 'You are wanted on the phone urgently, sir.' He picked up the phone in the briefing hut to hear Tom Gleave say, 'The *Scharnhorst* and *Gneisenau* are approaching the Straits.' When Esmonde put down the receiver, he ordered Rose to stop practice at once and the rest of the aircrews were warned.

The message came as a complete surprise to the Swordfish crews, who had been 'stood down' until dusk. Most of the airgunners were drinking coffee and reading in the Petty Officers' Mess. Twenty-year-old pilot Charles Kingsmill was having his hair cut when the order came to go to the briefing hut as fast as possible. When the crews arrived there, they found Esmonde on the telephone listening to the latest reports from the radar stations as the German battleships raced towards the Straits.

Wing-Cdr Tom Gleave came swerving up to the hut in an old Ford V.8. He said that there was still no confirmation from the Admiralty, who remained convinced that the battleships would not dare to attempt to force the Dover Straits in broad daylight. Was the Admiralty right? Or was Constable-Roberts?

Gleave and Esmonde sat beside the telephone waiting for it to ring again. Neither spoke. They both knew that if Constable-Roberts was right the Swordfish crews had little chance of survival.

There were seven pilots for only six Swordfish. In the briefing room, the two most junior pilots tossed for the right to fly on the 'Fuller' mission. Sub-Lt Peter Bligh called 'Tails' and won. Sub-Lt Bennett lost and was to remain on the ground. He owed his life to that tossed coin.

At 11.40 the phone rang. It was Constable-Roberts again. 'It's our friends all right,' he said. 'Beamish has identified them off Boulogne.'

Esmonde put down the telephone and turned to his aircrews. 'The balloon's gone up,' he said in a clipped, unemotional voice. 'Get ready!'

The RAF was alerted at the same time. The fighter aircrews were much quicker off the mark than the ground staff. They were anxious to get into the air, but they were delayed by staff muddles.

Flt-Lt Cowan Douglas-Stephenson – 'Stevie' – was on duty in the concrete watch office at Biggin Hill – the most vital fighter station in Southern England. American-born 'Stevie', who was married to Jeanne de Casalis, the 'Mrs Feather' of the BBC wartime radio show, remembers the day well. He said, 'Between 11.30 and 12.30 a.m. pilots of three squadrons of Spitfires arrived. Some of them were Czechs, Belgians and Poles. It was just like bedlam.

'No one knew anything except there was 'a flap on'. All they had was the call sign written in pencil on the back of the pilots' hands where it could easily be rubbed off. Everyone wanted to know what to do.

'I knew that the battle plan for Operation Fuller was in the locked safe. But the Intelligence Officer had gone away on twenty-four hours leave leaving the secret orders locked up. No one could find the key.'

The pilots milled around in the Watch Office until 11 Group got through to the Biggin Hill Controller, Bill Igoe, and gave him the order for the squadrons to take off for Manston and escort the Swordfish.

While this 'flap' was going on at Biggin Hill, Esmonde sat by the phone awaiting further orders. Occasionally he stood up to gaze across the frozen fields as though trying to imprint them upon his mind for ever. When the phone rang again, it was Number 11 Fighter Group saying, 'We intend putting in the Biggin Hill wing of three squadrons as top cover. The Hornchurch wing of two squadrons will act as close escort to beat up the flak ships for you.' The voice continued, 'Both wings have been told to rendezvous over Manston. What time should they be there?'

Esmonde glanced at his watch, 'Tell them to be here by twelve-twenty-five,' he said. 'Get the fighters to us on time – for the love of God!'

Then Constable-Roberts rang again. At Dover Castle both RAF and Navy felt that even with a heavy fighter escort, few Swordfish crews would return from this mission. No one wanted to give him a direct order to lead his men to their deaths. 'The Admiral wants to know how you feel about going in,' said Constable-Roberts. 'He wants it to be your decision.'

What could Esmonde, a regular officer, say? Although the Dover message was well meant it was worse than receiving a direct order. He made the only possible reply, 'The squadron will go in,' he said stiffly. 'Where is Jerry? What's his speed?'

'Hold on,' replied Constable-Roberts, 'they are about ten miles north-east of the Straits sailing at twenty-one knots. If you are satisfied with the fighter escort the Admiral says it is O.K. to go.' Then, a pilot himself, he added in a gruff voice, 'Best of luck, old boy.'

Esmonde and Gleave compared the reports of the ships' course and speed with their maps. The German ships were travelling so fast that Esmonde had had to make an immediate decision. With a top speed of only 90 m.p.h., his Swordfish would lose the ships if they did not take off at once.

He turned to his aircrews and said briskly, 'We will attack in sub-flights in line astern, height fifty feet. Intention: to hit and slow down any of the big ships. We will have plenty of fighter cover so you won't have to worry too much about enemy fighters. Once over the escorting screens of destroyers and E-boats, attack independently. Pick your target to your most convenient

110

dropping point. But make sure it is *Scharnhorst, Gneisenau* or *Prinz Eugen.*'

The crews doubled off to their Swordfish parked near the Margate Road. Esmonde, a small figure in dark blue naval uniform, wearing an orange-coloured 'Mae West' and swinging a flying helmet by its strap, was about to run after them when the telephone rang again. It was No. 11 Group reporting that some of the fighter escort might be a few minutes late.

Esmonde replied, 'We are taking off at twelve-twenty-five. I'll orbit out to the coast for two minutes.'

Gleave, whose voice trembled as he wished him luck, said afterwards, 'Although his mouth twitched automatically into the semblance of a grin and his arm lifted in a vague salute, he barely recognized me. He knew what he was going into. But it was his duty. His face was tense and white. It was the face of a man already dead. It shocked me as nothing has ever done since.'

Neither Esmonde nor any of his officers said anything. But battle-veteran Ginger Johnson exclaimed as he climbed into his rear cockpit, 'What flaming hell chance have we got?' No one answered him.

Esmonde's observer, Lt W. H. Williams, and his gunner, Leading Airman W. J. Clinton, also climbed into their cockpits. Esmonde was just about to follow them into the plane when a runner arrived with another message from the control room, 'Dover says the enemy's speed now estimated at twenty-seven knots.'

This was vital information. If the battleships were sailing at a higher speed than the first estimate the Swordfish must take off without delay.

It was 12.25 p.m. when Esmonde waved his arm to tell the planes behind him to take off. As the six biplanes lumbered into the air, Gleave stood alone in the middle of the snow-covered field at rigid salute.

At 1,500 feet off the Kent coast the aircraft circled over the sea waiting for their fighter escorts. Behind Esmonde's plane was Brian Rose with Lee and Johnson. Behind him and slightly above was Charles Kingsmill with Sub-Lt 'Mac' Samples as his observer and Leading Airman Donald Bunce his gunner.

Then came the second flight led by Lt Thompson with Sub-Lt Parkinson as observer and Leading Airman Topping at the guns. Behind them were Sub-Lt Wood and Sub-Lt Fuller-Wright and Leading Airman Wheeler. Sub-Lt Peter Bligh and Sub-Lt Bill Beynon with Leading Airman Smith were the last in the formation.

Eighteen young men in six slow, old aircraft, only capable of flying at ninety knots because of the weight of their torpedoes, were on their way to attack two battleships, a heavy cruiser, six large destroyers, thirty-four E-boats and a group of flak ships – apart from the massed might of the Luftwaffe.

At 12.29 p.m. – four minutes after the arranged rendezvous time – the Swordfish were still orbiting over the coast near Ramsgate. The weather was thickening up and there was not a fighter in the sky.

What had happened to the five Spitfire squadrons? Four of them did not arrive. Only ten fighters of 72 Squadron commanded by Squadron Leader Brian Kingcombe, a former Cranwell cadet, found the Swordfish.

As it was considered too cloudy for flying from Gravesend – a satellite airfield of Biggin Hill, where they were stationed – 72 Squadron had been 'stood down' after breakfast. At 9 a.m., they were suddenly called by Igoe from thirty minutes 'availability' to two minutes 'readiness' which meant sitting in their cockpits. Three times the 'scramble' was called off and they went back to the operations hut – only to be sent back immediately. These contradictory orders made them realize there was a 'flap' on but no one gave them any information.

Then came the final order, 'Scramble! Get to Manston to escort six Swordfish and intervene in a battle between German E-boats and British MTBs.' When Kingcombe, sitting in his cockpit, received the message he thought it odd to be asked to interfere in 'a small naval scuffle.' He was told nothing about the German battleships. The traditional security screen was still functioning. He remained puzzled when he heard similar orders going out to four other squadrons. Why was he being told to go as fast as possible to Manston to escort six Swordfish which were orbiting the airfield? It must be a big show.

Kingcombe and his pilots, by their own account, went 'balls

out right through the gate', taking only ten minutes to reach Manston. When Esmonde saw Kingcombe's Spitfires come streaking out of the clouds towards him it was 12.32 p.m.

The Swordfish and Spitfires circled for two more minutes but no more fighters arrived. Esmonde knew it was now or never. He waved his hand and dived down to fifty feet to lead his Squadron out to sea. Kingcombe, who still had no idea what the operation was about, led his Spitfires ahead at about 2,000 feet to protect them. The German ships were twenty-three miles away – fifteen minutes flying time in a Swordfish.

Aboard the *Scharnhorst*, Vice-Admiral Ciliax stood on the bridge eating German sausage and drinking coffee. He turned with relief and astonishment to *Scharnhorst*'s commander, Captain Hoffmann. Except for a few shells, which had landed a thousand yards away, and an attack by a handful of MTB boats which had been driven off by the E-boat and destroyer screens, they had sailed unchallenged through the Straits of Dover.

Where was the RAF? Where was the Royal Navy? Were they all asleep?

As he speculated about this, six ME 109s saw the wave-hopping Swordfish ten miles east of Ramsgate, in heavy rain and visibility down to four miles. As they swooped, Kingcombe's Spitfires, guns rattling, drove them off but a few machine-gun bullets and cannon shells ripped through the fabric of the Swordfish.

Kingcombe recalls, 'While making for a Messerschmitt I suddenly saw a beautiful bloody battleship and I thought to myself "I never knew the Navy had such a lovely boat". I was sure she was one of ours because she was heading straight for Dover. Anyway, no one had told me anything about German battleships being in the Straits.

'Not realizing she was only heading for the English coast because she was making a long zigzag in evasive action, I went down to 600 feet to give her a signal. When everything opened up on me I was still not worried for I knew the Royal Navy fired at anything which appeared too near their ships. When I swung off, followed by the rest of the squadron, the air was suddenly full of German aeroplanes, mostly cannon-firing FW 190s. They were nasty customers, who had only come into service at the end of 1941, and were a little faster than the 109 Messerschmitts. As I tried to beat the German fighters off the Swordfish, which were still lumbering along, I realized the "beautiful ship" was the *Prinz Eugen*.'

Now the British planes were approaching the main Luftwaffe fighter screen. They flew through layers of cloud like wedding cake, with German fighters patrolling at all levels. As soon as the Spitfires broke up one attack wave, another flight of Messerschmitts dived in between the two Swordfish flights. Twenty ME 109s circled for a mass dive to port but three of Kingcombe's Spitfires attacked and scattered them. Suddenly the ten Spitfires were lost in a whirling air battle with the German fighters.

As Kingcombe's courageous and experienced Spitfires began fighting furiously with the Luftwaffe, the Swordfish pilots sighted the German battle-fleet. It was a daunting sight. From just above wave level to 2,000 feet the whole sky swarmed with Luftwaffe fighters – the biggest number ever to cover a force at sea. Several Swordfish swerved wildly as some of the inexperienced pilots mastered a momentary impulse to flee.

Aboard the *Prinz Eugen*, the anti-aircraft gunnery officer, Commander Paul Schmalenbach, suddenly heard one of his look-outs shout, 'Enemy planes at sea level!' Just above the waves he saw six grey biplanes, split into two waves of three, approaching slowly, like clumsy birds. Schmalenbach reported them to *Scharnhorst* and *Gneisenau* ahead.

The Germans realized with a cold chill that here was their greatest danger of all – a suicide attack. When they were 2,000 yards away, every flak gun in the German fleet from the 4-inch guns to the multiple-barrelled guns manned by German marines, burst into flickering flame. With gold-trailing tracer shells and white stars of bursting flak around them, the Swordfish came on unswervingly.

Esmonde led his squadron over the destroyers while his gunner Clinton fired his machine-gun at the diving Luftwaffe planes. Tracers from destroyers and E-boats smacked into his cockpit. As more FW 190s dived on to the Swordfish, cannon shells smashed big holes in their canvas fuselage. It was miraculous they were still flying.

Tracer set fire to Esmonde's tail plane, and rear-gunner Clinton climbed out of his cockpit and sat astride the fuselage beating out the flames with his hands. When he clambered back, they were over the outer screen and the German battleships' main 11-inch guns came into action. Belching smoke and flame, they laid down a barrage which sent spray crashing into the low-flying, now limping aircraft. One shell burst in front of Esmonde and shot away his lower wing.

His Swordfish shuddered and dipped but still flew. With blood pouring from wounds in his head and back, Esmonde hung on to the controls holding his course steady for *Prinz Eugen*. Behind him lay Williams and Clinton. Both were dead.

In a last desperate effort, he pulled the Swordfish's nose up into the wind for the last time and released his torpedo. Then there was a red flash as a direct hit from Schmalenbach's guns blew his plane to pieces. As Esmonde's Swordfish crashed into the sea, German look-outs reported the track of his approaching torpedo. Captain Brinkmann ordered, 'Port Fifteen'. As Esmonde died, *Prinz Eugen* dodged his torpedo easily.

Admiral Ciliax's attitude mirrored the heroic futility of the attacks and the lack of any real sense of danger aboard the battleships. On the bridge of *Scharnhorst*, watching the Swordfish lumbering towards her, he remarked to Captain Hoffmann, 'The English are now throwing their mothball navy at us. Those Swordfish are doing well to get their torpedoes away.'

While all three ships steamed full ahead, firing with everything they had, the torpedo planes continued coming towards them dead straight, just skimming the waves. The Swordfish immediately behind Esmonde was piloted by Brian Rose. As Rose followed Esmonde into the attack, his observer, 20-year-old Edgar Lee, saw Esmonde crash into the sea. Then Lee saw the ships standing out clearly under the clouds, and tried to give directions through the speaking tube shouting, 'Now, Brian, now!' He did not know it had been smashed by gunfire. Rose, wounded in the back by cannon-shell splinters which shattered his cockpit, managed to hold on to the controls. Lee was too busy shouting directions to notice that Rose had dropped their torpedo. At the same time the main petrol tank was hit. Luckily it did not catch fire, but the engine began to splutter. Rose switched over to the 12-gallon emergency gravity tank, which meant they had about 10 to 12 minutes flying time left.

Rose, losing height, tried to pass under the stern of the *Gneisenau* but flew right over *Prinz Eugen*, nearly colliding with her mast. As they swerved away from her barrage, Lee looked round and saw gunner Ginger Johnson sprawled over his gun. He was dead. Then he saw blood running down Rose's side and realized he was also hit.

Yet Rose managed to bring the plane down on the ice-cold waves half a mile from the *Prinz Eugen*. Lee dragged out the yellow rubber dinghy and pulled Rose in. As he did so, the battered Swordfish sank, taking Johnson's body with it.

The third Swordfish in the first wave was piloted by Charles Kingsmill. Their first view of the Germans was when his gunner, Donald Bunce, saw a German destroyer tearing through the water. At the same time the Swordfish was attacked by German fighters and their cannon shells ripped through the fabric. Bunce fired his Vickers at them and then stood up to see if there were any more coming. When he went to sit down again his seat had gone. There was a big hole underneath and three-quarters of the fuselage was already a series of gaping tears and holes.

Suddenly, through the mist, his observer 'Mac' Samples caught a glimpse of a big ship which he thought was the *Prinz Eugen*. They staggered forward over the battle-fleet screen with everything coming up at them. It all seemed so unreal that they became almost detached. They watched the shells and bullets ripping through their wings as if it was happening to somebody else.

A group of Focke-Wolfes swooped on Kingsmill's plane. Bunce had never seen one before. When the first one dived on their Swordfish, he was uncertain whether it was one of theirs. He shouted through the voice pipe, 'What's this? Shall I fire at it?' Samples shouted back, 'Fire at any bloody thing!'

He was facing backwards so he could direct his pilot away from the planes diving on their tail. Both Bunce and Samples stood up screaming 'Bugger off, you bastards!' at the German planes. This was an automatic reaction to conquer their fear. They also shook their fists and made rude two-fingered gestures.

Then a cannon shell hit the fuselage between Kingsmill and his observer and exploded, wounding Samples. Bunce saw the pilot and the observer covered in blood, which began running over the plane. He continued firing and 'Mac' Samples still kept telling Kingsmill to try and dodge the attacking German aircraft – but he was too busy concentrating on the *Prinz Eugen*.

Kingsmill remembers, 'The tracer came floating gently towards us and then whizzed past. There were more and more large splotches in the sea as aircraft and ships fired at us and their shells burst into the waves. We were really in it now. Suddenly, I felt a sharp pain in my shoulder and my foot went squelchy. Oddly enough I didn't feel any more pain and managed to keep control of the plane. Samples got hit in the legs at the same time but Gunner Donald Bunce was unhurt. The sea was rough and I was not certain that my torpedo would run properly. I chugged along at fifty feet but could not at first get close enough to drop it.'

Kingsmill turned back to make another run across the intense flak sent up by the destroyer screen. As he flew once again towards *Prinz Eugen*, the German gun crews in sleek black anti-flash overalls continued to fire everything they had at him. To Schmalenbach and his gunners Kingsmill's Swordfish was coming unbelievably slowly – but it was still flying.

Samples felt a burning sensation in his leg and when he looked down at his black flying boots he was astonished to see that in one there was a neat pattern like buttonholes. It was only when blood started spurting out of them that he realized he had been hit by machine-gun bullets. He felt no pain – only surprised interest. Gazing at his leg drilled with holes, he did not notice Kingsmill drop his torpedo aimed at *Prinz Eugen* from 2,000 yards.

As Kingsmill's Swordfish, torn and shaken by flak, veered back once again over the destroyers, a shell sliced off the tops of two of the three cylinders of his engine, leaving him with hardly any power. He pulled the stick back, 'hanging on to the prop' to keep her aloft. With her fabric tattered like an old blanket, the plane began gradually sinking towards the water, when the engine burst into flames and the port wing caught fire. Both Kingsmill and Samples were wounded, but they were

117

still in control and Bunce kept firing and screaming insults at the Germans. Kingsmill tried to shout to Samples through the voice pipe, not knowing it was shattered, to say he was going to try and bring her back to base. Covered in blood, Samples managed to climb towards him and shout into his ear, 'We will never do it. Try and ditch near those friendly MTBs.'

He pointed to Pumphrey's MTBs, who were still in the area. Watching Esmonde's gallant Swordfish coming in wave-high, the MTBs realized that most of them would be shot down and the aircrews might need help if they ditched. So they cruised around out of range waiting to see what happened. The E-boats were also near. Kingsmill still kept his aircraft under control although she seemed to move as slowly as if flying through glue. As he staggered over the last E-boat, his engine finally died and he came down towards the sea.

Weaving a little above wave level, Sq. Ldr Kingcombe watched Esmonde and his Swordfish attacking in two 'vics' of three. He said, 'I went down to 100 feet, clipping the bottom of the clouds, and we managed to keep most of the German fighters off them. The Germans were firing heavy guns which threw up great mountains of spray like water spouts. The Swordfish flew straight into them. Mostly they were caught by the *Prinz Eugen*'s flak and I saw the leader and two others go into the drink. They caught fire and went diving in flames towards the water. By this time the FW 190s were swarming everywhere. I saw one go down after I had given him a burst. I claimed him, but unfortunately in the sudden 'scramble' I had forgotten to take the cover off my camera – so I could not prove it. By this time it seemed as though there were a hundred fighters, both RAF and Luftwaffe, in the air.'

While the Swordfish crews were dying so heroicly and uselessly, Brian Kingcombe's ten Spitfires equally courageously tried to prevent their massacre. Although they were jumped by dozens of German fighters, they gave an extremely good account of themselves. They had numerous dog-fights with Messerschmitts and Focke-Wolfes at odds of three-to-one.

Pilot Officer Ingham, Pilot Officer Bocock and Pilot Officer de Naeyer dived on some FW 190s, whose tracer was hitting one of the Swordfish. Her petrol tank blew up and the Swordfish dis-

1. The camouflaged warships in dry-dock in Brest harbour.

2(a). Vice-Admiral Ciliax addressing the battleship crews.

2(b). The *Gneisenau*.

3. German coastal artillerymen manning A.A. guns
during the break-out.

4(a). Swordfish torpedo-bombers of the type used by
Esmonde's 825 Squadron.

4(b) (*far left*). Lt-Cdr Eugene
Esmonde, leader of the Swordfish
attack on the German battleships.

4(c) (*left*). Leading Airman A. L.
'Ginger' Johnson, gunner on Sub-
Lieut. Brian Rose's Swordfish.

5(a). *Prinz Eugen's* heavy guns firing at the Swordfish.

5(b). Esmonde's Swordfish crashing into the sea.

6(*a*). Captain Helmuth Brinkmann on the bridge of *Prinz Eugen*.
6(*b*). The view from the bridge. These pictures are from a German
film taken during the action.

7. Captain (now Admiral Sir) Mark Pizey, on the bridge
of H.M.S. *Campbell*, flagship of the 21st Destroyer Flotilla.
From a contemporary painting by Douglas Wales Smith.

8(a). H.M.S. *Worcester* in dry-dock after the action showing damage to the port bow.

8(b). Damage to H.M.S. *Worcester*'s bridge.

appeared before they could stop the attack, but Ingham managed to get one FW 190 in his sights and give it a long burst. It hit the sea trailing black smoke.

Pilot Officer Rutherford was flying at sea level when he saw the Swordfish turn to attack the *Prinz Eugen*. Skimming the waves, four FW 190s flew beneath the Spitfires followed by eight more in a 'gaggle'. In the all-out fight which ensued Rutherford made a head-on attack on an FW 190 which was coming straight towards him. He roared to within fifty yards and hit the FW's engine, cowling and wings.

As the German plane lurched towards the water, three other FW 190s swooped on Rutherford, cannons firing. Ducking and weaving to avoid them he climbed into the low clouds. When he came out again he had lost the FWs – and also his own squadron. He came down to sea level to see patches of oil 300 yards away from where the first FW 190 had crashed into the sea. Near the oil he saw two men, clinging to a half-submerged dinghy. They were Brian Rose and Edgar Lee. At minute intervals, he made three 'Mayday' signals to summon help for them.

Kingsmill's burning plane, with the engine shot away, glided silently towards the water. The crew saw the second flight of three Swordfish, led by Sub-Lt Thompson, approaching the *Prinz Eugen* at 100 feet, and Kingsmill, unable to gain height, flew underneath them. This was the last time anyone saw these three planes.

Thompson's three Swordfish limped on, their fuselages tattered canvas ribbons, their crews wounded or dying. Still maintaining a steady course, they flew into the red and orange wall of exploding shells. The three Swordfish with their nine young aircrew were never seen again. One after another, they were blown to pieces. Not a trace of any was ever found.

As Kingsmill's Swordfish, with blood dripping through rips in the fuselage, came down to ditch near a couple of boats which Samples had thought were MTBs, they opened fire. They were German E-boats. Samples paid for his mistake by receiving a bullet in his bottom, but Kingsmill managed to turn his plane away and land down near some small British ships which were coming towards them. Kingsmill recalls, 'I managed to put her down in what I now immodestly claim was a perfect landing. It was very choppy with quite big waves, but I felt no feeling of cold at all.'

Wearing their yellow life-jackets, they tried to haul themselves out of the cockpits. Kingsmill and Bunce jumped into the sea because their dinghy had been destroyed in the burning wing, but Samples went down with the plane. He had forgotten he had a G-string hooked between his legs to prevent his falling out when the plane rolled and turned. It dragged him down with the plane and, half-drowning, he fumbled to free himself. It seemed like hours, although it only took a few seconds before he managed to untie himself and float exhausted to the surface.

From the German battleships, the brave Fleet Air Arm fliers seemed like far-away dots. The ships saw their torpedoes running but swung away and all of them missed. From the bridge of *Scharnhorst*, German fighters were seen shooting at two Swordfish which dived on *Prinz Eugen*. *Gneisenau* could be seen zigzagging and shooting down Thompson's flight of three.

As he watched the tiny smoking specks falling into the sea through his binoculars, Captain Hoffmann muttered, 'Poor fellows. They are so very slow. It is nothing but suicide for them to fly against these big ships.'

Everyone on the battleships' bridges felt the same. As they watched the forlorn attack, the English coastline could be dimly and intermittently seen from the German ships. Aboard *Scharnhorst* Wilhelm Wolf, watching the flames of the fleet's flak guns, thought: 'What an heroic stage for them to meet their end on. Behind them, their homeland, which they have left, with hearts steeled to their purpose, is still in view.'

Navigator Giessler said, 'Such bravery was devoted and incredible. One was privileged to witness it. Although they were shot down by our anti-aircraft fire before they could get into position to release their loads, they knowingly and ungrudgingly gave their all to their country and went to their doom without hesitation.'

The heroic, incredible, Swordfish attack was over. As the last of the six torpedo planes blew up and splashed into the sea, the German fighters gave a victory roll over the ships before resuming their patrol. It was 12.45 p.m. They had only taken off twenty minutes before. The Germans could not believe it was finished. *Prinz Eugen*'s flak commander Schmalenbach said, 'We expected them to be the first wave of a massive attack by hundreds of planes and my gunners waited tensely for it to happen. But nothing else came.'

There were only five survivors out of eighteen who had flown into the hail of fire. Brian Rose and Edgar Lee were crouched in their dinghy shivering from the freezing spray. With stiff fingers, Lee managed to fire a rocket, but when they saw an MTB approaching he was convinced it was a German boat. Then they heard English voices, and one of Hilary Gamble's MTB crew jumped overboard into the icy sea and tied the dinghy alongside their boat, while other sailors swarmed down to lift up the airmen. A few minutes later Rose was wrapped in a blanket and Lee, wearing a towel, was sipping the one drink he detests – rum.

A mine-sweeper saw Kingsmill's crew crash and raced over to them. They threw down a rope climbing net from the deck. When Bunce was trying to push Samples, who was badly wounded, on to the net, someone called out from the ship, 'If you're all right, sailor, climb aboard and leave him to us!' As he began to climb up, several of the ship's crew dived into the water and began hauling Kingsmill and Samples up the net.

They dragged Samples up last. When they laid him on deck Kingsmill and Bunce were already below in the rolling ship. He was shivering with cold and shock. There was no more room below for him and they had no more blankets. To prevent him dying of exposure, a big sailor lay on top of him to try and warm him up. The sea was very choppy and every now and again as the boat gave a lurch he said politely to Samples, 'Excuse me, sir, I am not used to these small ships. I have always served on bigger ships.' He kept leaving the shivering observer to stagger to the side and vomit violently. Then he would come back and lie on him again. Samples began to dread his return; the smell of vomit was worse than the cold and his wounds.

Samples recalls, 'I was very upset about my shivering. I was only 23 and thought it would look as if I were frightened. But I will never forget the most pleasurable experience of my life. When I got to Ramsgate they put a semi-circular cage with a

121

radiant heater over the lower half of my body in hospital. I stopped shaking like a leaf when the warmth and feeling came back. It was a sensation that has never been equalled. Being so young I was terribly embarrassed when they tended to my wounds, and nurses stood by whilst doctors picked the German E-boat shrapnel out of my bottom.'

While Esmonde's Swordfish and Kingcombe's Spitfires were giving the Germans their first real taste of opposition, where were the rest of the RAF fighters? The other four squadrons – two from Biggin Hill and two from Hornchurch – either took off too late or lost their way in the mist. When those Spitfire squadrons finally arrived, it was nearly 1 p.m. and the Swordfish battle was already over.

Two Spitfire squadrons from Hornchurch – 64 and the 411 Canadian – were ordered to rendezvous with the Swordfish at 12.30 p.m. But 64 Squadron did not arrive over Manston until 12.45 p.m. to find the Swordfish gone. Ten aircraft set course for Calais, patrolled for a short time but saw nothing and flew back to their base in Essex.

The Canadian 411 Squadron, led by Sq. Ldr R. B. Newton and Wing-Cdr Powell, found the battleships after the Swordfish had been shot down and were fired upon by flak ships, but did not engage in any other action.

The other two Biggin Hill squadrons of twenty-six fighters who were supposed to join Kingcombe's ten Spitfires in keeping the German fighters off the Swordfish were also a vital quarter of an hour late. When they climbed to attack the Luftwaffe umbrella, the Swordfish had already been shot down.

One of them, the 401 Canadian Squadron, reached the ships at 1 p.m. German fighters tore towards them, and Pilot Officer Ian Ormston shot down one ME and damaged another.

Biggin Hill's third squadron, 124, although airborne at 12.20, also missed the Swordfish but had dog-fights over the Channel with the Luftwaffe.

The squadrons behaved with great bravery, but their attacks made no difference to the outcome of the Swordfish battle. They had missed the Swordfish through a combination of inefficient ground work and bad weather, causing them to lose their way.

Kingcombe's 72 Spitfire Squadron's log entry said, 'First big

offensive of the year. Ten Spitfires at 12.18 escorted six Swordfish in an attack on the *Scharnhorst*, escorted by light craft, in the
Straits of Dover. 72 Squadron's score was the largest of any
squadron.'

As the Spitfires turned back to England to refuel, the five
Swordfish survivors rescued from the sea were being taken back
to Dover and Ramsgate.

The only uninjured survivors were observer Edgar Lee and
Gunner Donald Bunce. Edgar Lee was ordered to report personally to Admiral Ramsay who signalled the Admiralty, 'In my
opinion the gallant sortie of these six Swordfish constitutes one
of the finest exhibitions of self-sacrifice and devotion that the
war has yet witnessed.'

Shortly after the Swordfish attack, three more MTBs under
Lt D. J. Long left Ramsgate to intercept the battleships. It was
an unsatisfactory engagement on both sides. Due to bad weather
and engine trouble none of the three boats found the ships.
Long fought a battle with the E-boats and the destroyer *Friedrich Ihn*, who chased him off – but not fiercely enough. *Friedrich
Ihn*'s captain, Lt Cdr Wachsmuth, was criticized for not pursuing Long's boats more vigorously.

The destroyer flotilla's report said, 'The destroyer *Friedrich
Ihn* brought on itself the fire of the English coastal artillery and
switched the attention of the batteries from the big ships by
drawing their fire. *Friedrich Ihn* carried out the task allotted to
her by fighting off the English MTBs with great success. As a
result the British MTBs did not succeed in reaching the German
battleships. However, it is incomprehensible that at 2.18 p.m.
the destroyer did not successfully attack the two English MTBs
coming towards her. This would have been the right thing to
do.'

Now the Germans were through the Straits unscathed, and
were beginning to run up the Belgian coast. All of them had the
feeling that, far from the battle being over, it had hardly begun.

The Admiralty had flung six old Fleet Air Arm biplanes in a
doomed attack on the ships. Surely now the greatest battle-
fleet in western waters was racing to sink them? In fact, all
there was in the Home Fleet base at Scapa Flow that day were

the new battleship *Duke of York* and the three heavy cruisers, *London*, *Sheffield* and *Liverpool*. At sea in the area were the aircraft-carrier *Victorious* and heavy cruisers *Berwick*, *Shropshire* and *Kenya*. Together they could have made an annihilating attack. Instead, they remained aloof while the Royal Navy launched its last attack against the German battleships. It was to be made by Pizey's six 20-year-old destroyers.

The RAF had not really entered the battle yet. At 2.30 p.m., nearly 700 bombers and fighters were beginning to take off from airfields all over Britain for a massed air attack. Unfortunately, because of the confusion, they were taking off piecemeal.

Meanwhile, Admiral Ramsay was sitting on the navigating counter in Dover Operations Room swinging his legs when the phone rang for him. He kept saying, 'Yes sir, no sir.' He put down the phone and said, 'That was the Prime Minister. He wanted to know how they had managed to get through.'

Flt-Lt Gerald Kidd, who had been called in from Swingate Radar Station said, 'I could tell him why. It was simply due to the fact that there was no forethought, no co-ordination whatsoever. I am going to write a report on it. I don't care if I am court-martialled.' Ramsay paused for a moment and then said, 'Go ahead. Somebody must say so.'

When Churchill telephoned Dover Castle, Nora Smith with the rest of the afternoon shift had already started tracing the battleship plots for future reference. She made two copies which later were shown to important visitors. Churchill was to be one of them.

9

Admiral Ciliax leaves his Flagship

February 11 was the last night of the stand-to for the six destroyers in Harwich. On the morning of the 12th, the operation was to be abandoned and the destroyers were to return to Sheerness. Looking at the charts on that evening Pizey said, 'As tomorrow's the last day, I've got the Commodore's agreement to go out at 6 a.m., to exercise the ships in pairs in the wide swept Channel.' In fact, he admits that at the back of his mind was the thought they might be more useful at sea if the Germans did come through. As the captains of the six destroyers met for the last time in Harwich harbour, it looked to them as though the alert was all over. Four hundred miles away in Brest, Admiral Ciliax and his captains were ready to cast off within three hours.

On 12 February, when the six destroyers slipped their cables and began to head out of Harwich harbour before dawn, it was the start of a cold misty winter's day. It was barely light when *Campbell*, with Captain Mark Pizey and his navigator, Lt Tony Fanning, on the bridge with him, cleared the boom. Strung out behind them were *Vivacious*, *Worcester* and *Walpole*, followed by the 16th flotilla leader, *Mackay*, with *Whitshed*. They were accompanied by six Hunt Class destroyers with 4-inch A.A. guns to protect them from German aircraft while they exercised.

In the centre of the flotilla was *HMS Worcester* inevitably known in the fleet as the 'Saucebottle'. On her bridge were Lt-Cdr Colin Coats, a 39-year-old grey-haired regular R.N. officer, who had spent most of his time in destroyers, and his first lieutenant, curly-bearded Richard Taudevin, who had an RNVR wartime commission. With them on the bridge was the

125

Australian ship's doctor Lt David Jackson. As he watched the silvery shape of the destroyers being swallowed up into the mist, the doctor shivered slightly, for he was cold even in his thick jersey and monkey jacket. He was glad they were due back in harbour by tea-time.

The practice shoot was to be with their 4·7 guns at a towed canvas target. After the first series of shoots off Orfordness, it was *Worcester*'s turn to tow the high-speed target for the other destroyers.

It was nearing the end of the forenoon watch when the yeoman of signals aboard *Campbell* handed Captain Pizey a signal from the C-in-C Nore, Vice-Admiral Sir George Lyon, which read: 'Enemy cruisers passing Boulogne. Speed about twenty knots. Proceed in execution of previous orders.' Signals began flashing from the flagship *Campbell*, ordering the destroyers to abandon the target shoot, alter course, and join him at full-speed.

It was 11.58 a.m., and off-duty officers were sitting in *Worcester*'s wardroom when an officer came clattering down the companion-way and shouted excitedly, 'Have you heard the news? They're out and we are going after them.'

'Who's out?' inquired someone uninterestedly from behind a magazine.

'The *Scharnhorst* and *Gneisenau* – they are coming up the Channel.'

The signal lamps and short-range radio were still flashing messages from destroyer to destroyer. Pizey signalled the Hunt Class destroyers: 'Must leave you behind.' This was because they could only keep up a maximum speed of twenty-five knots against twenty-eight to thirty knots for Pizey's flotilla. In an ordinary operation, he would have kept down to twenty-five knots, but this was too slow if he were to be in time to intercept the enemy. *HMS Quorn*, flotilla leader of the Hunt Class A.A. destroyers, flashed a farewell message as she turned to obey orders and lead her destroyers home to Harwich.

Aboard *Campbell*, Fanning plotted the German positions as given by the Admiralty, and Pizey realized the interception could take place at the Hinder Buoy as planned. This meant skirting the British minefields and sailing through the narrow swept Channel in single line.

On arrival at North Hinder Buoy the four destroyers of 21 flotilla were to station themselves on the starboard bow while 16 flotilla under Captain Wright stationed themselves to port. Upon the signal 'attack' they would simultaneously launch their torpedoes. Although this plan was drawn up specifically for a night action, Pizey felt he had no alternative but to adhere to it.

Chief Engineer Hugh Griffiths of *Worcester* was writing letters in his cabin when he felt the ship shudder as the engines began to rise towards full speed. When Bill Wellman the torpedo-gunner dashed into his cabin and said, 'We're off after the *Scharnhorst* and *Gneisenau*!' Griffiths did not believe him. He had been sleeping in his boots for over a week at five minutes readiness and he replied, 'Don't be silly, Bill. It's just another bloody false alarm. We'll be home for tea.'

As he said this, a messenger arrived asking Griffiths to see the Captain on the bridge. Climbing on deck, he could see *Campbell* and *Vivacious* ahead beginning to breast the waves as their speed rapidly increased. Steaming beside *Worcester* was *Mackay*, while in her wake were *Walpole* and *Whitshed*. All the old destroyers shuddered and thumped as they slowly crept up towards their maximum speed of thirty knots. They looked a brave sight, but every ship was over twenty years old and their torpedo tubes had to be hand-worked into position for firing.

Mackay's crew were piped on to the mess deck to be told by Captain Wright that two or three German ships had come out of Brest and they were going to try to intercept them at the mouth of the River Maas. He wished the ship's company good luck and dismissed them.

Charles Hutchings, an AB writer, went to his battle station on 'Monkey island,' four feet above the bridge. He was operating a sight setter which fed information to the guns. It was Hutchings first action, and he was very tensed up until an experienced Scots bosun told him, 'Treat it like practice.'

Aboard *Worcester*, Douglas Ward, a burly 24-year-old gun-layer, was helping to clear the after 4·7 gun, when all hands were piped to an early lunch of corned beef, mashed potatoes and tea. Everyone on the mess deck had now heard the news and were very excited at the prospect of 'having a go at Jerry'. They were not apprehensive as they assumed their role to be just a part of a big attack. Although Pizey and his commanders knew differently, many of the crew firmly believed they would be supporting British battleships steaming out of Scapa Flow, and would be safe under the protection of their great guns. Some of the older, battle-experienced petty officers did not share the optimistic views of the wartime-enlisted sailors. They had been in naval actions before and knew what sudden butchery they could bring.

Then at 1.18 p.m., an hour after he had received his first order, Captain Pizey received another message from the Admiralty. The original signal telling him to intercept the German ships, giving their estimated speed as twenty knots, was based on reports from Spitfires over the Channel and radar. Now, after waiting for over an hour, a more accurate plot of their position was reported from Dover, saying their radar plot had faded at 1.12 p.m. When Navigator Fanning worked this out he calculated that the German warships proceeding on the same course were making nearly thirty knots.

Pizey was the victim of yet another failure to react quickly enough. Why the Admiralty should have so easily accepted the original estimate of speed is inexplicable as the German battleships' cruising speed was known to be twenty-eight knots – and in fact they were capable of thirty-two knots under pressure. Why should they not be cramming on every ounce of speed in their desperate dash up the English Channel? Yet nearly an hour passed before Pizey's destroyers were given details of their real speed.

When he received this report on the bridge of *Campbell*, Pizey had to think very quickly. If he continued on his present course he would miss them. But the only direct course meant going right through the mined area. Yet it was his only chance of intercepting the Germans.

He took less than five minutes to make his decision. At 1.24 p.m., he sent a signal saying: 'Speed 28 knots, course 090.' This meant he had decided to risk damage to his destroyers in the minefield even before he met the Germans. He had charts of the minefields with the rows of mines marked, and there was a narrow channel about a mile wide through which he decided to lead his destroyers. If they navigated carefully the only danger was floating mines. This risk he calculated he had to take. His decision to change course and go through the minefield was described by the C-in-C Nore as, 'One of the soundest appreciations of the action.'

When Pizey gave orders to change course he could not increase speed beyond twenty-eight knots. *Campbell* and *Mackay*, larger and more powerful, could make two to three knots more, but if they did so they would be unable to keep the flotilla together. Even so, one destroyer, *Walpole*, who was last in line, fell out because her old engines could not stand the pace. Her Captain, Lt-Cdr John Eadon, signalled she was unable to go on as her main bearing had burnt out. She was going to try to limp back to Harwich.

Pizey's new plan was to intercept the German battleships off the Hook of Holland. At 1.35 p.m., just as they were entering the minefield, the Germans became aware that the little destroyer flotilla was sailing towards them. A cloud-dodging Junkers 88 appeared and dropped some bombs near *Mackay* and *Worcester*. She missed – but she reported their presence.

Five minutes later, Admiral Ciliax on the bridge of *Scharnhorst* with Captain Hoffmann was handed a signal: 'From JU 88. One cruiser and five destroyers in grid square AN 8714, course 095 degs., high speed.'

Was this report accurate? Were they by any chance capital ships? And why were they so near? Ciliax rightly guessed that a force had been patrolling at sea off Harwich and been ordered to the attack. When the reported position of the British warships was checked on the charts, it was calculated it would be two hours before they could make contact. By that time the Germans would be in a more favourable position to deal with them – or even avoid them altogether.

They were now at the northern end of the Channel and the weather was beginning to deteriorate fast as had been forecast – and hoped for. But there were corresponding disadvantages. Poorer visibility rendered navigation difficult and they had difficulty in finding the mark-boat, which was out of position. Off the Belgian coast there was a depth of water of less than ten fathoms. Although Group West had given them an experienced pilot, who knew these waters thoroughly, a temporary speed reduction was necessary because mine-sweeping was still in progress in this area.

Tension grew. Double look-outs scanned the misty horizon and dark sky. Minutes slowly ticked by, but except for the rattle and explosion of dog-fights overhead nothing happened. The expected second wave of torpedo bombers did not arrive.

At 2 p.m., the ships were through the dangerous channel and Ciliax ordered the ships to go to twenty knots. As they did so, some Spitfires and German fighters could be seen from the German battleships. Ciliax, watching the air battle from the bridge of *Scharnhorst*, remembered Hitler's prophetic utterance, 'The British will find it very difficult to assemble the necessary air forces for a co-ordinated attack within a few hours' notice.'

It was clear that Hitler was right. RAF attacks were spasmodic and unco-ordinated. Their fighters were the only planes reaching the German ships, and they attacked in such small groups that Adolf Galland's German air umbrella had no difficulty in dealing with them.

Still steaming at twenty knots, the warships entered the dangerous shallow waters off the Dutch coast. Fifteen minutes after the Junker sighting, the first mark-buoy at the far end of the sandbanks loomed up ahead of *Scharnhorst*. As soundings gave fifteen fathoms, the battleships' speed was increased to twenty-seven knots. The officers on the bridges of the battleships knew this was dangerously fast and waited anxiously until they were clear of the sandbanks and could resume formation.

At 2.11 p.m., when Pizey was in the middle of the minefield, 12 Hunt Class destroyers left ports in the Thames Estuary to support him. They were *Garth, Fernie, Berkeley, Eglinton, Hambledon, Quorn, Southdown, Meynell, Holdness, Cattistock, Pytchley* and *Cottesmore*. At 2.16 p.m., Commander C. de W. Kitcat in the *Eglinton* was ordered to patrol forty miles to the east of Harwich with six destroyers. At the same time Lt C. W. H. Farringdon aboard *Meynell* was ordered to patrol with five other destroyers near Number 51 Buoy, thirteen miles east-south-east of Harwich, and await further orders.

At 2.30 p.m., just over an hour after entering the minefield, all Pizey's destroyers were clear. At the same moment, a wireless message told Admiral Ciliax in *Scharnhorst* that Group North, under Admiral Wolfram based in Kiel, had taken over from Admiral Saalwächter of Group West in Paris.

In Group West, Commander Hugo Heydel, the first operations officer, had moved his charts back into the operations room. Commodore Friedrich Ruge, without whose mine-sweeping operations the break-out would not have been possible, was so pleased that the ships had steamed through his area without damage that he did something unprecedented. He ordered champagne for the operational staff.

At the same moment, *Scharnhorst* was off the mouth of the Scheldt near Flushing. Helmuth Giessler looked at his charts as they reached 'Point Delta' in their planned course. A messenger reported guard-boat Number Three was 4,000 yards away and the depth of water twenty fathoms.

Two minutes later at 2.32 p.m., there came a violent shock. The heavy ship seemed to lurch in the water and men were nearly flung out of the crow's nest. In the Luftwaffe Control Room radio apparatus came crashing down on people's heads and Lt-Col. Hentschel sprained his left knee and arm.

Staff Captain Reinicke, in the charthouse below the bridge, heard the deep grumbling noise of an underwater explosion. Then the shock flung him upwards and his head struck the metal ventilation casing just above the chart table. When he rushed on to the bridge he saw the ship was losing way. All the lights went out and soon she was lying rolling slightly in a choppy sea.

The *Scharnhorst* had struck a mine dropped by the RAF in eighteen fathoms of water. The generators ceased working and electric current failed throughout the ship. Water began to pour into the engine room, who reported they must heave-to for a time. She immediately sheered off to starboard, dropping away from the line of following ships. Captain Hoffmann ordered the main engines to be stopped and damage control parties sprang into action.

It was such a big explosion that Captain Fein on the bridge of *Gneisenau* following *Scharnhorst* at first thought his own ship was hit. Then he and his officers saw *Scharnhorst* ahead belching black smoke and gushing a large quantity of oil on the port side.

Prinz Eugen's crew also heard a violent explosion to port

followed by a heavy swell. Then a false warning of an approaching torpedo track made them change course and they lost sight of *Scharnhorst*. There also came a sudden deterioration in the weather. Visibility was less than a mile with light rain and the cloud ceiling down to 1,000 feet.

Aboard *Scharnhorst*, the quietness was eerie with the engines stopped after going full steam ahead for nineteen hours. They watched *Gneisenau* and *Prinz Eugen* race past them. They were carrying out orders that if one of the big ships was sunk or stopped, none of the others were to heave-to to render assistance. They were to sail on.

Aboard *Scharnhorst*, a young engineer officer, Lt Timmer, made a rapid inspection of the damage and reported to the bridge, 'Two double bottom compartments flooded and a large hole in the starboard side of the hull.' As Admiral Ciliax considered he could no longer continue his command from the disabled battleship, he decided to transfer his flag to one of the destroyers. Reinicke gathered up all his confidential papers and books and raced down to the quarter-deck to await the Admiral's orders. Col. Ibel signalled to Lt-Col. Dorando aboard *Prinz Eugen*: 'I am crossing over with staff to *Z.29*. Take over control of the fighters and tell the Commander.' He did this because all *Scharnhorst*'s radio connections had failed and the fighters could no longer be advised from her.

As the destroyer *Z.29* came alongside, pitching and rolling, Captain Hoffmann began to receive damage reports from his Chief Engineer, Walther Kretschmer. He reported that the engines were stopped because the shock of the explosion had shut all the automatic valves. But there did not appear to be much damage. Some wing cells aft were taking in water and turret 'A' announced a slight inrush of water. There was also some flooding in the port foc'sle.

Admiral Ciliax shook hands with Captain Hoffmann saying, 'I hope *Scharnhorst* will eventually make it. Follow the Squadron as best you can and put into the Hook of Holland or the nearest port in emergency.'

The seamen of both ships were dangling fenders, but there were great risks of damage. Ciliax, Reinicke and Luftwaffe Colonels Ibel, Elle and Hentschel lined up outside the rail of

Scharnhorst to make a jump for it. The sailors below in the destroyer stood ready in their wet oilskins to cushion their fall. In the mounting wind and rough seas, the destroyer tossed heavily and had trouble keeping alongside the more slowly rolling battleship.

Admiral Ciliax and his staff, carrying documents and registers, started to leap on to the destroyer's heaving deck. For Col. Hentschel, with his sprained ankle, it was a specially agonizing jump. While they were doing it, *Z.29* collided with *Scharnhorst*. When she pulled away with the Admiral safely aboard at last, there was a rending crash which left a jagged wing portion of her bridge hanging from the *Scharnhorst*'s superstructure.

Those of the ship's company aft were amazed to see their Admiral, who had been piped aboard with salutes, heel-clicking and barked orders from petty officers only a few hours previously, leave the ship with so little ceremony. One moment the figures of the Admiral and his staff were silhouetted against the rail. Then they were gone and the tossing destroyer, her superstructure and fo'c'sle dented and scraped by the encounter, had moved clear. The next minute, *Z.29* was dashing at more than thirty knots after *Gneisenau*, abandoning *Scharnhorst* astern in the mists and rain.

When the destroyer had disappeared into the gloom of the dying February afternoon, four torpedo boats – *T.13, 15, 16* and *17* – stood by the stricken *Scharnhorst*.

It was 2.40 p.m. when Ciliax, accompanied by Captain Reinicke, 'abandoned' ship. The impetuous departure of Ciliax, without waiting even five minutes for a report on the state of the ship, was typical of a man suffering from intermittent indigestion pains. He was always a man in a hurry.

Many aboard *Scharnhorst* saw Ciliax go with mixed feelings. Some were glad to see the testy Admiral depart. Others wondered what it all foreboded. The camouflaged destroyer was so patently mistress of the elements, while *Scharnhorst* was rolling helplessly in the North Sea swell – a sitting target for the vengeance of the English, which could not surely be long delayed.

It was obvious to all in *Scharnhorst* that unless they were able to get under way again the English would sink her. Look-outs kept an anxious watch for the RAF. She was only twenty-five miles to the south-east of Pizey's racing destroyers. The crew felt helpless; even the telephones on the ship were dead.

Below in the engine room, Chief Engineer Kretschmer with his devoted staff worked frantically on the automatic boiler controls, stopped by the shock of the mine. At 2.49 p.m. Kretschmer reported the boilers were operating again. Five minutes later he reported the port engine shaft was working. Less than half an hour after the explosion everything came to life. It was reported they had shipped a lot of water in their refrigerating room, but nothing vital was damaged. Had Ciliax waited for Walther Kretschmer's report, he could have remained on his admiral's bridge.

What was to be their fate? That was the unspoken question of many even after Walther Kretschmer got the screws turning again. There was a growing number who were fatalistic. They were beginning to realize from the immensity of the fighter cover, the size of the accompanying 'mosquito' fleet around them, and the elaborate course marked out with anchored craft that they – even their Captains and the Admiral himself – were all puppets moving along the invisible wires laid down for them. During it all Captain Hoffmann, respected throughout the fleet for his great qualities of seamanship, remained imperturbable and gave confidence to all around him. Even though the engines were working again, the mine had put out of action both the direction finder and the echo-sounding gear. While technicians worked to get the equipment going again, a torpedo boat was detailed to provide *Scharnhorst* with navigational help.

Even with this help, when they got under way again at twenty-seven knots it was not plain sailing. There were minefields to port and sandbanks to starboard. Yet Captain Hoffmann decided to risk maintaining his highest speed to try and link up with the other ships again, fifteen miles ahead of them.

While *Scharnhorst* battled with her mine damage, a smaller drama was being enacted in the operations room of Group West in Paris. No sooner had Ruge ordered champagne than a signal reported, '*Scharnhorst* has hit mine'. There was consternation. Then came the time – 2.32 p.m. She was two minutes out of their area. They had done their job. Ruge thankfully ordered another bottle.

.   .   .   .   .

134

While the German naval operations officers were toasting each other in champagne in Paris, a gigantic, confused air battle was hotting up in the murky skies off the Dutch coast.

The torpedo-carrying Beauforts, the RAF's most important ship-busting aircraft, were trying to reach the German battleships. But the struggle to intercept them was again being held back by ground staff incompetence.

At 11.55 a.m., when the Germans were at Cap Gris Nez and a quarter of an hour after Tom Gleave had warned Esmonde, a staff officer from Thorney Island telephoned No. 11 Group, asking for fighters to rendezvous with his seven Beauforts of 217 Squadron over Manston at 1.30 p.m.

The Hornchurch controller pointed out that his fighters were all required to escort the Swordfish, but if Thorney Island would have their aircraft over Manston at 1.30 p.m. he would see what could be done. Following this uncertain arrangement the Beauforts were ordered to take off.

The distance between Manston and Portsmouth is 120 miles. If they had left from Thorney Island at the same time as Esmonde took off from Manston, they could, by flying at twice his speed, have joined him to deliver a co-ordinated attack. But they were held up.

When the order to take off was given, it was discovered that two of the planes were armed with bombs instead of torpedoes, while a third aircraft developed a mysterious technical fault which could not be traced. Instead of immediately launching the four available planes, they were held back while the ground crews struggled for over an hour to make the other three ready.

Eventually, someone made a belated decision and the four torpedo-carrying Beauforts were ordered to take off for Manston. The three other Beauforts were ordered to follow as soon as possible. Owing to this delay on the ground, the four Beauforts, led by Pilot Officer P. H. Carson, did not take off until 1.25 p.m. – five minutes before they were due to meet the fighters over Manston.

The security curtain prevailed here too. Carson and his aircrews, flying in complete ignorance of the importance of their mission, were told to look for a German convoy. Nor did anyone at Thorney Island inform Hornchurch fighter control that the Beauforts would be late.

Yet in spite of the Hornchurch controller's doubts, the Spitfires arrived on time and circled above the airfield waiting for the Beauforts. After five minutes Tom Gleave telephoned Hornchurch saying, 'Why are your fighters circling over here? What are they waiting for?'

This was the first news they had that the Beauforts had not yet arrived. When they telephoned Thorney Island, to discover the torpedo bombers had only just taken off, it was hastily decided that the Beauforts should meet the fighters over the battleships. The Spitfires were contacted by radio and ordered to fly off towards the Germans.

Twenty minutes after the fighters had flown out to sea, Pilot Officer Carson arrived over Manston with his four Beauforts. The Morse kept crackling from Manston control telling him to take the same course as the Spitfires. But someone had blundered again. Thorney Island had forgotten to inform Manston that the Beauforts had recently exchanged Morse for radio telephone. Unaware of this, Manston persisted in trying to give new orders to the torpedo bombers. While they were being frantically signalled in Morse they could not receive, Carson's four Beauforts continued to circle the airfield diligently awaiting orders. Puzzled by lack of communication, but deciding he could wait no longer, Carson and another Beaufort flew off towards France to find the 'convoy'.

It was a sensible, courageous act – except he still did not know what he was looking for, nor where to go. Having had no further information concerning the position of the 'convoy' since he left Thorney Island, he searched an area of the French coast fifty miles behind where the Germans were steaming.

While further attempts were made from Manston to contact them in Morse, the two other Beauforts continued circling. As their fuel was running out, they landed at 2.45 p.m. – an hour and a quarter after the arranged rendezvous with the Spitfires. The two pilots went to the control room and asked, 'What's all the flap about? We were told to rendezvous with some fighters over here and follow them to our target. Where are the fighters? What is the target, sir?'

Station Commander Tom Gleave gasped, 'Has no one told you what you are here for?'

He hastily briefed them with the latest position, their Beauforts were refuelled, and the two pilots took off one and a half hours late. They flew across the North Sea straight into a whirling mass of FW 190s, Spitfires and Hurricanes. RAF fighters were diving, circling and firing at the Germans, while the Beauforts swooped down to wave height to find the battleships. At 3.45 p.m., they dropped their torpedoes but missed.

It was now four hours since the British forces had been ordered to attack, three hours since Esmonde and his men had died trying to torpedo the battleships. The German ships had now passed through the dangerous narrow channel which had given them so little room to manœuvre, and *Scharnhorst* had had enough time to patch up her damage. She was now steaming once again at near full speed to catch up with the *Gneisenau* and *Prinz Eugen*.

While the four Beauforts of 217 Squadron were circling uselessly over Manston, 42 Squadron was also running into trouble. Just as the German battleships were approaching the Dover Straits, the squadron landed at Coltishall from Leuchars at 11.45 a.m. It had been delayed by the weather and ground difficulties. Although the Coltishall controller, Sq. Ldr Roger Frankland, knew about the break-out of the battleships it was only on the 'old boy net'. Other senior officers were under the strictest orders not to divulge the reason for the operation to the aircrews. Said Frankland, 'I have never had an explanation of it. The Beaufort squadron were sent out to look for a convoy. I did not question this stupid secrecy at the time but now it looks bloody silly!'

Coltishall was a fighter base and three of the Beauforts landed unarmed. North Coates, 150 miles away near Grimsby, possessed a Mobile Torpedo Servicing Unit which was at once ordered to Coltishall. The RAF told the police of the urgency and they supplied a siren-wailing motor-cycle escort to clear the road. They need not have bothered.

The Mobile Torpedo Servicing Unit had not been called upon since the outbreak of war – over two years before – and was wrapped in a trance-like euphoria. If they had rushed the torpedoes and compressed air in half a dozen lorries, they could have reached Coltishall in three hours, but instead they crawled out of North Coates in a lengthy procession. This majestic slowness, aggravated by icy roads, caused the 'Immobile Unit' as it was later cruelly dubbed, to arrive at Coltishall just as Ciliax's battleships reached German waters.

This was only the beginning of the disasters that befell 42 Squadron. Apart from the tortoise-like behaviour of the Torpedo Unit, which immobilized three Beauforts, two aircraft developed mechanical trouble when the squadron landed.

Like 217 Beaufort Squadron from Thorney Island, the serviceable Beauforts were held back for the other five. They were delayed for the incredible period of two and a half hours. It was not until 2.16 p.m. that the nine operational Beauforts, led by Sq. Ldr W. H. Cliff, headed for Manston. A signal was sent to Manston to expect them at 2.50 p.m. They arrived only three minutes late.

According to their flight plan, given to them at Coltishall before they took off for Manston, they were to follow the 407 Canadian Squadron of Hudsons to the Dutch coast. These Hudsons were to provide diversionary bombing of the battleships to draw off the flak while torpedo bombers attacked. Both squadrons were to be protected by Spitfires.

When the nine Beauforts arrived over Manston at 2.53 p.m. for once the co-ordination was perfect. Eleven Hudson bombers were waiting in the air and a score of Spitfires circled above them. Obeying their orders, the Beauforts formed up on the tails of the Hudsons. But instead of leading them out to sea, the Hudsons turned tightly and formed behind the Beauforts. The Beaufort commander Cliff, still carrying out his orders, reformed again behind the Hudsons. The Hudsons once again turned and circled behind the Beauforts.

Why this ridiculous ring-a-ring-a-roses? The Hudsons were waiting for orders. Once again Wing-Commander Gleave and his staff tried frantically and unsuccessfully to reach them – by Morse, while the planes had just been fitted with radio telephone. No one had told Manston.

As Carson had done two hours before, Cliff decided he had had enough of this futile follow-my-leader, and led his aircraft out to sea. He was technically disobeying orders, as he headed towards the area where he had been told by Coltishall the 'German convoy' would be. Six Hudsons decided to follow him, hugging the tail of the last Beaufort. The other five Hudsons remained circling over Manston for another half an hour. At 4 p.m. they turned and set course for their home base at Bircham Newton. It was not their fault. No one had told them where to go, what to look for – in fact no one managed to communicate any orders at all.

Cliff led his Beauforts and the six Hudsons across the North Sea in thick cloud and light rain. It was not long before the Hudsons lost touch with him. Soon afterwards the Hudsons' radar began to 'blip'. Diving beneath the clouds, they sighted some German ships to starboard. They swooped through the flak and dropped their bombs on the E-boats and destroyers. Two Hudsons were shot down in this brave attack.

While the torpedo-carrying Beauforts were struggling against the continuing ground muddle, Bomber Command finally came to life.

Bomber Command was between commanders. Air Marshal Sir Richard Peirse had relinquished command at the beginning of January, and Air Vice-Marshal Arthur 'Bomber' Harris was in America and was not due to take over for ten days.

Since 4 February, 300 bombers had been ordered on a two-hour standby for 'Fuller'. But this had meant these bombers had to drop out of nightly attacks against Germany, which Bomber Command saw as their chief task. In view of this, the Air Ministry made a request to the Admiralty to remove the stand-by ordered on behalf of the Navy. The Admiralty would not agree, arguing that the break-out was more likely than ever.

In spite of this, Bomber Command decided to hold only 100 aircraft ready for 'Fuller'. They reverted to normal stand-by working with the remainder. But RAF staff officers omitted to tell anyone of this decision. As a result, when the German ships were reported after midday in the Straits of Dover, it was not until nearly three hours after the alarm that the first bombers were airborne.

Although 242 bombers were sent up, they proved practically useless. Courageous aircrews in formidable aircraft were sent on a mission in which everything was against them. The most operationally experienced bomber crews in the world, they were trained for high-level night bombing of static targets – not a needle-in-a-haystack operation of trying to find and hit fast-moving battleships in the poorest visibility. Also most of them had been bombing Germany the night before.

They set off in three waves. At 2.20 p.m., the first wave of seventy-three bombers took off. It was a hasty, disorganized attack, the planes flying either singly or in pairs. On this cold, overcast winter's afternoon, they swarmed out over the North Sea towards the Dutch coast with thick cloud hanging only a few hundred feet over the waves. When their perspex froze, it was difficult to see, and their heavily-iced wings made flying even more perilous.

Meanwhile, the three remaining Beauforts of 217 Squadron, which had been left behind at Thorney Island, arrived over Manston. The three pilots also knew nothing about the German battleships. However, the leader, Pilot Officer J. A. Etheridge, had sense enough to land and ask for orders. He was immediately briefed by Gleave and his staff and set off in the right direction. For once the instructions were absolutely accurate.

When his Beaufort broke cloud, he found himself right above the German battle squadron. Etheridge, ringed with a flak barrage, took a wide swing over the Dutch coast but his aircraft was hit in several places. His wireless operator had his arm broken by shell splinters, then a cannon shell shot away the torpedo release gear. Unable to launch his torpedo, he turned back for England.

The second Beaufort, piloted by Pilot Officer T. A. Stewart, was attacked by two Messerschmitts. As a cannon shell ploughed through the Beaufort's tailplane, Sergeant Bowen, his gunner, fired a long burst at one of them. The Messerschmitt went spiralling down towards the sea with smoke pouring from it.

The third Beaufort, piloted by Sergeant Rout on his first operational flight, flew low through the flak barrage to drop its torpedo. FW 190s pounced on his tail and he was wounded in the hand by a shell. His wireless operator had a bullet wound in the arm and leg, and his rear-gunner had been seriously wounded when a splinter from the shattered windscreen perspex hit him in the right eye. The aircraft caught fire, but despite their wounds the crew crawled about painfully and put out the flames.

As the two aircraft swept low over *Scharnhorst*, their wings and fuselages riddled with shell splinters from flak gunners, Captain Hoffmann watched from the bridge the two Beauforts split up to attack on opposite sides from astern. A torpedo was seen running, and Hoffmann ordered hard to starboard. When he did so, the Beaufort on the starboard side turned in towards the ships, flying low over her quarter-deck, sweeping her with machine-gun fire. The flak gunners on the port side, busily firing at the first plane, found bullets smacking on to the deck behind them. A hail of bullets struck the bridge of *Scharnhorst*, but no one was injured.

After this determined attack, both Pilot Officer Stewart and Sergeant Rout managed to bring their damaged planes back to Manston. Etheridge nearly did not make it. Near Ramsgate, anti-aircraft batteries, who appeared to be firing at everything coming in from the Channel, mistook his Beaufort for a German and he was shot up again. He staggered back to make a belly-landing at Horsham St Faith, Norfolk.

Meanwhile Carson had arrived back at Manston from his futile cross-Channel search. When he reported to Gleave in the control room, he learnt for the first time about the presence of the German battleships.

Carson then did a very gallant thing. Not waiting for the other Beaufort, which was refuelling, he took off alone to look for the Germans. It was raining hard and visibility was only three miles. German fighters, cruising around the North Sea looking for British aircraft, instantly swooped on his lone plane, but the mist helped him to dodge them.

When his radar picked up the German ships, he skimmed along the waves ahead of the outer screen of E-boats protecting the *Gneisenau*, while flak burst all around him and more fighters came at him, their cannons rattling.

Pulling the stick back, he lifted the Beaufort up a little to cross the masts of the German destroyers laying smoke along *Gneisenau*'s side, and then came down to wave height to drop his torpedo from 2,000 yards. A thumping noise reverberated through the plane as cannon shells smashed into his tail. As he turned to head back into the clouds, he did not know that *Gneisenau* had quickly altered course, and this lone attack narrowly missed crippling her. His torpedo passed only twenty yards from *Gneisenau*'s port side.

The bombers, through no fault of the aircrews, had an almost completely frustrating day. The experience of 40 Squadron Wellington bombers stationed at Alconbury, Huntingdonshire, was typical. The night before, they had taken off at 6.30 p.m. to bomb Mannheim, arriving back just before midnight.

Just before lunch, they were loafing around the mess or resting in their huts when they were called to the briefing hut for the 'Fuller' emergency. Four Wellingtons under Sq. Ldr McGillivray took off at 2.40 p.m. They flew most of the way over the North Sea in 'ten-tenths' cloud reaching up to 1,500 feet.

When the four Wellingtons reached the estimated position of the battleships, a German fighter approached to within 200 yards. As the Wellingtons swerved away, the fighter vanished into the clouds. The bombers continued to circle over the estimated position but their perspex became totally iced up. The de-icer failed in the Wellington piloted by Sergeant Hathaway, preventing him from seeing out of the cockpit. As he would have been a sitting duck for any German fighter in this state, he turned back to grope his way home.

Flying Officer Barr, twenty minutes late taking off, was not airborne until three o'clock. When he arrived over the target area he also circled round, but could see nothing through the thick cloud. Then the front gunner reported his guns jammed, so he too turned back. As he approached the English coast near Lowestoft, anti-aircraft gunners fired at him. The firing still continued as he roared over the roof-tops of Lowestoft, frantically giving three-colour recognition signals. But his rear-gunner, Pilot Officer Leavett, was hit in the back of the head by shrapnel. Barr made an emergency landing at Lakenheath with the bleeding, unconscious gunner in the back, and Leavett was rushed to the RAF hospital at Ely.

Another Wellington squadron, 241, stationed at Stradishall, had even worse luck. Heavy snow had delayed flying operations for a week, but as the snowstorms had abated they were warned on Thursday to be ready to bomb German targets that night. While they were preparing for this night operation, orders were received, 'Carry out Fuller.'

At 2.45 p.m., twelve Wellingtons headed towards the Dutch coast with cloud down to 500 feet. Formation-keeping was almost impossible and only one pilot saw what he believed to be German ships. He went down to 1,000 feet and dropped six 500-lb bombs but observed no results.

Another Wellington, flying at 300 feet under the thick cloud, saw the white wake of a ship. As it turned to pursue, a Messerschmitt came out of the clouds, its machine-guns spitting. The rear-gunner opened fire on the German and in the dog-fight both planes dived into cloud. The Messerschmitt vanished so the Wellington criss-crossed the area but could not find the ship's wake again. Most of the Wellingtons brought their bombs back. Their pilots reported, 'Nothing seen after prolonged search; and returned to base with all bombs.'

One failed to return. Aboard her were the senior officers of the squadron including its commander, Wing-Cdr Macfadden with Sq. Ldr Stephens and Flt-Lt Hughes. After they radioed that they were having engine trouble there was silence. The 241 log-book said, 'The squadron had a very unsuccessful day and lost the Commanding Officer.'

The Blenheim bomber squadrons had the same experience – a last-minute take-off in thick weather and a futile search for the battleships. In their case, the hazards were increased because some of the aircrew had not flown operationally before.

The experience of dark-haired, stocky Flt-Sgt Tom Betjeman, a pilot with 110 Squadron of Blenheims, stationed at Wattisham, Suffolk, was similar to the experiences and frustrations of several hundred bomber pilots.

Like most bomber crews, they had been on stand-by for a week, taking their meals in the crew room in flying kit. They knew 'something big' was in the air but they were not told what it was. Just after 11.30 a.m., they were called into the briefing hut by their squadron leader, who informed them that the *Scharnhorst* and *Gneisenau* had broken out and told them: 'Get cracking. This is what we have been standing by for.'

143

Betjeman, who had a fruit shop in Caterham, Surrey, before he joined up, was on his first operation after coming out of flying school. He led a typical wartime bomber crew. His navigator was a former New Zealand clerk named Noel Colyton and his 21-year-old ginger-haired gunner, Jackie Turner, was an apprentice draughtsman from Manchester.

On the airfield, ready loaded with two 500-pound bombs and two 250-pounders, was his Blenheim. As he climbed in, the armaments officer warned Betjeman that the bombs were set for eleven seconds delay. He said, 'Though conditions give 500 feet cloud don't dip below it to bomb – or you will blow your bloody selves up!'

For night operations against the Norwegian coast the bombers were painted black. Every one of them was very conscious that in daylight they would be an easy target when outlined against the grey clouds.

'Also the weather was terrible,' recalls Betjeman. 'It was the stickiest day I have ever seen. There were misty flying conditions and visibility was not more than three to four hundred feet.'

They took off in four flights of three. As Betjeman in the last three taxied into the runway, the other two planes in his flight went out of action with engine trouble. Flight Control ordered him not to take off alone. They kept calling him, but as he had switched off his radio telephone he did not hear them, and he took off into the low cloud.

He flew by dead reckoning just above the waves over a fairly calm sea. Although his navigator Colyton warned, 'Remember the Met. report gave icing conditions above 400 feet,' Betjeman decided to take a chance and climb into the cloud when they reached the target area. After about fifteen seconds, Air-Gunner Turner came through on the intercom to say, 'Lumps of ice are hitting my rear turret from the prop, Tom.'

This meant he must immediately descend to a warmer temperature. Coming down iced-up through thick cloud was very tricky for an inexperienced pilot like Betjeman. It would have been easy to panic, but he put her nose down very gently, and fortunately, as they came nearer sea level, the ice quickly melted. They 'stooged around' searching for the battleships but could not see anything except mist. Realizing their task was hopeless they turned for home.

Flying Officer Norman Nicholas was also on his first operational flight as the navigator of another Blenheim. On the third leg of a square search over the estimated position, he sighted six warships through a break in the clouds. Still trying to identify them positively as the German battleships, he directed the captain, Pilot Officer Hedley, towards them on a bombing run. As flak shells began to burst around them the air-gunner shouted, 'My machine-guns aren't working!'

Nicholas was determined to try and hit the German ships. But he failed to get a reasonable aim with his bombsight so he called, 'Dummy-run!' to the pilot. When they turned for a second run the clouds had closed in, and they could not see the ships anywhere. As they circled round searching, the air-gunner still could not get his guns to fire. They were defenceless against German fighters, so Hedley decided to return to base. As they flew back, Nicholas bitterly regretted not having taken a chance and released his bombs on the first run.

Most of the squadrons had a similar experience, or like Betjeman and his crew they returned having seen nothing. Out of the thirty-nine who claimed to have located the battleships, none dropped a bomb which did any damage. The others brought their bombs back or jettisoned them when attacked by German fighters. Fifteen bombers were lost. It was estimated that as many losses were due to flying too near the waves as from German attacks. The Germans lost seventeen aircraft.*

In addition to the bombers, every available plane in Fighter Command flew several sorties that day. Although 600 were available on paper, only 398 took off to attack the Germans. Seventeen of them were shot down. Altogether, with the 242 bombers and 35 Coastal Command Hudsons and Beauforts – of which five were lost – 675 aircraft took off to attack the German battleships.

No one can blame their aircrews for the failure of this massive attack. The bomber crews who found the ships attacked with lonely heroism on that grey winter's afternoon. In the

* This is from British sources. The relevant Luftwaffe records have been destroyed.

late afternoon one solitary Wellington shot out of the clouds in thick weather right over *Prinz Eugen* at 400 feet and flew through a hail of flak which practically ripped off her tail unit. As she dived over the destroyer *Hermann Schoemann* and dropped her bombs, she was badly hit and crashed into the sea. The German crews watched her burn with a long sheet of flame rising from the water.

This was just one of the bombers which did not return. No one knows who the pilot was but he upheld the honour of the RAF. His attack was as courageously carried out as Esmonde's and his Swordfish. He too deserved the VC.

Ciliax recognized the gallantry of the RAF when he reported: 'From about 12.45 until 6.30 p.m. massed and individual air attacks from planes of all types. Impressions: Dogged aggressive spirit, very plucky flying, great powers of resistance against light flak hits.'

He explained the lack of success of the attacks like this: 'The British were surprised, which led at the beginning to somewhat desultory and precipitate actions by their forces. During a period spanning one and a half hours after the first attack, no English aircraft succeeded in reaching the Squadron due to our excellent fighter cover. Not until our own fighter cover was badly handicapped by the increasing deterioration in the weather did the enemy aircraft succeed in penetrating to the ships.'

Adolf Galland paid this tribute to the RAF, 'Their pilots fought bravely, tenaciously and untiringly, but they were sent into action with insufficient planning, without a clear concept of the attack, without a centre of gravity and without systematic tactics.'

10

The Gallant Little *Worcester*

The British destroyer *Walpole*, steaming slowly on the edge of the minefield while engineers tried to patch up her main bearing, was an easy but ambiguous target. She had a canvas roundel with the RAF sign on the fo'c'sle, but it was hard to see from the air as it was very misty with low cloud and only two or three miles visibility.

Suddenly two RAF Wellingtons swooped out of the grey clouds and dropped bombs near *Walpole*. On their tails, a formation of Messerschmitts came roaring down the port side and chased off the Wellingtons. Tensely, the *Walpole* crew stood by their guns. They refrained from firing at their unusual escort of German fighters, who returned to circle diligently over the British destroyer when they had chased away the Wellingtons.

It was then they must have recognized the red, white and blue roundel. They were so obviously embarrassed by the discovery that they only fired a few token machine-gun bursts before, as one rating expressed it, 'They poked off into the glue.'

Her engineers having managed to repair temporarily her engines, *Walpole* began to move slowly through the water. She was not attacked again. She made Harwich in three hours at slow speed to meet the Hunt Class destroyers waiting on the other side of the minefields to escort her in.

At 2.45 p.m., when Pizey's other five destroyers were steaming at full speed, line ahead, a plane appeared from a cloud. As it approached, the gun crews trained their guns until orders were passed to them: 'Friendly aircraft ahead.' It was a Hampden. When the bomber dived in low between *Mackay* and *Worcester*, their look-outs switched their attention to the sky for German aircraft, knowing she was friendly.

Suddenly an officer on the *Mackay*'s bridge shouted, 'The Hampden has let go bombs.' At the same time Pizey muttered, 'Hell, we've made a mistake!' As he said it, bombs exploded astern of *Mackay* drenching the after gun crews with spray. Her gunnery officer, afraid the A.A. crews would open fire, shouted over their telephone system, 'Check, check, check. Do not open fire. Repeat. Do not open fire.' He added, 'This aircraft is friendly although he has a funny way of showing it.' But as they saw the bombs dropping, some of the destroyers too far away to identify it opened fire.

The Hampden was not finished yet. She turned and came in low again, this time over *Worcester*, straddling her with bombs. Watching the attack aboard *Campbell*, Pizey muttered, 'It looks like a Hampden – but it can't be!'

'Doc' Jackson was sitting in *Worcester*'s sick-bay trying to take his mind off the coming action by reading an article in a medical journal on the care of sick children, when he heard the bomb explosions rattling the ship's side. He raced on deck just in time to see more bombs falling between his ship and the destroyer *Mackay*. One of them sent spray over the bridge and Coats signalled to Pizey he was about to open fire. The reply winked back hastily: 'Don't do it. It really is a British plane.' As the plane disappeared into the dark low-lying clouds, the destroyers' A.A. gun-layers plainly saw the RAF roundels on its wings.

But these two episodes were only the curtain raiser to a giant mix-up in the air. As the five destroyers emerged from the minefield, they were attacked indiscriminately by both German and British planes. Flying in and out of low cloud together were ME 109s and Beauforts. Higher up in the clouds, flying wing to wing with Hampdens, were Dorniers and ME 110s. Still higher, Heinkels and JU-88s flew next to Wellingtons, Halifaxes and Manchesters, with Spitfires darting between them. Many British aircraft took their own destroyers for German, and on several occasions destroyers opened fire on Wellingtons and Hampdens before they were recognized as belonging to the RAF.

When Pizey and Wright saw the great mass of aircraft overhead, they wished the Hunt Class destroyers had been fast enough to accompany them, for their 4-inch guns could have done considerable damage. As it was, the five destroyers fired their 3-inch A.A. guns and machine-guns at the German aircraft.

The weather grew increasingly bad. It was blowing hard with a heavy westward swell and waves were breaking over the gun crews as they stood at their posts. Visibility suddenly decreased from seven to four miles, which was a relief to the destroyer captains since it would help to mask their attack.

They had two pieces of good fortune. One was the mine which stopped *Scharnhorst* and slowed her down, thus keeping her out of the destroyer action. The other was *Campbell's* up-to-date radar. Three weeks before being ordered to Harwich, *Campbell* was refitting in Chatham. Originally, she was fitted with a fixed aerial type of radar with a range of 4,000 yards, which could only pick up ahead. While they were refitting, Captain Pizey inspected a 271 set which was due to be fitted to another ship. This was not only a more powerful radar with a range of twelve miles, but was a rotating set which meant it could pick up objects in any direction. As the ship for which it was intended was not ready to receive it, Captain Pizey persuaded the dockyard superintendent to get Admiralty approval to let him have it. This radar then replaced the 4·7 gun director on the back of the bridge. It had to be installed in such a hurry that electricians were still aboard putting the finishing touches to it as *Campbell* sailed from Chatham to Sheerness. A leading telegraphist aboard *Campbell* was an enthusiast about radar. It was only his knowledge that enabled them to make it work quickly.

At 3.17 p.m., when the destroyers were twenty-two miles from the Hook of Holland, this new radar performed perfectly. Two large 'blips' began to show on the screen, indicating ships nine and a half miles away. As they went full ahead, the sea became even rougher and the destroyer decks were awash with big waves. Then a look-out shouted 'Gun flashes ahead!' This was the German battleships firing at RAF planes. It was just after 3.30 p.m.

On the starboard bow, *Campbell's* bridge officers saw gunfire flickering through the grey curtain of cloud on the horizon. Through binoculars, the German ships could be seen as black blobs silhouetted against the darkening sky. They were steaming fast four miles away on a course converging very slightly with their own.

The cry came, 'Enemy in sight!' and *Campbell* hoisted her battle ensign on the yard-arm. Through mist and rising spray they could see the big White Ensign battle flags sprouting on the masts of the other destroyers.

Aboard *Whitshed* the bosun's mate commented, 'Isn't it glorious to see the battle flag flying!' His views were shared by many young wartime ratings who had never seen action before. It was indeed an inspiring historic sight – five old British destroyers thumping and rolling as they steamed through the mounting waves to attack the pride of the German Navy. They did not know then that *Scharnhorst* was out of range.

At 3.42 p.m., amid gun flashes and A.A. tracer, the German warships could be clearly seen in line ahead from *Campbell*'s bridge. They were now so near that many of the German aircraft flying over them thought the approaching British destroyers were friendly and fired off their recognition signal – four balls in the shape of a diamond.

Aboard *Worcester*, gun-layer Douglas Ward peered through his telescopic sights, and saw one German battleship looming very large. Within a short time she became so clear that he did not need his optical viewer. He could see her quite plainly over open sights.

With RAF bombers diving on them and Spitfires and Messerschmitts battling overhead, the German commanders were so worried about the aerial threat that Captain Fein now commanding the squadron aboard the leading ship, *Gneisenau*, was unaware the British destroyers were approaching at high speed.

At 3.45 p.m., standing on the bridge of *Gneisenau*, he saw shells bursting near with the greenish-yellow smoke typical of British ammunition. For a moment he was uncertain what was going on, but suddenly a look-out shouted, 'Enemy in sight on port bow!' As a line of grey silhouettes came steaming out of the mist, Fein ordered his gunnery officer Kahler to open fire. He also radioed Group North at Kiel: 'Am in action with enemy destroyers.'

But was the destroyer attack a feint? He ordered the German destroyers forward to see if there were any bigger ships waiting to attack as soon as he went into battle against Pizey's destroyers. He also ordered his own ship and the *Prinz Eugen* to zigzag. This was mainly because the RAF were delivering a fierce attack on *Prinz Eugen*, whose flak guns were blazing away at the planes diving on her. The attack was so intense that Commander Paulus Jasper, her gunnery officer, had gone himself to the main flak position to direct operations.

At 3.43 p.m. the operational telephone rang from the bridge warning him that British destroyers were approaching on the port side at top speed. He ran to the foretop and gave the preliminary order to the big guns: 'Prepare to open fire.' Then Jasper made out a line of shadowy shapes which he took to be four destroyers.

At the same time, Senior Midshipman Bohsehke, in charge of the forward heavy gun position, saw four British destroyers steaming from the stern on a parallel course. *Campbell* came on with flashes coming from all her guns, and Bohsehke and Petty Officer Gustav Kuhn tried to identify her. Both thought *Campbell* had such a high superstructure that she was probably a cruiser. Commander Jasper thought she had three funnels.

Then British destroyer shells began to explode around *Prinz Eugen*, their red-hot shrapnel hissing into the water. As *Campbell* ran parallel to *Prinz Eugen* at full speed, Bohsehke managed to get a 'fix' on her. When Jasper gave the order, there was a tremendous flash and crash as Bohsehke opened fire with a full 8-inch salvo. As the big shells burst around her, *Campbell* still came on, taking advantage of the smoke screen laid down by the German escort vessels.

There came a series of further blinding flashes as the *Gneisenau* began to fire her big 11-inch guns as well as the 5·9s of her secondary armament, which alone were big enough to deal with the destroyers.

At the same time, Captain Brinkmann of *Prinz Eugen* signalled, 'Am in action with cruisers and destroyers.' An action signal of this nature is always given top priority in any navy. But in this case there was such confusion in her signal room that it was not transmitted. Signals were in the hands of a first lieutenant assisted by a midshipman, neither of whom were very experienced. During the voyage, the signals room dealt with 800 messages, but there was such trouble decoding that important messages were reaching the bridge hours late. As a result of this, the German Admiralty did not know *Prinz Eugen* was in action.

When the destroyers approached, *Gneisenau* was 5,500 yards ahead of *Prinz Eugen*. Fein, obeying his orders to save his ship at all costs, fired his guns at the shadowy shapes of the destroyers. Although *Gneisenau* was still in the fight she disappeared from *Prinz Eugen*'s sight, which led Captain Brinkmann to believe he was fighting the battle alone.

Aboard *Prinz Eugen*, while Bohsehke's heavy guns were firing, the flak guns were also in continual action. In the Luftwaffe fighter operations room, Lt Rothenberg and Lt von Kuhlberg kept reporting RAF aircraft on all sides. The specially installed quadruple 2-cm guns scored many hits. Their shells were seen to explode against several RAF aircraft, but they continued to fly despite being filled with holes. They seemed to absorb the small shells but Lt Paul Schmalenbach, the flak commander, wondered if they all got back.

Meanwhile Pizey's five destroyers were still racing forward at thirty knots, replying with their own guns and firing pom-poms at attacking German aircraft. Shells began to fall very close, straddling them. Pizey held his course, waiting for the right time to launch his torpedoes. He stood on the bridge of *Campbell* watching the German aircraft and ships as calmly as if he were on manœuvres, leaning forward every second or so to give orders to his navigator or the yeoman of signals.

Aboard *Whitshed*, Ted Tong, being one of the tallest men in the crew, stood on a steel table with one arm round a stanchion hauling up shells for the 4·7 after-gun. He had hoisted up several dozen shells when he heard a yell from the gun crew above. 'There they are!' and the guns started firing. The ship rumbled and rocked with explosions, but Tong still could see nothing. Even those on deck could see very little through the blinding spray and splashes of bursting shells, but as *Mackay* turned towards the Germans, Hutchings on duty above her bridge saw two shapes glinting a beautiful silver in a sudden patch of sunlight.

It was getting towards dusk as the destroyers went into open battle order to attack. Waves broke green fore and aft and even officers on the bridge were drenched with spray. The torpedo crews, knee deep in water as the destroyers rolled heavily, tried to train their tubes. Flotilla-leader *Campbell* was followed by *Vivacious* with *Worcester* last of the line.

On their starboard beam were *Mackay* and *Whitshed*, who were to attack first. As he hauled round to starboard to launch his torpedoes, Captain Wright in *Mackay* saw a big German ship steering directly towards him. He recognized the *Prinz Eugen*. But she was not going to attack. Her commander, Captain Brinkmann, had altered course thinking *Mackay* was a German destroyer. For two minutes *Whitshed*, rolling in the great seas, followed *Mackay* towards the German ships under heavy fire. Visibility was still bad and the destroyers came under attack from everything the Germans had, but by a miracle there were no hits. Neither Kahler on *Gneisenau* nor Jasper on *Prinz Eugen* had their range. The nearest German shells fell a quarter of a mile away from *Mackay* and *Whitshed*.

It was 3.45 p.m. when *Mackay* and *Whitshed* launched their torpedoes together from 4,000 yards. As *Mackay* launched hers, *Prinz Eugen* again altered course. This was not to avoid what she still thought was a German destroyer, but to dodge an RAF plane that was trying to bomb her.

Hutchings watched *Mackay*'s torpedoes drop into the sea like a diver making a belly flop, and as they began to run she swerved sharply away. With the ship shuddering and turning at full ahead, Hutchings had to cling to the two brass handles of his sight-setter to keep upright.

Aboard *Whitshed*, Tong heard the gun crews shouting, 'We are attacking the *Prinz Eugen*. We can see her. I think we have hit her!' But *Whitshed*'s torpedoes also missed *Prinz Eugen*, as German shells fell into the sea around the destroyer, the near-misses rocking the ship. Immediately after she had fired, cloud descended to nearly sea level and the German battleships disappeared from the destroyers' view in a rain squall.

At this moment Pizey decided to attack. In his report he said, 'As we closed to 3,500 yards I felt our luck could not last much longer. The ships were being well straddled.'

What finally decided him was a heavy shell fired by Kahler's guns aboard *Gneisenau* which failed to explode, bounced off the waves and then dived under *Campbell* like a porpoise. Pizey turned to navigator Fanning and said, 'Pilot, we are turning. What retiring course do you recommend?' Fanning had already worked this out, and the course was instantly radioed to the two destroyers astern. This was so that the ships would all turn together, firing their torpedoes simultaneously to give the greatest arc of fire. There was hardly a second's interval between Pizey's decision on the bridge of *Campbell* and the information being received by the other destroyers. As the torpedo gunners waited tensely to receive their orders by voice pipe and telephone, Pizey, half-blinded by spray on the bridge, said tersely, 'Torps, we go in to attack the enemy with torpedoes . . . now!' The yeoman of signals on the bridge called down to the radio room, 'Give the executive signal.' This was three short dots and a long in Morse. As the Morse signal bleeped to the other destroyers, Pizey ordered, 'Turn to fire.'

It was forty-seven and a half minutes past three when *Campbell* and *Vivacious* turned to port and fired together from 3,500 yards – about two miles. *Campbell* launched six torpedoes but *Vivacious* only three, because half her torpedo tubes had been removed to fit a 3-inch anti-aircraft gun.

Midshipman Bohsehke aboard *Prinz Eugen* saw *Campbell* fire her torpedoes and called out a warning. Captain Brinkmann at once turned the ship hard to starboard away from their foaming wakes. At the same time, *Campbell* was once again straddled by shells from Bohsehke's forward guns, and every other gun the cruiser could bring to bear.

The foretop was obscured by smoke blown forward by a heavy stern wind, so the German gunners could not see where their shells were landing. As the shells ringed his ships, Pizey was watching for the result of his torpedo attack. When he saw German destroyers appearing ahead of the *Gneisenau*, he hoisted the flag signal: 'Disregard.' This meant; 'Act independently,' which gave individual ships freedom to either attack the destroyers or take evasive action.

But one destroyer had not yet attacked. While cascades of water from high waves and near-misses were showering over her,

Worcester, shuddering from her labouring engines, pressed even closer than the other two destroyers. She steamed so near that as she ran parallel with the two German ships, the officers on her bridge could clearly make out their triangular masts and massive grey shapes. Lt-Cdr Coats, a very brave and determined man, muttered through his teeth, 'I am going to sink one of those damned ships.' He passed the message to his crew, 'Everyone must do their best.'

In front of him towered the leading battleship of the Squadron – the *Gneisenau*. Coats steamed closer, ignoring the shells which were now raining down on him as the German gunners began to get the range of his tiny destroyer. Their broadsides cut a foaming swathe through the water fifty feet ahead of him.

But smoke and *Prinz Eugen*'s torpedo-dodging course changes made firing and observation difficult for the German gunners. Then, as *Worcester* was still holding a steady course towards her, Petty Officer Kuhn managed to get a 'fix' on the destroyer's muzzle fire. None of the German gunners could tell through the mist whether she was a new destroyer or one of the four at which they had already fired.

Although it was only a matter of seconds before the German guns must register a hit, Coats still stayed on course, firing back. Some of his shells aimed at *Prinz Eugen* burst harmlessly in the high waves. Douglas Ward fired one round from his after 4·7 gun, and then his second shot misfired. In the excitement of battle someone had forgotten to put in the cordite.

It was three minutes since *Campbell* and *Vivacious* had fired. It seemed like three years. The ship was lurching and shaking and everywhere there was a shattering, overpowering noise. It was impossible to tell which were their guns firing and which were German shells exploding.

On the bridge, a young sub-lieutenant with a pistol-type instrument in his hand waited for the order: 'Fire One.' Then he would press the trigger which fired the torpedoes electronically. Torpedo-gunner Wellman had his own sights below. If the bridge did not give the order to fire, his duty was to pull his own lever and fire the torpedoes himself. The bridge ordered a deflection of 25 knots for the torpedo firing. By voice tube and telephone this order was given to Wellman, who acknowledged it.

Worcester steamed on into the hellish cauldron, the *Gneisenau* a grey mass towering before her. But the usual count-down went calmly on – '40, 30, 20' – reporting the degrees to go before the 'fish' went off. The orders were repeated continually, so there could be no misunderstanding.

She began to heel over heavily to starboard before making her big turn to port to launch her torpedoes, while in the sea near her slanting deck there were dozens of fountains from shell splashes. She was now so near that Bohsehke in the forward gun position on *Prinz Eugen* ordered a flattened trajectory, which could hardly miss her.

Coats, about one and a quarter miles away, running broadside to the German ships, was just about to give the order to fire when there was an ear-splitting crash. Three heavy shells exploded on *Worcester* at almost the same time, with a cloud of white smoke and orange flashes.

One burst abreast of the 12-pounder gun, and all the gun crew were either killed or wounded. Just forward of the 12-pounder was Gunner Wellman, with the ratings manning the torpedo tubes. Deafened, their faces blackened, they dodged the splinters shaken but unhurt.

Forward of the torpedo tubes on the starboard side a hole was driven which extended from half-way across the deck to below the water-line, completely wrecking and flooding the No. 1 boiler room. Fragments of shell penetrated No. 2 boiler room, making another large hole from the deck half-way to the water-line.

Another direct hit landed on the starboard side of the fo'c'sle deck about fifteen feet from the sick-bay, drilling it full of holes and knocking out Dr Jackson and his sick-bay attendant, A. J. Shelley. It also tore up her decks, smashing the lower part of the bridge and wrecking the radio room. Miraculously, neither Cdr Coats nor his officers were hurt, even though below the bridge boxes of ammunition for the Oerlikon guns began to explode.

The third shell exploded on the water just short of the ship level with the wardroom, completely wrecking it and blowing to pieces some of the supply and repair party. The three shells which hit the ship were so heavy that some of the crew thought they were from shore batteries firing from the Dutch coast.

Worcester had still not fired her torpedoes when Bohsehke's shells hit her. The sub-lieutenant on the bridge still continued giving orders to prepare to fire but Wellman on the torpedo deck, deafened and dazed, could not hear him because of the noise. When the Oerlikon ammunition started exploding, Wellman thought the bridge had gone and muttered, 'We will have to fire the torpedoes ourselves.' Still not being able to hear the bridge, he did his duty and went ahead and fired.

When they jerked over the side they were 2,500 yards from the *Gneisenau*. Yet, although the *Worcester* had steamed so near to the *Gneisenau*, her three torpedoes passed harmlessly astern of her and ahead of the *Prinz Eugen*, which was dodging seven bombs RAF planes had just aimed at her.

The noise was appalling. There were so many explosions that it was impossible to make out whether they were being hit again or not. The ship was completely curtained by shell splashes. That concealment momentarily helped to save them from further punishment. All sight of the German ships was lost and it was difficult to see what had happened to the torpedoes.

Coats, still unhurt on the bridge, recalls, 'It was three minutes after *Campbell* had fired that I launched my torpedoes. As I went in zigzagging to avoid the German shells, it was the longest three minutes of my life. The other destroyers had vanished making me feel very lonely. When I fired my torpedoes I saw black smoke coming up from the water. I thought it was a hit from one of my torpedoes, but it was a bomb exploding near *Gneisenau*. I felt shattered and useless as I realized my torpedoes had gone well astern of *Gneisenau* and ahead of *Prinz Eugen*.'

After the three shells had disabled her, *Worcester* made an almost complete circle, her engines silent, drifting to her port broadside to *Prinz Eugen*. It was like target practice for Bohsehke's gunners. Two of his shells scored direct hits to be followed by two more from the *Gneisenau*. The four heavy shells ripped through the disabled destroyer, smashing her guns and tearing more great gaping holes in her side.

One shell from *Prinz Eugen* went through her bows, exploding in the paint locker and starting a fire. When someone shouted, 'Fire in the fo'c'sle!' the sea was so high that at first the waves seemed to put it out, but it flamed up again.

As Chief Engineer Griffiths came on deck to report his boilers useless, there was a puff of brown smoke and large jagged splinters whistled across the deck. A shell hit the base of the forward funnel, making a hole about four feet across and breaking the mast six feet above the deck. It fell backwards and leaned, swaying crazily, against the top of the funnel, with the rigging hanging loose. Commander Coats's mind went back to Nelson's day when grapeshot tore down the rigging and he muttered to Lt Taudevin, 'This is just like old times.'

Worcester, drifting beam-on exposed to point blank fire from the two German ships, was clearly seen by Petty Officer Hehenberger on the range-finder in the foretop of *Prinz Eugen*. He watched *Worcester*, on fire and apparently stopped, disappear into the black smoke of more heavy bursting shells. When the smoke cleared, other men on the foretop of *Prinz Eugen* glimpsed her for a short time through the haze before, battered by Bohsehke's shells, she seemed to disappear beneath the waves. Master-gunner Emmanuel Pietzka, on the stern flak gun, also saw *Worcester* burning in a vast cloud of smoke. A few seconds later, she could no longer be made out – only smoke and surging water. The sight reminded him strongly of the sinking of Britain's biggest warship, the *Hood*, which he had observed from the same position in *Prinz Eugen*.

Coats shared the view of the German gunners. As he gazed from the bridge at his battered burning ship, he decided she would sink at any moment. She was wallowing down by the stern with a list of 20 degrees to starboard. The quarter-deck was awash and she was rolling sluggishly. The main compartments were so full of water that every time she rolled it felt as if she would not right herself again. So he gave the order: 'Prepare to abandon ship.' As one of the young ratings descended the starboard ladder from the bridge, shouting out the order, he was hit by a shell splinter.

As a result, a garbled version of the order spread rapidly round the ship. Deafened by the guns and bursting shells, the crew thought the order had been given 'Abandon ship'.* Carley floats were thrown over, the whaler was lowered, and a few men began jumping overboard to swim or hang on to floats which drifted near the ship.

But *Worcester* did not sink. She was probably saved from complete annihilation by a tiny bit of luck – *Gneisenau*'s heavy guns went out of action. A shell which was being rammed into a heavy gun jammed and the cartridge case became twisted, stopping the moving ammunition belt.

Worcester was still afloat but now with a fire in the paint store which the crew tried to get under control with buckets of water. The forepeak, the locker-room, the wardroom, the after-magazine, the shell-room and the after-stores were all flooded. A newer destroyer would have sunk but her older, closer frames probably saved her. But she was finished and out of the fight.

Nightmare scenes were taking place aboard her. When the shell shattered the lower bridge, destroying the ammunition locker underneath it, the force of the explosion also jammed the water-tight doors of the radio room below the bridge, and the men inside were roasted like turkeys.

The helmsman, with a shattered hand, still kept trying to steer. Another sailor next to him in the wheelhouse was a mass of blood and bone.

One young sailor in a gun turret had his arm blown off and picked it up sobbing and tried to push it on again. As the gun was still in action, a Petty officer knocked him uncon- scious. It was not only the kindest thing he could have done, but it also prevented panic spreading among the young gun crew, several of whom were also wounded. The unwounded gun crews continued to fire until they ran out of ammunition. Ward and his mates still tried to fire their gun, but the ship began to settle so rapidly into the water that they could no longer get a bearing.

Worcester's guns fell silent. All that could be heard were the screams of the wounded, the hiss of steam escaping from the

* As a result of this disaster aboard the *Worcester* the Royal Navy finally decided to cancel the order 'Prepare to abandon ship' as it could so easily be misinterpreted in the din of modern battle.

broken boilers and shouted orders as she swung helplessly in the waves.

At the same time the Germans' big guns stopped raining death on to *Worcester*. Through his binoculars, Captain Fein of *Gneisenau* watched the blazing destroyer wallowing in the heavy seas. She seemed gradually to be settling into the water so he gave the order to cease fire. He said, 'I watched our guns score direct hits on the English destroyer and it seemed to me that she heeled so far over under their impact that she nearly capsized. I ordered our guns to cease firing, as there seemed no point in wasting shells on a ship already sinking. No ship of that size could be hit so heavily and survive.'

No more British destroyers could be seen from either ship. *Worcester* had presumably sunk in a cloud of black smoke and the others had vanished into the mist. Midshipman Bohsehke aboard *Prinz Eugen* fired once again at long range at a dimly recognizable ship and also at the gun flashes of another ship astern. Then Gunnery Commander Jasper ordered: '*Halt, Batterie, Halt!*'

It was 3.56 p.m. The destroyer action was over after eleven minutes. The shelling of *Worcester* had only lasted three minutes.

The official German report said: 'Both *Prinz Eugen* and *Gneisenau* opened fire with their heavy naval guns. The English destroyers turned on a parallel course, engaging the main formation in a running gun battle. They were firing torpedoes at the same time as the German ships were attacked from the air by torpedo carriers. After the first direct hits on the enemy destroyers – three of the hits seen from the *Gneisenau* caused fires – the *Prinz Eugen* sank one destroyer and set another on fire. The enemy turned away sharply in order to engage while passing and were almost immediately out of sight in the mist.' The German report was incorrect – only *Worcester* was damaged.

From the point of view of the German warships, it had not been a satisfactory action. Both Fein of *Gneisenau* and Brinkmann of *Prinz Eugen* regretted they were not armed with torpedoes. If they had, they believed they would have had a good chance of finishing off the destroyers more easily than with the heaviest gunfire. But they had no warheads aboard, as Group

160

West had ordered them to keep all explosive material to the minimum.

The *Worcester*, hit seven times by heavy shells, was a smoking shambles and seemed certain to sink. The decks were slippery with blood and the bridge was spattered with brains and chunks of torn red flesh. Blood and trickling green paint from the damaged paint shop flowed round shattered bodies in oilskins about the decks. A sailor came staggering out on deck trying to hold his guts in with his hands.

The unwounded survivors of the crew waited helplessly for German destroyers to approach and finish them off. None came. They were sweeping ahead of their battle squadron, scouting for British capital ships, which were in fact hundreds of miles away in Scapa Flow.

As both the doctor and the sick-bay attendant were knocked out for a time, the rumour went round the ship that everyone in the sick-bay had been killed. But Dr Jackson and his assistant dazedly picked themselves up as a sailor staggered through the door and fell unconscious. After they had lifted him into a bunk the doctor scrambled up on deck. He was still so dazed that he forgot his equipment and had to go back to grab as many dressings as he could. He stuffed two bottles of morphine into his pocket and picked up a torch, as all the lights had failed and it was becoming dark. Some slightly wounded men from 'A' and 'B' gun crews appeared, grinning apologetically, at the door.

Only when he climbed on deck did he realize the battle was over. The noise had ceased, to be replaced by an eerie quiet as the ship rolled sluggishly surrounded by towering waves. He realized that he and the rest of the crew were almost totally deaf. Officers and men were going round shouting at each other – the sudden cessation of the bombardment having failed to register.

The doctor crawled about the blood-stained decks shoving morphine into the wounded and dying men. After attending to a man on 'B' gun, he went to a bad casualty in the wheel-house. Then he went down to the waist of the ship and worked his way along the upper deck. A lot of wounded men were lying or sitting under the pom-poms and beside the empty torpedo tubes, where Bill Wellman, miraculously unwounded, was attending to them.

Beside the 12-pounder gun, some men were lying so still that the doctor knew he need not stop. He went on to the after-superstructure, where there were some dreadful casualties among the men of the supply and repair party.

A leading stoker, his stomach ripped out and his arm torn off, staggered to the side to drown himself because he knew he was finished. Chief Engineer Griffiths pulled him back on to the deck and the doctor tried to operate on him, but he died a few minutes later.

Then Griffiths saw First Officer Dick Taudevin hurrying along the deck and said to him, 'This is a fine old pot mess. Why are you running about so much?' Taudevin replied, 'I am trying to stop some silly buggers from jumping overboard. They think the order has been given to abandon ship.'

While Jackson was doing what he could for the wounded, Lt Taudevin appeared at his elbow and said, 'Thank heaven you are all right, Doc. We are not abandoning ship. Tell the wounded.' Then he went calmly aft and, in as firm a voice as he could manage, he told those wounded who were conscious to stay under cover and sit down.

No one has a clear recollection of what took place on those smoking, bloody decks littered with the wounded hoarsely calling for help. There was terrible confusion and one or two cases of panic. While some men with shattered legs were dragging themselves along the deck on all fours, other wounded lay moaning quietly on the slanting decks. One or two staggered to the rail and threw themselves overboard. They were either trying to save themselves from the sinking ship by reaching the floats or drown themselves deliberately, as they knew they were so badly wounded they only faced a painful lingering death.

Amid the confusion, Chief Engineer Griffiths saw Engine Room Artificer Hayhoe shutting off the steam throttle and shouted, 'What the hell are you doing?' Hayhoe replied, 'There is no steam, Chief. All the boilers have gone except Number Three.'

Griffiths and Hayhoe climbed down to the damaged Number One boiler room. There were only two hatches so just the two of them went down, for if the ship suddenly began to sink a third might have no time to climb up.

162

The hole in the ship's side near the engine room, although four feet long, was well above the water-line. The sea was still pouring into Number One boiler room, but there was steam in the gauges and the steering gear was undamaged. At the same time, Stoker P.O. Dawson reported that Number Two boiler was also badly damaged but Number Three was intact.

The ship's list was increasing and Griffiths knew if he did not get her underway soon she would sink. Normally the way to correct a list is to flood the opposite compartment, but they were shipping water so fast from the bow damage that the decks were only two or three feet above the waves. Any more flooding would certainly have capsized her.

Standing waist-deep in water in the flooded engine room Griffiths had a hasty conference with Hayhoe. Ships' boilers must use the purest distilled water, and in normal times Admiralty experts constantly examine the water-carrying gear for purity. Now this had all gushed away. There was only one way they could keep the ship moving – to use salt water. But would the boilers continue to work or would salt bubbling up with the steam soon choke the pipes?

They managed to patch up the large hole by stuffing it with hammocks and putting in their only collision mat. Griffiths then ordered a hose slung over the side and the bilge pump rapidly pumped in twenty tons of sea water.

To lighten the ship, the crew were frantically throwing everything overboard. Lockers, sacks of potatoes – even the heavy range-finder was unscrewed – were thrown into the sea. The crew also wrapped the wounded in blankets and put them on the quarter-deck or under the break in the fo'c'sle. P.O. Gordon started cutting off the rigging which hung dangling over the decks from the shattered mast.

Campbell and *Vivacious* were searching for German destroyers ahead of the battleships. As his other ships vanished in the mist, Pizey decided that in the circumstances the safest course to steer was 180 degrees, which meant turning completely back on his tracks in the hope of making contact with the flotilla. Shortly after turning on to the new course, Pizey saw a ship ahead of him which he thought was the *Prinz Eugen*. As they drew nearer, he realized it was the *Worcester*, damaged and apparently stopped. She was two miles off *Campbell*'s port beam with smoke and steam pouring from her. Floating in the water near her were men clinging to floats. It was 3.57 p.m., and the Germans had just ceased firing.

When *Worcester*'s crew saw *Campbell* and *Vivacious* approaching, they thought they were the German destroyers they had been expecting to come and finish them off. With all their guns out of action they waited for the end. *Campbell* tried to reach *Worcester* by short-wave radio, but along with practically everything else her radio had gone. She could only signal by lamp. It was not until *Campbell* began shouting to her by loud hailer that *Worcester*'s dazed crew realized she was friendly.

When *Campbell* and *Vivacious* steamed out of the murk, the men on the Carley rafts gave the thumbs-up sign and started to paddle towards them. As they drew alongside *Campbell*, men swung overboard to try and pick them out of the sea.

It was at this moment that Sq. Ldr Cliff with his torpedo-carrying Beauforts from 42 Squadron arrived on the scene. They ran straight into the great air battle which was still raging. Luftwaffe fighters were trying to shoot down RAF bombers as they dived through flak clouds thrown up by the *Gneisenau*, *Prinz Eugen* and their escort ships. Although the Germans had broken off the action because they could no longer see the British destroyers, both sides were clearly visible from the air. They were so near to one another that some of the Beaufort pilots thought the British destroyers were escorting the German ships.

As the Beauforts came down to wave height to drop their torpedoes, the heavy shells from the German ships smacked into the water between the planes.

Through the shell bursts Cliff saw a ship which he believed to be *Scharnhorst*, with a column of smoke pouring from her funnel. He flew over a destroyer and came down to within 1,100 yards of the ship to release his torpedo. As he banked steeply to port he saw another destroyer. A minute later he signalled base that he had dropped his torpedo, seen it run, but could not observe the result.

Following Cliff through this fierce barrage came Pilot Officer Birchly, who sighted two destroyers and a bigger ship which he also believed to be *Scharnhorst*. He flew over the destroyers to within 800 yards of the ship before dropping his torpedo.

The third Beaufort of the flight was piloted by Pilot Officer Kerr. He too saw a large 'ship', which he was sure was the *Scharnhorst*, with four destroyers near it. Kerr came down to eighty feet off the water to drop his torpedo. Air-Gunner Sergeant Smith fired back at the destroyers, which were sending up clouds of flak bursts towards him. Both his wireless operator, Sergeant Waller, and his gunner, Sergeant Smith, reported that the warship was 'listing badly with smoke pouring from her bows'.

Pilot Officer Archer in another Beaufort also saw a big ship with a large superstructure and a short funnel which he too took for the *Scharnhorst*. As he dropped his torpedo his plane was hit by a shell which ripped through the port engine. Another made a hole in the tail and blew the perspex off the rear turret, wounding Sergeant Betts, the gunner, in the face and arm. Shrapnel grazed the leg of radio operator, Sergeant Cain.

But as the Beauforts pressed home their attack at nearly wave height, one of them made what might have been a tragic mistake. In the air and sea mix-up, one pilot mistook *Campbell* for a German ship. When Pizey saw the torpedoes drop, he thought they were aimed at the *Prinz Eugen*, which he knew was hidden near by in the mist. Then his alert Asdic operator reported: 'Torpedo at green forty-five approaching on a steady bearing.'

To his horror, Pizey realized it was coming at him. It could not have happened at a worse moment, for nearly a dozen of his men were hanging over the side on ropes trying to rescue the *Worcester* ratings before they drifted away in the freezing water. He realized there was only one thing to do to save his ship and its crew – go full speed astern. It was an agonizing decision to have to make, because it meant temporarily abandoning men in these icy waters.

As *Campbell* went astern her wake washed over the floats alongside and men were thrown into the sea. Some too wounded to swim managed to grab lifelines thrown to them. But some died from exposure in the very cold water.

Before *Campbell* had gathered any appreciable stern way her Asdic operator reported: 'Bearing growing ahead.' This meant the torpedo was going across *Campbell*'s bows – and would therefore miss. Pizey recalls, 'It did not take a second before I gave the order: "Full ahead." This stopped the ship's way and we were able to continue to pick up survivors. Some of them were floating in the water in a bad way. It was a dreadful sight. But, thank God, most of the badly wounded who had been put into the whaler and on to the Carley floats seemed all right. We were able to get them on board.'

It was not only the RAF who made mistakes in the mêlée. So did the Luftwaffe. At the same time as Pizey was dodging the RAF torpedo, the German destroyer *Hermann Schoemann* was firing frantically at a Dornier 217 which dropped two bombs near her. When the German bomber turned to rake her with machine-gun fire, the destroyer's flak guns tried to shoot her down.

Then another Dornier swooped over the destroyer *Z.29* with Admiral Ciliax and his staff aboard. As she approached for a bombing run, the flak gunners stood ready anxiously watching her. Just as they were about to open fire, she recognized them and swerved away. Firing off the recognition signal of five red stars, the plane vanished into the clouds.

While both British and German ships were fighting off attacks by their own planes, *Worcester* was waterlogged and rolling badly. But Chief Engineer Griffiths was now confident that, if he could get the after-boiler working he could get her under way. Pizey signalled her by lamp: 'Intend taking you in tow.' When Douglas Ward was ordered by the bridge to find a tow rope, he reported that it had disappeared in the wreckage. Coats signalled Pizey. 'Towing gear not available.' Pizey replied: 'Stand by. We will pass our own towing gear.'

It was still touch and go for *Worcester*. As she reached the end of her roll, she seemed momentarily to stand still. Coats realized that if she listed a fraction of a degree further she might turn turtle. She was also drifting so badly that *Campbell* had to turn and pass her bows to try and toss the towing gear aboard.

As *Campbell* was about to throw the gear, Pizey saw she was moving away from him. At first he thought his helmsman had miscalculated. Just as he realized she was moving under her own power a signal flashed across: 'One engine room connected up.'

Slowly *Worcester* began to make steam. The engine knocked and the pumps and dynamo repeatedly stopped, but somehow Griffiths and his men managed to start them again. Coats signalled Pizey: 'The only way I can make steam is by using salt water, but I can make my own way home.'

At 5.18 p.m. she began to move slowly, and Coats went to the wrecked chart-room under the bridge. Most of his navigational aids had gone. The ship had taken such a battering that the gyro-compass had been smashed and the magnetic compass was unreliable. When *Campbell* gave him his position and a course for home, he told Taudevin to take over as officer of the watch while he was in the chart-room helping the navigator.

With smoke pouring from her after-funnel and steam issuing from a great rent in her starboard side, *Worcester* began to move slowly away from *Campbell*. At first she made only a knot or so through the heavy seas, but gradually gathered speed. When it was clear she could proceed on her own, Pizey decided to carry out the instructions of the C-in-C Nore that all ships which had fired torpedoes were to return to Harwich to re-arm and refuel. When they left Harwich, they had enough fuel to last two or three days. Running as they had been, at full speed ahead, they now had fuel for only ten hours. *Campbell* went off with *Vivacious* at twenty knots – the maximum they could make in existing weather conditions.

This left *Worcester* to make her own way home.

.

11

'*Scharnhorst* in urgent need of help'

The official RAF report that only thirty-nine found the ships is obviously an underestimate. There seems little doubt that many of the missing planes found them and were then shot down into the water.

After wireless signals from *Gneisenau* telling of a battle with an 'enemy cruiser and destroyers' – Captain Pizey's force – were picked up by *Scharnhorst*, still lagging in the rear, heavy attacks by the bombers which the RAF had now thrown into the action began to increase.

T.13, the leading torpedo boat protecting *Scharnhorst*, was riddled with splinters when bombs fell all around her. Smoke poured from her hatches and she stopped. *Scharnhorst* and her escort steamed on leaving her to her fate. She limped towards the Hook of Holland, escorted by another torpedo boat.

As the winter darkness fell, the RAF attack developed so fiercely that the flak guns became red hot. Sailors tried to cool them by throwing buckets of water over them, but several guns jammed and one 20-mm gun-barrel burst.

The *Prinz Eugen* had her only casualty during these attacks. Curiosity killed Senior Artificer Erich Kettermann, who was below decks on repair work. He left his station and went up to the deck to see what was happening. As he opened an armour-plated door he was struck by a shell fragment and killed instantly.

The third Beaufort Squadron, twelve aircraft of No. 86 stationed at St Eval, Cornwall, was not yet in action. They were so late leaving Cornwall that they did not arrive at Thorney Island until 2.30 p.m. There they were told they would be fitted with torpedoes at Coltishall, although it was primarily a fighter base. This order was technically correct – only no one had checked that the Mobile Unit had not arrived. Their squadron leader spoke to Flt-Lt Kidd on the phone saying, 'I have landed at Coltishall and there are no torpedoes there. What the hell are people playing at?' He was ordered back to Thorney Island.

It was not until 5 p.m. that the Beauforts arrived over Manston to find no fighters awaiting them. They circled for a few minutes then set off alone. At 5.41 p.m. they reached the reported position of the Germans given to them at Thorney Island hours before.

This information was, of course, completely out of date, as the German ships were now fifty miles away northwards. Searching low over the misty sea, the squadron saw four German minesweepers who fired at them. It was now getting too dark to see anything, so they turned and headed for home. Two did not make it. It is thought that flying low in the darkness, they flew into the water.

Apart from these planes, the Beaufort pilots who found the ships attacked with the utmost courage.

The surviving RAF air-crews themselves had no illusions about how the battle had gone. The entry in the 217 Beaufort Squadron log for 12 February read: 'Terrific flap. *Gneisenau* and *Scharnhorst* out of Brest heading towards North Sea. How they managed to get this far is one of the minor mysteries of the war. Late this evening still in a muddle.'

By seven o'clock that evening, the Beauforts of 42 Squadron had landed at North Coates. The operational record book reported, 'Nine aircraft led by Sq.-Ldr Cliff took off to attack the German fleet in the Channel. Seven torpedoes launched. Pilot Officer Dewhurst failed to release his torpedo. Flt-Lt Pett failed to find the battleships.'

Concerning Sq.-Ldr Cliff's attack, the 42 Squadron log reported: 'The Beaufort sighted one destroyer and one large cruiser, believed to be the *Scharnhorst*, at 16.06. There were large columns of smoke forward of the funnel.

'A second destroyer was sighted to starboard with a speed of 10–12 knots. The torpedo was released at the battleships from

1,200 yards inside the destroyer screen. When they turned to port they sighted another destroyer 100 yards on the starboard beam. The torpedo was seen to run but the result not observed. Landed at North Coates 18.50.'

The attack delivered by twenty-eight torpedo-bombers had not only failed but very nearly sank Captain Pizey's destroyer. Yet no one can blame the pilots who had flown off in dribs and drabs with totally inadequate information. It was the result of inefficiency on the part of the ground staff and lack of liaison between all commands.

That evening the only surviving Swordfish air-gunner, Donald Bunce, made his lonely way back to the sergeants' mess at Manston, which he had left just before lunch. There he wrote this terse, undramatic report in his log-book, 'Torpedo attack against *Scharnhorst* and *Gneisenau*. Attacked by fighters (FW 190s) and forced into sea.'

The only other unwounded survivor, Edgar Lee, after reporting to Admiral Ramsay, was driven back to Manston where as senior surviving officer of the Swordfish squadron he had a lot to clear up before being sent on immediate leave. Tom Gleave shook him by the hand. He said nothing. What was there to say to a man when thirteen of his comrades were dead and three others wounded?

That same night Gleave sat in his office and wrote his first report on the Swordfish massacre. He admits he was in tears. In his outer office a young WAAF sat sobbing over her desk. She was the girl-friend of one of the naval fliers. He addressed his report to Air Vice-Marshal Trafford Leigh-Mallory, Chief of 11 Group, for forwarding to the proper naval authorities. In stilted service prose, he told of the courage of the Swordfish crews:

'Concerning pilots and crews of 825 Squadron which operated from Manston against *Scharnhorst*, *Gneisenau* and *Prinz Eugen*, attached is the report of Sub-Lt Lee. As Officer Commanding this station to which 825 Squadron was attached for operational purposes, and having been fully acquainted with their operational activities and the circumstances attendant thereto in respect of the above operation against enemy warships, which resulted in the loss of the entire squadron and seventy-five per cent of their crews, I respectfully submit that it would not be presumptuous on my part to express an opinion on the manner in which Lt-Cdr Esmonde and the crews under his command carried out their duties on this occasion.

'I discussed the operation with Lt-Cdr Esmonde prior to the squadron taking off at 12.30. His pilots and crews present at this meeting displayed signs of great enthusiasm and keenness for the job they were about to undertake, and it was no doubt due to Lt-Cdr Esmonde's leadership that such a fine spirit prevailed. Nothing more was heard of the squadron until the five survivors were brought ashore. The German battle-cruisers were undoubtedly protected by a terrific barrage of flak, and covered by one of the biggest fighter screens ever seen. Against this, the determination and gallantry shown by Lt-Cdr Esmonde and his pilots and crews is beyond any normal praise. I am of the opinion that Lt-Cdr Esmonde is well worthy of the posthumous award of the Victoria Cross.'

It was the first time in history that an RAF officer had recommended a naval officer, not even part of his command, for Britain's highest decoration. Gleave later had only one bitter regret. He felt he had written his report too hastily. If he had considered it a little more he would have recommended more V.C.s for the Swordfish crews.

The Admiralty, who must take the main responsibility for the useless massacre, said of Esmonde: 'He was free to act as he thought best and believed he might succeed. That he was taking tremendous risks he knew but he was prepared to face them as he had faced other risks many times before.'

But Admiral Ramsay and his staff officers at Dover were not prepared to shrug off the deaths of 825 Squadron as an inevitable casualty of war. In a personal message to the Fleet Air Arm base at Lee-on-Solent Ramsay wrote: 'I cannot help but regard the miscarriage of the plan to provide fighter escorts for the Swordfish as a major tragedy of this war. Until the time they took off I had thought all arrangements were proceeding satisfactorily. Had I known that the fighter escorts might not keep their rendezvous I would have told Lt-Cdr Esmonde to remain on the ground. Indeed I would have forbidden the flight as an order.'

Nearly everyone involved felt personal resentment at every

aspect of the operation. This applied particularly to the RAF. It ranged from Sq. Ldr Brian Kingcombe's remark, 'I have never known anything so bloody silly as all that mystery about the *Gneisenau* and *Scharnhorst*' to Flt-Lt Gerald Kidd, radar commander at Swingate, who, encouraged by Admiral Ramsay, sat down that night and wrote a report of the action so critical that he realized he might be court martialled for it. Instead it reached Churchill.

As the last British aircraft turned back for England and night fell, in some ways the most difficult part of the voyage lay ahead of the German ships. Though they had sailed through the Channel safely they were still a long way from home – and it was the darkest night anyone remembered. It hid them, but the channel along the Dutch coast known as Easy Street turned out to be not so easy as all that. There were sandbanks to starboard and the port side was thick with British mines. To add to their difficulties, *Scharnhorst*'s echo sounder and direction-finder, damaged by the mine explosion, were still out of action. Captain Hoffmann coming into the *Scharnhorst*'s chart-room said, 'Only God and courage can help us now!'

As the German ships struggled along the Dutch coast towards the Kiel Canal, one last line of attack remained to the British. The fast minelayer *Welshman* and squadrons of RAF bombers had already strewn mines along the French, Dutch and Belgian coasts. These were now reinforced by twenty aircraft – eleven Hampdens and nine Manchesters – from Bomber Command who took off to drop mines in the mouth of the Elbe.

When *Scharnhorst* was off the Hook of Holland, steaming in twilight through seas whipped up by a force seven south-westerly wind the *Friedrich Ihn* appeared steaming slowly. She was followed by torpedo boat *Jaguar*, black smoke pouring out of her badly smashed superstructure with one dead and two wounded aboard her. She had been hit in a dusk attack by the RAF.

Then directly in *Scharnhorst*'s path two destroyers loomed up with a cutter between them. The look-out shouted a warning as the cutter appeared directly in front of the battleship's mighty bow wave. Just in time, the order was given to reduce speed so as not to cut the boat in half or capsize her in their wash. Then the look-out suddenly exclaimed, 'The Admiral's in the cutter!' It was true. From the bridge they could make out Admiral Ciliax standing in the stern.

Captain Hoffmann recognized one of the destroyers as the *Z.29*, which had taken the Admiral aboard. Although a great cloud of steam was pouring from her engine-room hatches, she had not been hit by the British. One of her own A.A. shells had burst before leaving the barrel of the gun, and a fragment of the broken gun had cut through the deck, killing one man and severing the main lubricating oil line to the turbine bearings. As repairing the oil pipe and switching over to another tank would take at least twenty minutes it would mean their falling back, and Ciliax might lose touch once again with the squadron. While the ships were still visible in the growing dark he had to decide quickly.

He was in the cutter transferring to the second destroyer *Hermann Schoemann* when *Scharnhorst* nearly ran him down. The sea was now so rough that the crew of the cutter were ordered not to try to return to *Z.29*. They climbed aboard *Hermann Schoemann* with the Admiral and the small boat was sunk by gunfire.

At 6.16 p.m. the last British plane vanished into the darkness. Ten minutes later the last Luftwaffe fighters flew back to Dutch, Belgian and French airfields. From Le Touquet, Fighter Commander Adolf Galland signalled his congratulations to the Luftwaffe aircrews. Their job was over, the ships were now protected by thick weather and dense darkness. Only Vice-Admiral Ciliax aboard the destroyer *Hermann Schoemann* did not rejoice. He knew this might be the hardest part of the passage. As the night closed in, Giessler put on his green military sheepskin which was warm and comfortable for watch-keeping. It was a present from his father who had worn it during the First World War. Round his neck he wore a thick scarf which he called his 'white shawl'.

Near Terschelling the direction-finding system became operational again in *Scharnhorst* and Giessler checked his position on a positive bearing with radio transmitters ashore. But the echo-sounder was still defective and no further mark-boats were due to be sighted until nearly 8 p.m., when the Texel mark-buoy would provide a much-needed guide into the Friesian channels.

The strain of the past twenty-one hours was beginning to tell on officers and men now as they sailed without lights in the narrow channel, groping their way homeward on the final stretch.

At 7 p.m. there came the drone of high-flying aircraft obviously tracking the ship by radar. Once or twice planes were heard quite clearly in the black night. But the battleships were now considered fairly safe from air attacks.

At 7.15 p.m. the destroyer *Hermann Schoemann* came up at high speed with the Admiral's flag fluttering at her mast-head, and signalled *Scharnhorst* to follow her. Led by the destroyer, *Scharnhorst* was steaming at increased speed towards the mark-buoy when the weather took a hand. A fierce squall blotted the ships out from each other and *Scharnhorst* lost *Hermann Schoemann*'s stern light.

On *Scharnhorst*'s bridge everyone peered at the dark water ahead. As there was still no sign of the destroyer's light, Hoffmann ordered Giessler to turn on to the new course by dead reckoning. Just as the helm order was being given a look-out shouted, 'Small boat on the starboard quarter.' It was the mark-buoy. *Scharnhorst* was in the proper channel. Now all Giessler had to do was to follow the buoys through the channel.

The long day was ending. For the ship's company it was their second night at sea with twelve hours at battle stations. Now that the last British aircraft seemed to have vanished into the darkness Captain Hoffmann decided that the men could take a break.

At 7.30 p.m., as the port watch ended, the battleship returned to a modified normal working. For the first time since they left Brest, *Scharnhorst*'s mess decks had their tables down for the port watch to eat a hot supper instead of gulping emergency rations in gun turrets or battle stations.

The men, though tired, were still keyed up. Everyone was eager to tell his own story of the day's action. Gunners who had been in the main armament turrets and others who had been manning the lighter flak guns exchanged stories of the air and destroyer attacks. The members of the coastal artillery on board also gave their account of the ceaseless British air attacks.

Now everything seemed to be going like clockwork. At 7.34 p.m. *Scharnhorst* passed the Texel at almost exactly the time scheduled by Group West. Not only had they made up the two hours delay in setting out from Brest but also the time lost through striking the mine.

Gneisenau, making twenty-seven knots in waters where she should normally have sailed at ten, lost touch with *Prinz Eugen* in the same squall which separated *Scharnhorst* and the Admiral's destroyer. Then she also stumbled across the marker-boats lying off the Friesian Islands.

Eleven minutes later – at 7.55 p.m. – she shuddered and stopped as a sudden flash lit up the battleship followed by an explosion. She had also struck an RAF-dropped mine. Yet the mine explosion was felt less strongly on her bridge than *Scharnhorst*'s mine had been from 1,500 yards. The middle engine failed at once, and Captain Fein ordered the other engines stopped in order to prevent too great a pressure on places where there was an inrush of water.

She drifted in the tides only six miles from Terschelling as damage-repair parties went below to investigate. Their examination showed a hole on the starboard side but only trivial damage. Reports coming in very quickly showed him that there were no more serious consequences. The mine had evidently gone off at right angles some distance from the ship.

Half an hour later, with the hole in her bottom near the stern blocked by a steel collision mat and with water-pumps operating, *Gneisenau* picked up speed. But her navigational equipment had broken down and she had to creep through the shoals using a hand lead. At times there was so little water under her keel that she had to reduce speed to eight knots. If she tried to go any faster her propellers stirred up enough mud from the bottom to stop her. She steamed uncertainly through the same area where *Hermann Schoemann* and *Scharnhorst* were looking for each other.

Prinz Eugen, having lost *Gneisenau*, was also moving blindly along the Terschelling banks at eight knots. She reported that she had no position and asked for a bearing.

At 9.35 p.m., when *Scharnhorst* was ten miles from the Dutch coast between Terschelling and Schiermonikoog, the sailors aboard were still talking about the action. One man on the mess deck was dramatically describing with outstretched arms how a Wellington had banked away from the hail of flak fire, when there came a gigantic jolt accompanied by heavy vibrations which seemed almost to wrench limbs away from bodies. The explosion sent Captain Hoffmann hurtling against the helmsman on the bridge. It was followed by a series of sharp cracks and grating noises as sailors were thrown to the deck. The current failed and the lights went out. Fans and other electrical apparatus ceased to function and a great quiet descended. The engines once again stopped. *Scharnhorst* had struck another mine.

Then all the bells began to ring together and telephones and voice pipes which were undamaged reported, 'Helm jammed', 'Engines stopped', 'Gyro compass out of order', 'Electric light circuit failed'. When the blue night lights were switched on they revealed that the damage appeared to be much greater than that caused by the afternoon mine.

The starboard main engine was damaged and stopped and the other two were jammed. The dynamo room and most of the auxiliary machinery was out of action. Several compartments on the starboard side were flooded and thousands of tons of water were rushing in, giving her a starboard list of seven degrees.

With communications broken down officers groped their way through the ship with torches, trying to assess the damage. As torches twinkled in the darkness they revealed smashed pipes, lights torn from sockets – even the welded compass fastening had broken away. Many instruments were useless. The shock had put the delicate prisms of the big guns out of trim. As the rest of their elaborate gear was affected they had become useless. They could not even be budged by hand.

Scharnhorst, dark and dead on the water, began drifting broadside towards the coast. She was as helpless as *Worcester*. And the Terschelling shoals were perilously near. It looked like the end of the voyage. Yet in spite of the extensive damage, her position was not so critical as it had been in the afternoon. For she was within the Heligoland Bight and the inky black night protected her.

As the night became colder and flurries of snow began to fall on deck, aboard the destroyer *Hermann Schoemann* Ciliax retired to the captain's sea cabin, which had been put at his disposal. Col. Ibel, the Luftwaffe liaison officer, was also somewhere below. Captain Reinicke was puffing his pipe on the weather side of the destroyer's bridge when suddenly he heard the deep rumbling noises of an underwater explosion. As it was followed within seconds by vibrations against the destroyer itself he realized it was not at any great distance. It came from the direction of the *Scharnhorst*. There seemed to be more than one heavy detonation. Or were some of the noises echoes?

Captain Reinicke ran to call Admiral Ciliax. But Ciliax, who had also heard the explosion, bounded hastily out of his cabin excitedly demanding information. With their blue-darkened flashlamps the destroyer signalman called up *Scharnhorst*. They got no reply. It looked ominous. Had her boilers gone up this time? Was she sinking?

It was over five minutes before a lamp spelled out the report from Hoffmann in *Scharnhorst*, who signalled at 9.42 p.m.: 'Have hit mine.' Although his fears were quietened, Admiral Ciliax, impetuous as ever, asked angrily, 'Why have they taken more than five minutes to give us the answering signal?'

The answer lay in the mine itself. The signalman's lamp in *Scharnhorst* had been broken by the force of the explosion. It had taken five minutes to produce another lamp. As there was silence after this laconic three-word message, Ciliax again thought she had gone down.

It was touch and go. The battleship drifted to starboard two miles from the perilous shoals as Chief Engineer Walther Kretschmer and his crew once again inspected the damage. They found rudder damage and three bolts sheared on the starboard engine. But at 10.15 p.m. – thirty-five minutes after the big explosion – the indefatigable Kretschmer was able to tell the captain, 'Ship is ready with starboard shaft for fourteen knots and the middle one for sixteen knots. Port shaft still inoperative.'

Slowly she began to steam again. But no more signals came from her. There were no details of damage, only silence.

Hermann Schoemann zigzagged through the inky darkness with her searchlight switched on looking for the flagship. Not for the first time in the operation Ciliax had lost touch. When nearly an hour had passed without finding her, he was certain *Scharnhorst* had sunk and ordered the destroyer to turn and steer for the starting point to try and pick up survivors of her crew. A strong smell of oil fuel drifting on to the destroyer's bridge deepened his fears. When their searchlight revealed a thick layer of oil on the water, the destroyer followed the oil-trail towards the navigational channel.

They found no sign of any wreckage. Had she sunk leaving only this trace? Keeping his searchlight trained ahead, Ciliax ordered the destroyer to increase speed. As destroyer and battleship circled round each other in the darkness both their blinker signals failed to be seen. It was not until 10.39 p.m. that Ciliax on the destroyer picked up a message from *Scharnhorst*: 'Ready to proceed at twelve knots. Please pilot me as echo-sounder has failed.'

For some reason Ciliax did not realize she was sailing under her own power again. At 10.46 he broke silence to radio shore installations in code: '*Scharnhorst* in urgent need of help. Also tugs.' At the same time he asked for *Scharnhorst*'s position from the escorting torpedo boats.

Hoffmann noted in his log: 'I perceive from this that he is no longer in the picture over *Scharnhorst*'s position.' At 11.3 p.m. Ciliax cancelled his 'urgent need of help' message. This was because a few minutes earlier *Hermann Schoemann*'s searchlight had illuminated a dark shadow ahead – *Scharnhorst*.

Now the battleship kept close on *Hermann Schoemann*'s stern as they steamed together towards the channel and the pilot ship which would guide her into Wilhelmshaven. She proceeded at reduced speed, as the special mine-sweeper to clear the way would not be ready until 7 o'clock next morning. They did not want to take any unnecessary risks in this mine-infested area.

Scharnhorst was safe but in a bad way. She reported: '(1) Starboard and middle engines operational for fourteen knots.

Port engine temporarily inoperational. (2) Limited oil and water supplies but sufficient for returning to the River Elbe. (3) Greatly restricted supplies of shells including heavy A.A. shells. (4) Flooding causing no vital failures. (5) One man badly wounded.'

But what about the rest of the Squadron? If they had sunk the operation had failed. In fact *Prinz Eugen* and *Gneisenau* were also safe.

Just before midnight *Gneisenau* made contact with *Prinz Eugen* and was ordered to go with her to the coastal town of Brunsbuttel on the north bank of the Elbe, sixty miles north west of Hamburg. It was at the western terminus of the Kiel Canal, which connects the Baltic with the North Sea.

As the night wore on, the British admitted the Germans had made it. At 1 a.m. in London, First Sea Lord Sir Dudley Pound lifted the private telephone which connected him with 10 Downing Street. While embarrassed senior staff officers gazed intently at maps on the War Room walls he made one of the worst reports an English admiral ever had to make to an English Prime Minister.

Pound said, 'I'm afraid, sir, I must report that the enemy battle-cruisers should by now have reached the safety of their home waters.' Churchill growled, 'Why?' and slammed the phone down.

12

The Ships Crawl Home

While the German ships were steaming slowly through the black night towards the safety of their home ports, in another part of the North Sea *HMS Worcester* was crawling painfully like a wounded animal towards the east coast of England. With smoke pouring from the after-funnel, steam belching from a great rent in her starboard side and her engines noisily clanking and thumping, she went ahead at six and a half knots – until 7.15 p.m., when steam was lost for several minutes. At 9.30 p.m., after steam had been lost again, she began to move at three and a half knots, working gradually up to seven knots.

As the ship staggered through the night, 'Doc' Jackson still tried to tend the wounded. He performed emergency operations with his hands torn and bleeding, and his instruments blunted. All the time came the call, 'Over here, Doc, for God's sake!' Always there was a new call for help.

Eventually all the bad casualties had some sort of first aid. The next task was to place them in some reasonable comfort. The holes in the bulkhead between the cabin flat and the wardroom had been plugged with wooden leak stoppers and someone had managed to make the lights work. So the doctor decided to use this as a temporary sick-bay. But the cabin flat was at the bottom of a vertical steel ladder, which was very difficult to get a wounded man down, and many of them had compound fractures of the legs making it difficult to move them at all. While the doctor tried to cope with them, sick-berth attendant Shelley dealt with the minor casualties who were eventually coming aft for treatment after repeated orders.

Even the unwounded were still dazed and tense. When Gun-layer Douglas Ward went to report to the wheel-house he was told, 'Shut the door, you bloody fool! Someone will see the light.' He replied, 'There is no door, sir.'

Then he went to man the starboard Oerlikon and found the gun position a bloody mess of torn flesh where the crew of two had been killed. At least he thought there were two. He covered the pieces with an oilskin and stood watch.

The cook had been killed, but someone volunteered to go into the galley and open tins to make a stew, throwing everything into a pail. The crew ate it hungrily.

Commander Coats said, 'I think I would have gone stark raving mad if I hadn't had to concentrate on getting my ship home. It was a tragic disappointment. You cannot get any closer in daylight, and at least two of my three torpedoes should have hit the *Gneisenau*, but they missed and all these lives were wasted.'

It was bitterly cold. The wind was rising and the smoke from the funnel driving into the mist over the dark sea made everyone aboard the ship feel lonely and deserted.

This feeling was increased when Engineer Griffiths told the captain that if the ship stopped for any length of time there was a good chance she would sink. He was not being pessimistic. When the salt water in the boilers stopped the ship every hour or so, she immediately began to loll about in the waves. Every time she seemed to go farther over to starboard and hesitate before righting herself frighteningly slowly. Before she did so everyone thought, 'This is it. We are done. We are finished.'

After seeing all the wounded were fairly comfortable, Jackson climbed painfully up the shattered ladder to the bridge to give Commander Coats his report. After he had told him the number of wounded and dead he broke down. He opened his mouth but no further words came. Coats looked at the doctor and said gently, 'You had better get on with your job, Doc.'

It was a terrible tale. Out of the ship's company of 130, over half were either killed or wounded. The total of dead was seventeen and there were six men missing. According to Admiralty figures, there were eighteen seriously wounded and twenty-seven slightly wounded – though Dr Jackson claims to have dealt with nearly a hundred dead and wounded. Most of the slightly wounded were able to carry out their duties and help man the ship after being attended by Jackson.

He returned to supervise the more severe cases, whose ship-mates had gently carried them to such shelter as they could find. While he was doing this he realized the noise of the engines had ceased once more.

This time they drifted for an hour and a half, in heavy seas off the Dutch coast, alone, disabled and probably sinking. With everything in darkness and wounded men lying groaning everywhere the listing ship seemed doomed as she wallowed in the heavy swell. The seas curled and broke over her decks strewn with jagged wreckage and peppered with splinter holes.

The doctor's chief horror was what would happen to the wounded if the ship sank. He tried not to admit it to himself – but in those icy seas survival even for the unwounded would probably be brief.

But the destroyer did not sink. Just before midnight, Griffiths and his men started the engines again and she began to creep slowly forward. They were also able to pump out some water, making the list less dangerous.

It was a moonless night, but the wind began dispersing the mists to give reasonable visibility. Every attempt was made to preserve naval discipline. Making smoke in wartime was a terrible crime in the Royal Navy and while *Worcester* was crawling at seven knots across the North Sea with a 20-degree list, a sailor arrived from the bridge with a message for the Chief Engineer, 'Captain's compliments, but he would be obliged if you would reduce the amount of smoke.'

Griffiths sent back a message, 'Owing to the holes in the ship there is a complete air passage through the engine room and I cannot stop the smoke.'

With most of his navigational aids gone, the only way Coats could bring his ship home was to endeavour to steer back along the exact track on which he had come out, based on the magnetic compass course *Campbell* had given him. This meant he had to cross the minefield once again. This seemed a minor worry now. In their disabled condition, the tides and sandbanks were even more dangerous. And he was unable to signal, no one knew where he was or when he was likely to arrive.

After midnight silence fell on the ship, broken only by the

labouring of the engines and the creakings of the battered wreckage as she rolled in the rising wind. Except for those on watch everyone seemed to be asleep. Even the wounded were asleep and fairly comfortable. Four never woke.

The doctor still toured the ship seeing that all the wounded were well covered with blankets, especially those lying on deck. The badly wounded who could not be moved lay in ones and twos in all parts of the ship from the wheel-house to the engine room. The sick-bay was still too damaged to use and the lobby outside it smelt of burning and cordite fumes. But the little cabin forward gave shelter to a few men. Others lay in the galley.

While the captain was busy navigating the ship, First Officer Dick Taudevin came to him and said, 'We ought to bury our dead at sea. It will help to keep up morale. And all these dead will cause consternation when we arrive.'

Coats agreed. Following such an action, not only did it seem to him fitting to bury his sailors at sea, but he thought grimly to himself, 'As our return is still by no means certain at least some of us will get a decent funeral!'

The dead were wrapped in weighted hammocks and one after another pushed over the side to splash into the waves, while Taudevin hastily read out the burial service. The ship could not heave-to for a proper funeral service as she might have sunk.

In wartime, lighthouses and lightships were darkened, but the Admiralty ordered the Orfordness light on the Suffolk coast lit up as a guide to *Worcester* in case she were still afloat. As he had no other means of navigation, Coats had to depend on this light to confirm his position.

At four o'clock in the morning, the weary doctor fell asleep with his head on the captain's table. At the same time the look-out saw a lighthouse beam and Commander Coats realized he had arrived where he ought to be.

Just before dawn, a bleary-eyed Taudevin shook the doctor awake saying, 'We are just coming up to the Sunk.' This was the Sunk Light Float at the entrance to Harwich Harbour. It was still dark when they climbed on deck together and the doctor went round the wounded again. The sky began to turn to grey. Dawn broke on the port bow and they could see the low misty coast of England.

Although the sea was much calmer, because of their slow speed in the fast running tide, they were nearly swept on to the sandbanks as they approached the harbour entrance. As they cleared them, they saw a convoy steaming out of Harwich and Coats turned to Taudevin and said, 'Am I glad to see them!' A Hunt Class destroyer signalled: 'Do you need assistance?' A winking lamp aboard *Worcester* proudly replied, 'We have come from Holland and we can manage the rest of the trip alone.' The signal added a request for ambulances to be ready to take off her wounded.

Refusing all help, *Worcester* steamed slowly up to the anchorage. She struggled into the harbour, listing heavily, full of holes with steam trickling from them. Her broken mast was still leaning against the funnel and her torn, smoke-blackened battle ensign flying from a broomstick over the bridge, as all the ships in the harbour sounded their sirens. Whistles piped as they cleared lower deck and fell in aft to pay tribute to her. They stood cheering as *Worcester* drew abreast. When they approached nearer to land her crew also saw lines of sailors and Wrens standing cheering outside Shotley Sick Quarters. The *Worcester*'s crew did not reply. There were too many dead.

Two waiting tugs were laid off until she was ready for berthing. All through the night Griffiths had wrestled with the oil pump, which had repeatedly broken down. But somehow he had managed to patch it up. Yet as the first hawsers were thrown across from Parkstone quay at Harwich the pump broke down again. This time he could not start it. It had packed up for good.

Then the ambulances began taking off the seriously wounded and the four men who had died during the night. Those four were given out as the official number of dead. In fact, they brought the total of dead to twenty-seven. There were only fifty-two unwounded survivors.

For the last time the doctor went wearily to his wrecked sickbay, littered with torn bandages. His jacket was stiff with dried blood up to the elbows. The tops of his white sea boot stockings and the knees of his trousers were blood-soaked. The two lower jacket buttons were missing and he saw one of them battered and slightly splayed lying in the cabin. He instinctively picked it up and slipped it into his pocket.

It was only when he was lying in a hot bath in a Harwich hotel that the significance of the battered button dawned upon the doctor. For in the corresponding position on his stomach was a circular bluish-green bruise, two inches across, where the button had stopped a piece of shrapnel.

Last off the ship was Commander Coats, who pulled down the blackened battle ensign and carried it ashore.

Because of the magnitude of the disaster the crew were kept incommunicado for days. Douglas Ward, whose namesake E. Ward had died of wounds on the ship, was so worried in case there was a mix-up with the telegram that he obtained special permission to go to the police station to get a message through to his wife to say he was safe.

Chief Engineer Griffiths was afraid that his wife would think he was a casualty. To avoid giving her a shock he asked the Post Office to send her a greetings telegram. They did not do so. When she received an ordinary telegram she was so afraid of the news it might contain she asked her landlady to open it.

The rest of the flotilla was back at sea. *Campbell* and her sister destroyers had returned to Harwich by midnight to take on torpedoes to replace those fired, and replenish their ammunition. The destroyers searched all night but found no further trace of the German ships. This was fortunate for the Germans because the two battleships were partially crippled and all three still vulnerable.

Scharnhorst was ordered by Group North to make for Wilhelmshaven, Germany's chief naval base. As she made her way there at 3.50 a.m., a cipher message was received on *Scharnhorst* from *Gneisenau* reporting that, although damaged by a mine, she had reached the Heligoland anchorage with *Prinz Eugen* and they were both making for Brunsbuttel.

Though so near safety the Germans still had to face a period of near-disaster. Until they could reach the German ports all three captains were still worried about mines and air attacks. Yet no tugs or pilot boats were available to meet them after their gruelling voyage. It was one of the most inexplicable scandals of the operation from the German point of view.

Group North had made no arrangements and left them all night hanging about outside the harbours. It was almost as if they did not expect them to make it. Nor had they been supplied with any special charts of the approaches to the German coast. Captain Fein of *Gneisenau* recorded in his log: 'It would have been very useful in this situation to have had a chart prepared on a large scale for the navigational approaches of the Elbe, like the one given by Group West for the navigational approaches of harbours of refuge.'

After lengthy signal exchanges, Fein established that no pilots were available. Due to thickening ice and the uncertainty about his position, he decided he dare not sail into the Elbe without a pilot. Afraid to make a radio signal in case it alerted the British, he sent a small ship, barrier breaker *138*, up the Elbe with the order to meet him at daybreak with pilots.

Although there was danger from the air, he considered that if he steamed to and fro on a dark night with poor visibility the danger of mines was greater, so he decided to anchor.

Prinz Eugen, following *Gneisenau* into Brunsbuttel, was also in the same dangerous situation. Fein signalled by lamp to Brinkmann that there was no pilot but that one had been ordered for first light in the morning. While *Gneisenau* dropped anchor east of her, *Prinz Eugen* sailed at slow speed up and down all night. Her commander, Captain Brinkmann, refused to anchor, fearing torpedo or bomber attack more than Fein feared mines.

It was not until dawn that tugs and ice-breakers with pilots came out and *Gneisenau* and *Prinz Eugen* began to enter Brunsbuttel roadsteads. Even so the situation was still perilous.

Renewed air-raid warnings shortly before the tugs arrived made Fein afraid that the British would now, without regard to the consequences, employ all available aircraft to wreck the ships in the river estuaries. As a south-west wind was still blowing and high tide had still about two hours to run, it was not a good moment to try and bring the battleship into port. But in view of the alarms, Fein decided he must try and go in. He did not feel able to take responsibility for remaining at anchor and possibly being hit by bombs or torpedoes without at least making an attempt to secure his ship in the locks.

As *Gneisenau* slowly edged towards the mole her stern swung strongly in the current towards it. Fein ordered: 'Emergency – full speed astern!' But as his ship backed away from the mole she began to drift towards a wreck that was lying at the entrance. Fein hastily tried again to bring her to a stop in order to manœuvre her clear. But he did not succeed in doing so. The racing tide smashed *Gneisenau* against the wreck.

He tried to go astern to disentangle his ship but did not succeed at first. Then the tide and wind came to his rescue, and with a rending crash the ship swung clear. The starboard propeller shaft tunnel was flooded. It had already been making water as a result of the mine explosion but they had been able to control it. Now the engineers feared this new situation might be dangerous. So Fein anchored outside the locks to await slack water and more tugs. Once again no tugs came, so he weighed anchor and *Gneisenau*, cautiously using only her middle and port propeller shafts, slowly reached safety at last.

Prinz Eugen, following astern, almost ran into the same wreck lying at the harbour entrance, but managed to get clear at the last moment. Then she too tied up at Brunsbuttel North Locks.

Aboard *Gneisenau* and *Prinz Eugen* most of the crews slept for the first time in twenty-four hours. But officers paced their quarter-decks wondering what was the fate of *Scharnhorst*. There was still no news of her. Hooters and fog-bells were rung in Wilhelmshaven at two-minute intervals to guide *Scharnhorst* to the anchorage.

Group North failed her as they had the two other ships. At 6.43 a.m., the tug *Steinbock* met her but in spite of frequent calls no pilot boat came out, so the tug tried to pilot her in. At 7.00 a.m. *Scharnhorst* arrived at lightship 'Fritz', where she took aboard the coastal artillery guard party. At 9.30 a.m. another tug arrived with Admiral Ciliax aboard. He and his staff were returning to the flagship.

The cold was intense. The winter mists of Brest had given place to the sub-arctic conditions of a North German winter as *Scharnhorst*, twice mined, her crew red-eyed with fatigue after twenty-three hours almost continuously at action stations, came creeping at last past the Jade towards Wilhelmshaven.

When they arrived off Germany's principal naval base the sea was freezing hard and the ice was packing into great cakes. Watching the thick ice and the fast running tide, *Scharnhorst*'s navigator, Helmuth Giessler, realized that now the battle was not only against the British – who might find them again now it was light – but against the weather.

It would not be high water at Wilhelmshaven until noon. Only then would the tugs be able to take her through the difficult sluice gates into harbour. Then the message came from Naval Group North: '*Es gibt keine Schlepper*' – 'There won't be any tugs.' Without their assistance *Scharnhorst* might have to remain outside the harbour, exposed to attacks.

Captain Hoffmann stood on the bridge contemplating sea and sky from which an attack might be expected any minute and took his last great decision. He turned to Giessler and said calmly, 'I will take her in – without tugs.'

With the ship's telegraphs constantly ringing and a half a turn of a screw here and a half a turn there, Hoffmann began to guide his ship towards the sluice. Directed by his skilled hands, the great battleship began slowly to crunch her way, foot by foot, through the ice floes towards the waiting lock gates. With the screws barely turning and the exhausted men on the bridge holding their breaths, the sharp prow of *Scharnhorst* entered the sluice gates with only inches to spare. As her sleek, shark-nosed hull crept past the groups of longshoremen standing among the ice-encrusted bollards on the jetty, they broke into loud cheers.

The seamanship Captain Hoffmann had learned since the day he entered the German Navy forty years before prevailed. When she tied up, he nodded briefly to the officer of the watch, Wilhelm Wolf, who rang through to Chief Engineer Walther Kretschmer, 'Finished with engines.'

As Giessler began to fold up his charts a signal from Ciliax was tapped out to Admiral Saalwächter in Paris. It said: 'It is my duty to inform you that Operation Cerberus has been successfully completed. Lists of damage and casualties follow.'

It was over. The *Scharnhorst* had come home.

·   ·   ·   ·   ·

One of the first to go ashore was Colonel Max Ibel, the Luft-waffe liaison officer aboard *Scharnhorst*. 'I have had enough,' he told Admiral Ciliax. 'What is my bill for the ride ?'

Later in the morning Ciliax received reports from his des-troyer captains as one by one they sailed into the German estu-aries. The German losses were seventeen Luftwaffe planes, two torpedo boats, *Jaguar* and *T.13*, damaged by bombs, two dead and several German sailors seriously wounded by bomb splinters and machine-gun fire. That was all.

In the afternoon, the Admiral who had sat in the same cabin in Brest nearly forty-eight hours earlier writing his doubts about the operation's success, made this entry in his war diary : 'The enemy betrayed his surprise, to the advantage of our formation, by throwing in his air forces precipitously and without plan. For the failure of the enemy air force to reach the target during the afternoon and evening in spite of the extreme deter-mination shown in their first torpedo attack, we have to thank the ship-borne flak and the fine services of our fighter cover.'

The attack of Esmonde's Swordfish was described by him as, 'The mothball attack of a handful of ancient planes, piloted by men whose bravery surpasses any other action by either side that day.'

At 2.15 p.m. all hands were piped aft to hear an address by Admiral Ciliax. It was not received with much enthusiasm. The sailors felt it did not come well from the Admiral who had just that morning retaken possession of his Admiral's quarters. There was a definite feeling in *Scharnhorst* that Ciliax had left them to drown if necessary. Although that might have been just the ignorance of sailors, there was no doubt that the peppery 'Black Czar' had almost totally failed to command the operation. This was mainly due to his jumping aboard the destroyer *Z.29* too quickly when his flagship hit the first RAF mine in the after-noon. But an even more puzzling decision was when he did not reboard her but the destroyer *Herman Schoemann*, when his own flagship, steaming normally, almost ran him down in the cutter.

Two hours later, the Fleet C-in-C Admiral Schniewind, who made it his business to be at Wilhelmshaven when the

Scharnhorst tied up there, also harangued the weary sailors. These speeches by Ciliax and Schniewind were delivered aft on the quarter-deck where 2,000 could be mustered. Both admirals stood under the long barrels of Turret 'C' for 'Caesar' on the traditional *'Palaverkiste'* – Speaker's rostrum.

By 4 p.m. the camouflage netting was being unwound and a tired ship's company were making *Scharnhorst* snug and safe for the night at her Wilhelmshaven anchorage.

Captain Hoffmann was still writing his report in his day cabin, when a visitor rushed in without knocking and flung herself into his arms crying, 'Papa, papa!' It was his 17-year-old daughter Elly who had heard the news and come on ahead of her mother, due next day from Bremen. As the orderly brought tea and Captain Hoffmann sat back to listen to the family news, she gave him one item which was especially welcome – his son Heinz, a U-boat officer, was safe and well.

The next day all Germany rejoiced over the feat, but officers and men of all three ships were too tired to share in the exultation.

In England, the first news of the break-out was given in a story in the early editions on Friday, 13 February. The *Daily Mail* said: 'One of the fiercest and most mysterious duels in the Straits of Dover was fought out yesterday between British and German long-range guns and between RAF bombers and fighters and German interceptor aircraft. Wave after wave of our own bombers crossed the Kent coast to attack what is believed to have been a German convoy passing through the Channel.

'Last night Berlin radio revealed that Swordfish torpedo bombers with heavy fighter protection had taken part in the battle, but no clue as to the identity of the target was given. The official German news agency claimed seven Swordfish were shot down in battles off the coast and the formation was turned back.'

The next editions carried a stop-press: 'The *Scharnhorst, Gneisenau* and *Prinz Eugen* with heavy sea and air support were attacked near the Straits of Dover – official.'

At 1.40 a.m. a joint Admiralty and Air Force communiqué

190

gave some details of the action. It said: 'The German ships strongly escorted by surface vessels and aircraft were making a break from Brest to Heligoland. Attacks were pressed home with the greatest determination and hits are believed to have been made on all three ships.'

13

The Whitehall Whitewash

The resentful anger that already reigned in Dover Castle was soon to spill over into a major row that shook the nation, causing a crisis of confidence in Churchill's wartime government.

Most of the RAF officers blamed the day's disaster upon the fact that very few pilots really knew what they were looking for. These included those in 42 Beaufort Squadron, who had nearly torpedoed Captain Pizey's flagship *Campbell*.

Sq. Ldr Roger Frankland, controller at Coltishall recalls, 'They tried to torpedo our own ships because of ridiculous secrecy. I have never heard anyone so rude as the leader of 42 Squadron of Beauforts on the phone to a group captain. He was hopping mad. He said, "I was sent looking for a convoy. Why was I not told about the bloody great battleships?" '

His complaint was echoed by most pilots. At some airfields the confusion remained until after dark. Late that evening one fighter pilot sergeant landed at Martlesham after a North Sea patrol and said in amazement, 'What's going on? I have just seen a huge battleship.' He had found himself over the battleships but did not know what they were – because he had still received no briefing.

The blame must lie right at the top between 11 Fighter Group Commander Air Vice-Marshal Leigh-Mallory and Coastal Command Chief Philip Joubert. Both of them were career officers of the old-fashioned type, slightly out of touch with the sudden emergencies of World War II air warfare. Leigh-Mallory was not personally very popular and many officers called him a 'pompous, ambitious fuddy-duddy'.

While the squadrons wrote their gloomy entries in the records one officer did more – Flt-Lt Kidd was as good as his word. He and Sq.-Ldrs Igoe and Oxspring were the three RAF officers who had realized instantly that the ships sighted were the German battleships.

Kidd sat up all night preparing a furious report attacking the whole British defence. He criticized the handling of the entire operation, particularly condemning the High Command. His letter read: 'I have the honour to request that consideration be given to the following views and to the alternative applications that follow them:

'The passage through the Straits of Dover of an enemy squadron in defiance of our sea and air power is tantamount to the infliction upon us of a major defeat. That defeat is the more serious in that it is in essence a naval one and follows closely upon the loss of the *Repulse, Prince of Wales, Barham* and *Ark Royal*. The confidence and hopes of Englishmen down the centuries has been focused upon our sea power. To us no joy is greater, no memory more lasting, than that of a naval victory and no bitterness, no loss of pride, can equal that which follows naval defeat. The effect on the public not only here but abroad of this latest successful challenge to our naval supremacy will be profound.

'It has been a common fault of ours in recent years to put too much blame on others, to put too much reliance on our friends, particularly the United States of America, and to give too little credit to our enemies for their power and their cunning. We have won victories over many in the past; we did not do so by belittling them and their efforts but by defeating them.

'Reverse has followed reverse in this war and after each, excuses have been made. "The Norwegians and Dutch would not collaborate with us", "The Germans violated international law", "The Belgians betrayed us and the French deserted us"; Sollum and Halfaya were described as places of no strategical importance, yet much British blood was shed in the attempt to recapture them. In Greece we were defeated because we had no airfields, in Crete we were driven out because the enemy operating from Greek airfields made Malemi and the other Cretan aerodromes untenable. Malaya was lost, it was stated, because of the defection of the Siamese. Why the need for all this humbug? The plain fact is that we are never ready anywhere, we do not organize, we do not plan ahead. The wastage in manpower and in the national industrial effort has been and still is nothing short of a gross scandal.

'The inertia, that corrupt and sordid paralysis that gripped the members of the House of Commons when Baldwin first declared he would "accept full responsibility" still prevails, and is to be found everywhere in the government of our affairs, it has crept through Government department after department and has seeped into the Services themselves. It has been likened to a dead hand, a hand that damps the ardour of the citizens, that numbs all effort and that is beginning to chill all hope itself. Let us rouse ourselves and grapple with realities while there is still time.

'Why did the German battle-cruisers get through? Let a straight answer be given and as much benefit as possible be derived from the occurrence. The answer is not that the plan to stop them was badly executed or that it miscarried; the real trouble is that there was no plan at all. We relied far too much on a hasty improvisation. The conclusions drawn from a day spent in the Naval Operations Room at Dover are as follows:

'(a) No adequate comprehensive plans were made to ensure destruction of the German battle-cruisers in the event of their leaving Brest. There is no excuse for this negligence on the part of the War Cabinet and on the part of those serving them.

'Plans should have been devised to provide against every conceivable contingency. Our Intelligence Service had given ample warning that the ships were about to leave and that it was probable they would sail up the Channel. At least seven destroyers had passed through the Straits of Dover on their way South to Brest during the three weeks immediately preceding the departure of the big ships. There had been increasing enemy shipping activity in the Straits of Dover prior to the 12th February 1942, and this activity, particularly noticeable in connection with minesweeping, reached its peak on the night of the 11th February. Three plans should have been made, one to cover the enemy convoy located moving west from Brest, another to provide for the enemy being located leaving Brest, or just having left Brest and proceeding east, and a third to be put into execution should the enemy succeed in making good his escape from Brest undetected and being located either by aerial reconnaissance or otherwise on his way up channel. These plans should have been sub-divided to guard against varying weather conditions. The attack, wherever it might take place and whatever the conditions that might prevail, should have been properly co-ordinated. Strict control over the parts played by the three Services should have been exercised and the maximum benefit derived either from the presence of the large enemy ships in narrow waters close to our air and sea bases or, if they went the other way, from their enforced absence from the protection of shore-based fighters. The fact remains that at no time was the enemy subjected to a really heavy and sustained weight of attack capable of impeding his progress.

'(b) There was no adequate aerial or sea reconnaissance, both of which should have been a matter of daily routine.

'(c) There was a lack of some properly appointed body whose duty it should have been to collect from all sources, assimilate and pass out to those concerned, information concerning the three ships or any one of them. The jamming by enemy interference of our radio location on the morning of the 12th and the reports of weather favourable to the enemy to effect a breakthrough might, if concentrated in the hands of such a body, have alone given a sufficient indication of the enemy's intentions. This body could have done invaluable work during the course of the action by making sure that all services, groups and units received the same information and that each knew what the other was doing. Had the Naval Staff of Dover known earlier of the circling plots seen by location stations, some action would in all probability have been then and there originated, which would have led to the discovery of the enemy squadron sooner than it was in fact made.

'(d) The presence of the ships was perceived at 10.45 a.m. and was at such extreme range that it was immediately concluded that if the ships were not the battle-cruisers, then it was something very exceptional and almost certainly worth attacking. No attack, however, was carried out until over an hour and three-quarters later, and then by very light naval forces only operating without air support.

'(e) This was the chance which Fighter Command had been waiting for for over a year, for there existed a state of affairs

195

that they had done their utmost to provoke during that time, that is to say a large number of enemy aircraft flying well within the range of our fighters and at both a numerical and strategical disadvantage. Yet nevertheless the effort of our fighter squadrons was made far too late, and when it came it was badly directed, in so far as many of the squadrons failed to reach their objective, although it was being plotted by the most accurate means known to science. By the time the attack was made, much of the tactical advantage that had been ours had slipped away and we were forced to operate nearer the enemy's bases than our own.

'(f) Coastal Command before as after the escape failed utterly to appreciate the situation. This failure may to no small extent be attributed to the lack of a precise plan of action common to the services and commands, but the fact remains that upon them greatly depended the chance of obtaining early warning of the departure of the ships, and also of an early attack upon them being executed. Yet it was 16 Group who complained that the attack was made by the Swordfish aircraft, "without waiting for the Beauforts". Battles are not won by procrastination, and the low speed of the Swordfish aircraft made it impracticable for them in the circumstances to carry out a joint attack with the Beauforts, which were over twice as fast. The Swordfish attacked when they did so that advantage could be taken of the accurate information of the position of the ships then available, and so that they might operate near their own coast and as close to their base as possible. The suggestion that the attack should be postponed is indicative of the failure to grasp the salient point that speed was an essential feature of the operation. Coastal Command, charged with the responsibility of keeping guard, let the Germans go and bungled the subsequent attack.

'(g) It was reported that pilots of Beauforts which landed at Manston to obtain more torpedoes were told supplies were not available. A number of Beaufort pilots ordered into action had never fired a torpedo. Such a state of affairs defies comment and only seems to lay stress on that need for forethought, the lack of which characterized the entire proceedings.

'(h) Owing to lack of co-operation between the Navy and Air

Force, the naval light forces attacked without air support, a support which would have greatly facilitated their task.

'(i) Of the fighter squadrons – eleven in all – detailed to assist and protect the Swordfish only one squadron made the rendezvous and others did not even find the ships. The Swordfish, when actually making the attack, were almost unescorted and were subjected to the concentrated A.A. fire of every German gun that could be brought to bear.

'(j) It is quite untrue that bad weather enabled the German ships to escape; the weather, anyway until 2.45, four hours after the first plot had been received, was not such as should have affected our operations adversely to any appreciable extent. The weather reports which the Germans obtained were equally if not more readily available to us. If the enemy knew the weather favoured the attempt, we also should have appreciated that the conditions were such as would proffer the chance he needed, and we should have tightened our watch upon him and made our dispositions accordingly.

'(k) Again owing to the absence of a clear-cut plan, our forces were scattered and unprepared and their efforts were ineffective. At no time was their combined weight felt by the enemy. We dissipated our power in a series of costly and ill-conceived attacks against a powerful and fully expectant enemy. The enemy had as usual planned carefully ahead, we had not. Of over 250 bombers employed only 37 located the target and some of these are believed to have bombed our own ships. All this despite the fact that the most accurate information as to the position of the enemy was available at Dover. Of the fighters we sent out, the value of a high proportion was lost as they were not as efficiently controlled as they should have been. There were too many water-tight compartments, too many persons and units trying to act independently of one another, each relying on his or their own source instead of on the best source of information which should have been supplied by some central organization.

'(l) Thirty-three rounds was the Army's contribution to the battle, and they were only able to supply this after inquiring whether they would be hampering the sea or air attack. These inquiries at the last moment and while the enemy were literally at our gates show the pitiful absurdity of the whole situation and emphasize once again the pressing need to think ahead.

'(m) These battle-cruisers will sink many of our ships and will cost many of our sailors their lives. Our prestige at home and abroad has sunk to a new low level and the repercussions caused by such a calamity cannot yet be foreseen. Worst of all, perhaps, is the tragic loss of many irreplaceable airmen and sailors in an abortive action. Theirs was great and lasting gallantry called for and rendered fruitless by that reckless gamble in their lives, which was necessitated by the indolence of those in whom they trusted.

'This reverse, like many others that have occurred in this war, is attributable to lack of imagination, energy and intelligence on the part of the people who carry our burdens in great affairs. They are heavy burdens and we need great men to carry them.

'Our pressing need is for reform and reorganization. What we should have done in peacetime we must do now in the heat and fury of the battle.

'(a) There must be a properly representative Imperial War committee in the deliberations of which the heads of the services can participate. A long-term home and overseas strategy must be worked out and put into execution without delay. Above all, we must take the initiative in as many spheres of action as possible and not lose it. Sub-committees with full freedom of action must be appointed to take care of operations subsidiary to the general Imperial plans. One such sub-committee should have been charged with the job of taking care of the German battle-cruisers at Brest and should have constituted the nerve centre of the attacking organization. All information should have been received and collated by them and all orders emanated from them; thus would it have been with certainty established that one body had the whole picture that only now, long after the enemy has escaped, is being laboriously pieced together.

'(b) There must be much closer liaison between the services and by the commands and units which they comprise. The right hand must always know what the left hand is doing. Very numerous instances can be quoted illustrating the complete lack of understanding that exists between Commands, the operational areas of which overlap.

'(c) Coastal Command is to all intents and purposes subservient to the Admiralty. The Command should be abolished and most of its work carried on by a Royal Naval Air Force, the remainder becoming the responsibility of Fighter Command. The presence of Coastal Command is redundant and seems merely to increase delay and confusion.

'(d) Men should be found for the jobs not jobs for the men. The right men must be in the right places before the right time, then and then only can our maximum war effort be developed and the might of our great potential strength be realized, executed and made to tell.

'The skill, the courage and the faith of our men is a national asset that has been many times squandered. Their example stirs me to write as I do and to state that I cannot any longer continue to shelter idly behind such bravery as was theirs. I have the honour, therefore, to request that:

'(a) I be permitted to resign my commission and to take up again the political campaign as Independent Candidate for the Chichester Parliamentary Division that I abandoned when war appeared to me inevitable, and which seems to offer me a better chance to serve my country than I now enjoy.

'(b) As an alternative, I be permitted to resign my commission and take a place with those of our seamen in the Royal Navy or in the Merchant Navy whose peril is now so much increased.

'(c) This letter be forwarded to the Air Council that such benefit as lies in what I have written may be taken for the public advantage.'

Kidd showed his report to Ramsay who said, 'I couldn't agree more. But who will believe us? They are bound to look for a scapegoat. It will be me – but what can I do?'

He was wrong concerning himself, but the day's defeat was followed by inter-service recriminations which reflected the bitterness which the Channel break-out let loose in Whitehall. Referring to the attack on *Campbell* and *Vivacious* by Beauforts while they were picking up *Worcester*'s wounded, a letter from the Admiralty to the Air Ministry said: 'We think that the unwarranted attack on H.M. destroyers by three Beaufort torpedo bombers on 12 February demands explanation. The Senior Officer's report is herewith attached.'

The Air Ministry, probably with a more realistic approach but with an utter lack of tact, replied: 'Low clouds, poor visibility and generally bad weather conditions prevailed and a certain amount of confusion was inevitable. The three aircraft concerned believed the target to be enemy warships.'

The fury of officers like Kidd over defeat was not isolated. The nation was ashamed and affronted. Every Englishman's mind went back to Sir Francis Drake and the Spanish Armada. *The Times* thundered in an editorial: 'Vice-Admiral Ciliax has succeeded where the Duke of Medina Sidonia failed. Nothing more mortifying to the pride of our sea power has happened since the seventeenth century.'

This was the most depressing factor of the German battle-ships' break-out. It spelled the end of the Royal Naval legend that in wartime no enemy battle-fleet could pass through what was proudly called the English Channel.

National and provincial newspapers joined with *The Times* in voicing indignant protests that this humiliating disaster had been permitted to happen. The London national newspaper, *News Chronicle*, said in an editorial: 'This story, though one of individual courage and steadfast devotion to duty, is not one which reflects much credit on those primarily responsible.' In the Commons it was said that 'it was the war's greatest blunder'.

While the English newspapers roared their disapproval, the German Navy was delighted with their victory. Forty miles west of Trondheim the German battleship *Tirpitz* was hiding in a fiord. At noon on 13 February, while her officers were having lunch in the wardroom, a radio broadcast announced: 'Under the orders of Admiral Ciliax, the *Scharnhorst*, *Gneisenau* and *Prinz Eugen* left Brest on the night of 11/12 February. With the protection of the Luftwaffe they passed through the Channel and the Straits of Dover. They have now reached German ports.' This news was received with great enthusiasm aboard *Tirpitz*.

The Germans also had an added piece of enjoyment when, on February 24, an intelligence memorandum was circulated to naval personnel. It gave a translation of *The Times* editorial, comparing the exploit with the Duke of Medina Sidonia. They enjoyed it very much in Wilhelmshaven, Kiel and Wolf's Lair in East Prussia.

The end of the British side of the story is told in a brief little note in a Coastal Command log-book at 4.25 p.m. on 13 February which read: 'Brest is going back to ordinary priority once a week.'

But the RAF soon recovered its sense of humour. On the day after the break-out, when three 'blips' were detected of ships sailing westwards towards the Channel, someone remarked, 'Do you know what that is? It's the buggers coming back!'

The RAF were alone in treating the affair with light-hearted retrospective cynicism. In the forty-eight hours after the German battleships had sailed safely home, the nation grew steadily angrier.

The *Daily Mail* said: 'The reasons for the escape of the German warships are still being debated – in every home, in every club, in every inn throughout the land. That *someone* was to blame is the only certainty. Again the suspicion arises that there is a lack of necessary co-operation between the Air Force and the Navy.

'The incident is symptomatic. Public reaction to the many "explanations" is one of weary resignation. And that too is symptomatic.

'It is symptomatic of the general feeling that there is something wrong with Britain's war direction and this feeling is crystallized in an almost universal demand for removal from high places of the tired and the incompetent.'

So Churchill, although totally out of sympathy with the public outcry, took an unprecedented step to protect his administration. On the following Monday – a wet, winter's day four days after the break-out – three men sat behind a long desk in Whitehall to perform a difficult task. They were to preside over the only judicial inquiry ever held into the conduct of a battle.

The three members of the Board were its president, Mr Justice Bucknill, Air Chief-Marshal Sir Edgar Ludlow-Hewitt, Inspector-General of the Royal Air Force, and the Naval member, Vice-Admiral Sir Hugh Binney.

Mr Justice Bucknill said, 'The Board's terms of reference are

201

to inquire into the circumstances in which the German battle-cruisers *Scharnhorst* and *Gneisenau*, in company with the heavy cruiser *Prinz Eugen*, proceeded from Brest to Germany on 12 February, 1942, and on the operations undertaken to prevent them.' The terms of reference were signed by Winston S. Churchill, Minister of Defence. The real objective of this solemn tribunal was to whitewash the Navy and the RAF, and help restore confidence in Churchill's government.

It had no power to compel admirals to attend. Vice-Admiral Binney hoped to persuade the Admiral Commanding Submarines, Admiral Sir Max Horton, to give evidence before the Board on this question. For the Board was not satisfied that Sir Max had drawn enough submarines from other areas to deal with a possible break-out. Horton refused to appear, saying: 'If I can't find out what is wrong in my command without setting up a panel of so-called experts, then I'll resign from the Navy and raise chickens.' This attitude was typical of the autocratic autonomy which Service Chiefs claimed for themselves in this period of the war.

The inquiry was a long parade of senior officers offering excuses and lame justifications for their own part in the disaster. Most of the witnesses knew it. As a result of his report, Gerald Kidd was called before the Bucknill Tribunal. After his evidence, Admiral Ramsay said to him during lunch at the Senior Services Club, 'It is a waste of time. You might as well turn round and go home. They are not even making any notes. All they want is a whitewash.'

Coastal Command, responsible for reconnaissance patrols – 'Stopper', 'Line SE' and 'Habo' – produced witnesses to explain why German battleships had been at sea fourteen hours before they were spotted off Boulogne. Their explanation? A blown fuse in 'Stopper', a damp plug in 'Line SE'.

Sir Philip Joubert, who had his three squadrons of Beaufort torpedo bombers in the wrong place, explained, 'The enemy broke out of Brest unobserved owing to the darkness of the night and the breakdown of radar.'

The Board wanted to know why, when Victor Beamish sighted the battleships, he did not use his radio to warn Fighter Command. The Navy particularly criticized this hidebound inefficiency of Fighter Command. When Royal Naval warships sighted the enemy they were under orders to give instant information about his position, course and speed – as Nigel Pumphrey's MTBs had done. Admiral Binney, commenting on the practice of keeping quiet about sighting the enemy, said: 'If a ship waited until returning to port before telling anyone it would be ridiculous.'

Yet the Board's view was that Beamish made the right decision. In his case any blame attached did not matter, for a month later he was killed when his Spitfire was shot down in a dog-fight over the Somme estuary. His body was never found.

The fact that at the same time Sq. Ldr Oxspring did break the silence rule and was ignored by 11 Group was carefully hushed up. Concerning No. 11 Group of Fighter Command, the Bucknill Tribunal said:

'Unfortunately No. 11 Group, who were responsible for the 'Jim Crow' reconnaissance, were not sufficiently alive to the fact that the German ships might be coming out about that time. True, they knew that operation Fuller was in operation but some of the witnesses said they had not been informed that there had been any breakdown in the night patrols, and in consequence their minds were not especially directed to the possible significance of the radar plots; and they were slow to order investigation by additional reconnaissance. Had these plots been investigated as soon as their character came under suspicion, it is possible that the enemy Squadron would have been sighted an appreciable time earlier than it was.'

If No. 11 Group had been efficient they could have given at least two hours additional warning. The weather was clearer then and bombers might have attacked successfully with armour-piercing bombs.

Wing-Commander Constable-Roberts reported that No. 11 Group had said they had supplied fighter escort when Esmonde had taken off. He was supported by the written report of Flt-Lt Gerald Kidd.

Kidd told the Tribunal that Manston informed him that the Swordfish had taken off and were circling the airfield. At the same time, Hornchurch reported that their fighters were over

Manston. When Manston said there was no sign of the fighters, Kidd asked the woman on the end of the line at Hornchurch to speak to the controller. She said he was busy on the plotting table. When he said he wanted to check with the controller where the fighters were, the woman replied the controller did not know. When Kidd persisted, he was finally informed the fighters had failed to join the Swordfish.

This is when he began to be angry. Had Hornchurch told him the fighters were going to be late he would have tried to keep the Swordfish orbiting to wait for them. Admiral Ramsay had only permitted Esmonde to take off on his suicide mission because he believed five fighter squadrons were on their way to escort the Swordfish. But the Bucknill Tribunal ignored the fact that four squadrons failed to arrive in time.

It was apparent that after the Germans had successfully defied the might of the Royal Navy and the RAF, there could only be excuses from the British services. As Hitler had foreseen, they had been unable to 'conceive and execute lightning decisions'. Bomber Command even made the typically bureaucratic complaint that their operations were limited because there had not been 'reasonable notice'.

Admiral Ramsay was one of the few who was open and honest. He frankly admitted he felt bitter at his own failure to anticipate more accurately the Germans' arrival in the Straits. Ramsay said, 'The main feature which influenced all operations was the failure to detect the enemy heavy ships at daylight on 12 February. Had they been sighted then there would have been ample time for our main striking forces to get off and make attacks in the narrow waters of Dover Straits. We would have had maximum advantage, and would have been able to use our numerical and tactical air superiority, combined with accurate knowledge of the enemy's path on the radar plot. Failing other information during the night, a successful dawn reconnaissance to the westward of Dover Command would have given two hours extra warning of their approach.

'The main hope rested on the expectation that the passage would be made before daylight. This would have afforded the most favourable conditions not only for the Swordfish aircraft but also for coastal craft and destroyers. In the event, these forces had to attack in daylight without the advantage of potentially overwhelming fighter support which never developed. Little hope could be placed in daylight torpedo attacks from surface craft, for these now actually went to sea under much more unfavourable conditions than had been anticipated.

'Some measure of success from recently laid minefields had also been hoped for, but the enemy had employed a large number of minesweepers to search a selected route, although actually the heavy ships were known to have passed over two of them.'

Like his air liaison officers, he was critical towards all three commands of the RAF – Coastal, Bomber and Fighter. His report was smothered in secrecy. No mention of it appears in the published records of the inquiry.

The Admiralty must take much of the blame. The Germans sailed triumphantly, untouched past Dover while the Royal Navy refused to move battleships out of Scapa Flow.

First Sea Lord Admiral Sir Dudley Pound was insistent that he would employ his battleships in only the safest waters. He had his reasons, but this decision perhaps erred too much on the side of caution.

The Fleet Air Arm also faced a vital question. Why did twenty-four Swordfish remain on the ground at Lee-on-Solent that day? Official explanation – there was not a single trained pilot, observer or gunner at Lee-on-Solent. Was this true – or was it another bureaucratic answer?

The RAF command was equally to blame. After the Swordfish attack, three hours elapsed before Coastal Command put every available aircraft into the air, throwing squadrons of torpedo bombers from Scotland to Cornwall into the battle – but too late.

The Tribunal sat for twelve days. Their findings reached the Prime Minister at the beginning of March 1942. When he read it, security descended like a fog blanket. Although it was claimed to be a complete 'answer' to any carping criticism, not even Members of Parliament were allowed to have more than minor information on the true facts.

The Bucknill Report, Command Paper 6775, was produced in Parliament by Deputy Premier Attlee on 18 March 1942.

He stated in reply to a question that the report had been received, but its contents could not be made public since it contained information which would be of value to the enemy. He added, 'The general findings do not reveal that there were any serious deficiencies either in foresight, co-operation or organization.' The House was not sàtisfied. Neither was the Press.

Evidently deeply stung by the criticism, Churchill quoted to the House an Admiralty statement of 2 February 1942, ten days before the warships broke out: 'At first sight this passage up the Channel appears hazardous for the Germans. It is probable, however, that as their heavy ships are not fully efficient they would prefer such a passage, relying for security on their destroyers and aircraft which are efficient, and knowing full well that we have no heavy ships with which to oppose them in the Channel. We might well therefore find the two battle-cruisers and the eight-inch cruiser with five large and five small destroyers, also say twenty fighters constantly overhead – with reinforcements within call – proceeding up the Channel. Taking all factors into consideration . . . the Channel passage appears to be their most probable direction if and when they leave Brest.' Churchill said, 'I have read this document to the House because I am anxious that Members should realize our affairs are not conducted entirely by simpletons and dunderheads as the comic papers try to depict.'

The Report was not 'tabled' until 1946. Even when the details which had been kept hidden for four years were revealed, they were not sensational. The determined smoke-screen made sure that no details of the mishandling of the German break-out reached even the peacetime public. For the official account contains more misinformation and downright rubbish than most government documents. It is difficult to believe that some of the facts had been deliberately falsified even in such a perilous time as this mid-war period. But it is such a farrago of omissions and evasions that the tribunal must have skimped their inquiries.

The period in which this happened must be taken into account. It was right in the middle of the war. The British public were despondent enough about defeats from Dunkirk to Singapore without being dismayed further by revealing the full facts of the inefficiency which allowed the German battleships to sail unscathed past the cliffs of Dover.

The Report said:

'The *Gneisenau* and *Scharnhorst* were located at Brest after shipping raids on 28 March 1941. The 8-inch cruiser, *Prinz Eugen*, which left Norway in company with the *Bismarck*, joined the battle-cruisers in Brest after the loss of the *Bismarck*. She was first seen in dry-dock there on 4 June.

'A photographic reconnaissance on 29 and 31 January 1942 revealed the arrival in Brest of two destroyers, five torpedo boats and eight mine-sweepers.

'The Admiralty always maintained that the most likely and safest course for the battle-cruisers when they left Brest was to break up the Channel to German waters. They would either do this or they would break into the Atlantic. Or they might go to the Mediterranean to Genoa or go north about the British Isles to return to German waters.

'On 2 February the Admiralty reviewed the position and drew up an appreciation that the ships would most probably proceed up the Channel. This was supported by indications like the concentration of torpedo boats, E-boats, mine-sweepers and other light craft along the coast from Le Havre to the Hook.

'The strong possibility was that the enemy ships would seek to pass the narrows at Dover under the cover of darkness. The distance from Brest to the Straits is 360 miles. During the winter months they could leave Brest shortly before dusk and run up the Channel in the dark, reaching the Straits about dawn. Or they might leave Brest to lie up in Cherbourg next day to run the Straits the following night.

'The enemy's occupation of the continental seaboard from Norway to Spain had rendered the participation of our own heavy ships in the operation impracticable. [In other words, the Germans might risk it but the Royal Navy would not.]

'Concerning executive order Fuller, on 3 February the Admiralty ordered the C-in-C Nore to have six destroyers with torpedoes on six hours notice in the Thames estuary to operate under the orders of the Vice-Admiral, Dover. Two fast mine-layers, the *Welshman* and the *Manxman* [the *Manxman* was in

207

fact not employed] were put on readiness and six Swordfish were sent to Manston. The submarine *Sealion* was ordered to join two submarines patrolling off Brest. Three squadrons of Beauforts were also put in readiness. One was at Leuchars, Scotland, to operate against the *Tirpitz* at Trondheim. One squadron was at St Eval in Cornwall. The third squadron was split up between St Eval and Thorney Island, near Portsmouth. The Beauforts from Leuchars were ordered to Coltishall in Norfolk.

'From 10 February, 100 bombers were ordered to stand by and 11 Group of Fighter Command was also warned. [Three hundred bombers were stood down without the Admiralty being informed.] On 11 February two more German destroyers entered Brest, making four.

'On 11 February a photo reconnaissance showed all three ships out of dock and six destroyers in harbour.

'The submarine, *H.M.S. Sealion,* saw no big ships while she remained in the vicinity of Whistle Buoy until 19.00, and then withdrew on the tide from this most dangerous patrol. She sur- faced south of Whistle Buoy and remained there until 20.35, but saw no enemy squadron. [In fact she left at 2 p.m. and was thirty miles away on the night of 11 February.]

'On the night of 11/12 February "Stopper" Patrol off Brest was ordered on a 12 hour patrol from 19.40 to 07.00 next day. The first aircraft took off at 18.27; when it encountered a JU-88 it switched off the radar equipment, and when it switched on again at 19.20 the radar was unserviceable. It had blown a fuse which they could not repair, so they returned to base. The crew trans- ferred to another aircraft and the patrol resumed at 22.38 and proceeded until 23.43. A third aircraft took over between 23–36 and 03.10. A fourth from 02.45 to 07.01. There was nothing seen, but there was a gap of three hours in "Stopper" from 19.40 and 22.38.

'"Line SE" Patrol was between Ushant and the Ile de Bréhat. It was ordered between 19.40 and 23.40 on 11 February. The aircraft reached its starting point at 19.36, when its radar be- came unserviceable through an obscure fault of unusual character which is still under investigation. It remained on patrol but reported the fault at 21.13 and was ordered to return. No relief plane was sent. If it were not for the technical failure of both their patrols they had an excellent chance of sighting the German squadron.

'On 12 February morning two Spitfires over Boulogne sighted E-boats leaving harbour. Under the standing order not to use wireless telegraphy, they immediately returned to base to report.

'Two Spitfires took off at 10.20 to sweep from Boulogne to Fécamp. Fifteen miles from Le Touquet, Sq. Ldr Oxspring sighted 20–30 vessels in convoy. He landed at Hawkinge at 10.50 and the information was passed to Dover and 11 Group. [He had given the alarm over the radio at 10.20 a.m., half an hour earlier, and no one in 11 Group took any notice.]

'Sgt Beaumont, who was with Sq. Ldr Oxspring, said he saw a vessel with a tripod mast and superstructure. When handed a book of German silhouettes he picked out a German capital ship.

'At 10.42, unconnected with the shipping reconnaissance, Group Captain Victor Beamish and Wing-Cdr Boyd, when attacked by Messerschmitts, flew right over the German squadron. They observed WT silence until they landed at 11.09 and informed intelligence at 11 Group Fighter Command.

'At 10.00–10.15 surface vessels appeared on the radar detector set at Beachy Head. There were telephone delays and the line was engaged, which held up the transmission of the information which did not reach Dover until 10.40. At 10.50 enemy shipping was detected by radar at Fairlight and passed to Dover.

'The Swordfish were ordered to be airborne at 12.20 to carry out an attack at 12.45. The rendezvous for their fighter escort was 12.25 over Manston. Owing to unforeseen delays the fighters did not get there in time.

'Two squadrons from Biggin Hill Wing arrived at Manston late and proceeded towards the target. Hornchurch Wing also missed the Swordfish at Manston and they searched over Calais without success. At 12.00 six Swordfish accompanied by ten Spitfires left for the target. Ten miles off Ramsgate German fighters appeared and battled with the Spitfires.

'On the morning of 12 February there were 36 serviceable Beauforts available. There were seven planes of 217 Squadron from Leuchars in Fife, 14 of 42 Squadron at St Eval, 15 of 86 and 217 Squadrons, except for three which were sweeping the

Bay of Biscay, from Thorney Island. Four of them which were in an advanced state of readiness proceeded to Manston at 13.40 led by Pilot Officer Carson, but they arrived too late to rendez-vous with the fighters. When they reached Manston, owing to the large number of aircraft circling the base, the Beaufort formation split up. [The report does not mention the mix-up of WT and RT orders.] Having obtained a fix, Carson reached the position of the German battle-cruisers at 16.40. Visibility was bad and he dropped his torpedo at 1,500 yards but was damaged by flak. A second pilot found the Germans at 18.00 and attacked.

'The two remaining Beauforts of the original four circled the aerodrome for some time and landed at Manston and set off again. Shortly after 15.00 they found the Squadron and at 15.40 their torpedoes were observed running. The three other planes left at Thorney Island flew to Manston and at 15.00 set course for the target. The visibility was so bad they made their attack singly and one was destroyed by fighters or anti-aircraft fire.

'The Leuchars squadron was delayed because of a snow-bound aerodrome but 14 serviceable Beauforts eventually arrived at Coltishall at 11.45. Three were without torpedoes and arrange-ments were made to send them to Coltishall but they did not arrive in time. Two had engine trouble, leaving nine which were ordered to Manston to pick up a formation of Hudsons who were to attack as a diversion. They arrived at Manston at 14.53 and accompanied by five Hudsons set off for the target at 15.34 [again without any radio orders]. Owing to the bad visibility they became separated and the Hudsons bombed the ships before the torpedo attacks began. Two Hudsons were lost.

'At 16.04 the Beauforts sighted the German ships and attacked in one flight of six and one of three. Seven torpedoes were dropped but heavy anti-aircraft fire prevented observation of results. [Nothing said about the near-sinking of Pizey's flagship *HMS Campbell*.]

'*The St Eval detachment*. At 12.20 Beauforts from St Eval were ordered to Thorney Island. Then they were ordered to rendezvous at Coltishall by 17.00 to pick up fighter escort. At 17.01 they picked up ten fighters over Coltishall and set course for the Ger-man Squadron. At 17.41 they were over the estimated position of the ships. At 18.05 they saw German mine-sweepers. Visibility was only 100 yards and it was raining heavily. The formation split up and lost sight of each other and darkness prevented their chance of effective action.

'*Destroyers.* The destroyers stationed at Harwich were *Campbell, Vivacious, Mackay, Whitshed, Worcester* and *Walpole.* They were all 20 years old.

'At 11.56 Captain Pizey in *Campbell* the flagship set off. At 15.17 Pizey saw two large ships on his radar at nine and a half miles. At 15.43 he came under heavy fire from the German ships. But they fired their torpedoes and *Worcester* fired her torpedoes from 2,400 yards. She was badly hit by the German shells and set on fire but managed to limp back to port.

'At 11.27 242 bombers set off and continued to fly throughout the afternoon. Thirty-nine attacked, 188 failed to find the ships and fifteen did not return. Twelve aircraft succeeded in laying mines which eventually damaged the *Gneisenau* and *Scharnhorst.* [In fact, the damage was done by mines laid much earlier.]

'*Fighter Command.* 11 Group had 21 Spitfire squadrons and four Hurricane squadrons. Also three squadrons from 10 Group and six squadrons from 12 Group took part in the battle. In all thirty-four fighter squadrons launched the most intensive fighter attack. Most of the attacks were launched at 14.05–15.05 to cover the Beaufort torpedo attacks. Out of a total of 398 fighter planes, 17 were missing.'

The Report then set out its conclusions.

'*Co-ordination of plans.* Was there any lack of proper contact between services and command? It must be remarked that there is such a thing as too much co-ordination. If the Germans came up the Channel the Assistant Chief of Naval Staff predicted it would be "A simple battle – all forces should be thrown into action at the earliest possible time".'

Then came a small note of criticism: 'Co-ordination was not entirely successful. For example, in the provision of escorts for the Swordfish. But later co-operation between the commands seems to have been complete [unfortunately, too late]. In these circumstances we have no suggestion to make for improvements of arrangements which already exist for the purpose of ensuring adequate liaison and co-operation between services and commands, which in our opinion proved on the whole to be satisfactory. There is no lack of evidence of co-operation or the will to co-operate.

'It must also be admitted that in addition to the short notice when information was received on the presence of the German ships they were to some extent caught by surprise. The general opinion of those dealing with the problem was that they would pass through the Straits at night. In addition, it must be remembered that an attack by destroyers or a handful of MTBs in broad daylight against capital ships, not themselves under heavy fire, was an adventure hitherto hardly regarded as justifiable.

'The Air Ministry, in receipt of the message that the German ships were in the Channel, sent to Fighter and Coastal commands this message: "*Scharnhorst* and *Gneisenau* reported in Channel sixteen miles west of Le Touquet at 11.5. Plus abnormal enemy air activity. Maximum available forces to be employed as early as possible to destroy the enemy ships and aircraft. This unique opportunity to be exploited to the utmost."

'After spending 15 days on this inquiry this Board is impressed by the countless acts of gallantry that came to their notice and the evident determination of all our forces to press home their attacks.'

The only other faint note of criticism was contained in this paragraph: 'Apart from the weakness of our forces, the main reason for our failure to do more damage to the enemy was the fact that his presence was not detected earlier and this was due to a breakdown of night patrols and the omission to send out strong morning reconnaissance. All operational orders said they would pass through in darkness.'

It is a collector's piece of officialese and double talk. Nearly 700 fighters and bombers – the entire force at the disposal of the RAF – had been flung into the battle without success because they were too late and completely unco-ordinated. Thirteen young Fleet Air Arm pilots had been sent uselessly to their deaths. Twenty-seven young sailors had been killed and eighteen seriously wounded aboard the destroyer *Worcester* when she took on a German battleship and cruiser single-handed – a piece of pitiful heroism which need never have happened if the Navy had brought in bigger ships.

Security was so rigid that hundreds of other young RAF pilots took off with no idea what they were looking for. One RAF squadron leader had reported by radio that German battleships were in the Channel – and been ignored. Another officer, a group captain, had not even broken radio silence in spite of the great urgency. Some RAF torpedo planes, taking off in confusion, had attacked and nearly sank our own destroyers. RAF night reconnaissance patrols over the Channel returned and were not replaced, leaving a gap of three vital hours. Except for hitting three mines, the battleships reached Germany untouched under the noses of the most battle-experienced air force and navy in the world.

The unpalatable truth which Churchill dared not reveal to the angry and disturbed British public was that some of his service chiefs had proved themselves tragically incompetent. For Hitler had been right. The carefully prepared German dash uncovered a lack of liaison and organization. Looking back, it makes one apprehensively wonder what might have been the outcome if the Führer had gone ahead with his plans to invade Britain.

The break-out of the battleships was a supreme example of meticulous German planning and efficiency defeating the hasty last-minute improvisations of the British.

Perhaps the main trouble was the short-sighted arrogance on the part of the British forces. Admittedly there were disasters against the Japanese in the East. But the Army had escaped miraculously from Dunkirk and the RAF had won the Battle of Britain. The Royal Navy had a centuries-old tradition of paramountcy behind it. The Admiralty simply did not regard a German dash up the English Channel as a serious possibility. Hence their pitiful dispositions. In the case of the newer service, the RAF at this time of the war reckoned to have the Luftwaffe on the run. They were flying on increasing number of fighter sweeps over France and every night mounting an even more devastating bomber offensive over Germany.

This somewhat smug attitude in all services as well as the petty rivalries, even among commands, were the basic reasons for the disasters of the day. But how could Churchill tell the nation that – particularly as it included incompetence at his beloved Admiralty?

Fighter Command Chief Sir Sholto Douglas commented later: 'At the time I was at a loss to understand the reluctance of the Royal Navy to have units of the Home Fleet ready to send out into the North Sea. The prizes to be gained in an action with ships of the importance of the *Scharnhorst* and the *Gneisenau* and the *Prinz Eugen* would have been worth bringing some of our bigger ships into action in time to intercept the German warships while they were still at sea. As it was, the enemy warships got away with it, even though they did hit some mines which failed to do more than slight damage, and they all made the safety of their home ports.'

The Germans had their complaints too. German Navy Chief, Grand Admiral Erich Raeder, was equally critical of the Luftwaffe. He wrote in his report: 'The Navy opinion was that with sufficient air defence the big ships could remain stationed in Brest even if British battleships were stationed at Plymouth and Portsmouth. The Luftwaffe could have considerably eased the task of the German ships by attacking British air bases. But as was constantly shown the Navy was dependent here upon the goodwill of the Luftwaffe.

'Numerous reports about the air attacks on Brest deeply impressed the Führer. He followed them continuously with concern and did not look with any favour on the operations of the big ships. This feeling, without doubt, was reinforced by Göring, who emphasized to the Führer again and again that there was just no sensible way to protect the big ships in Brest against air attack. In fact it did not lie in Göring's power nor in his wish. He therefore robbed us of a chance to do something worthwhile in convoy raiding.

'At the end of 1941, when the question of the transfer of the ships to the North Sea came up, the Führer produced a number of arguments for stationing the ships in Norway. Many reports of landings in Norway by the British in the spring played a considerable part in his case. Added to this, the ships in Brest were being damaged and remained inactive. When the question of a break-out was looked into, the Iceland passage was deemed unfavourable because the British, noting the absence of the ships from Brest, would have enough time to bring out their Home Fleet and concentrate it in the North Sea. Therefore if it were to come to a break-out, it must be through the Channel which would bring surprise. At the beginning of 1942, when we prepared to sail through the Channel, we hoped that the break-through might not be noticed by the enemy, but we were also prepared for a short sharp battle and an exchange of shots.'

24

But Who Really Won?

In spite of the whitewash of the Bucknill Tribunal some officers were secretly sacked or posted away. Admiral Ramsay was not a scapegoat as he had gloomily predicted – but a lot of other people were. They were not sacked, as that would have undermined public confidence, but kicked upstairs to harmless jobs. One of them, Air Marshal Sir Philip Joubert, C-in-C of Coastal Command, was removed to Mountbatten's staff in Ceylon with the backwater job of Director of Information and Civil Affairs. Others known to be hostile to the official 'whitewash', were posted away. Wing-Cdr Constable-Roberts was exiled to Scapa Flow, but managed to get a squadron in North Africa shortly afterwards.

Gerald Kidd applied to go on the Dieppe raid, but instead had a message to report for what he regarded as a 'stooge job'. As he had heard a rumour that he would never get another operational job as a result of the report he had put in, he sent a letter to Air Vice-Marshal Leigh-Mallory to protest about being posted away without explanation. He said, 'There is a rumour that there are orders I am not to be involved in any further operations along the south coast. I want to protest against this.'

He also requested to see Leigh-Mallory. Much to Kidd's surprise, he agreed to see him one evening at 11 Group at Uxbridge. His manner was unfriendly as he said, 'What do you want, Kidd?' Kidd replied, 'Why have I been taken off the Dieppe raid?'

Leigh-Mallory said abruptly, 'Sit down, Kidd.' He then produced a copy of his report and said, 'This is balderdash, bunkum and bilge. I strongly resent being ordered by the Air Council to answer a letter from a junior officer.'

Kidd replied stiffly, 'I am sorry, sir, that you regard it that way.

216

But the facts are correct. I wrote it after what was to me a tremendous shock and a great sense of personal loss.'

Leigh-Mallory repeated, 'I want to make it quite clear that I resent a junior officer criticizing me.'

Kidd answered, 'It is not intended as a criticism of you. It is a general criticism.'

In clipped tones, Leigh-Mallory said, 'Take paragraph E., which reads, "This was the chance which Fighter Command had been waiting for for over a year ... nevertheless, the effort of our fighter squadrons was made far too late and when it came it was badly directed, in so far as many of the squadrons failed to reach their objective."

Kidd replied by drawing his attention to the fact that his report made it clear there was 'no lack of courage and desire to defeat the enemy'.

Leigh-Mallory said, 'I agree with everything except the paragraph that affects me. We could have won a resounding victory, but I could get no co-operation from Joubert of Coastal Command. It was as if we were fighting a different war.'

Having made this astonishing confession to a junior officer, he became suddenly genial. The interview ended on friendly terms, when he introduced Kidd to his staff over a drink. He also promised to promote him – and kept his word.

There were several other echoes of the day's defeat. At Biggin Hill Fighter Base, Flt-Lt Cowan Douglas-Stephenson always kept a personal log giving details of every event that happened on the airfield from the condition of the runways to individual take-offs. He said, 'I was posted shortly afterwards to Hornchurch. Later when I returned to Biggin, I found the pages from Saturday, 3 January, to Wednesday 25 March, 1942 had been cut out with a razor blade. Why? Every other entry was intact.'

Stephenson is still convinced this was a deliberate act by someone in authority to lose the record of what took place at one of Britain's most vital fighter airfields that February day. They cut out a much larger section so that the excision of 12 February would not appear too obvious.

Barely a month after the break-out on 17 March 1942, the *London Gazette* gave details of RAF awards for the action. They included a DFM (Distinguished Flying Medal) to Hudson pilot, Flight Sergeant J. W. Creedon of 407 Royal Canadian Air Force Squadron, 'who made a daring low-level attack on a German destroyer escorting the *Scharnhorst* and *Gneisenau*. Creedon came out through cloud to 400 feet and sighted a destroyer directly below him. Diving through fierce flak to 200 feet he released his bombs which straddled the German warship. As he turned away to climb back into the clouds, he was attacked by a JU-88. But when Creedon's rear-gunner opened fire with his turret guns the German sheered off.'

For his gallant single-handed attack Pilot Officer Carson of 217 Squadron received the somewhat inadequate decoration of the DFC (Distinguished Flying Cross). The *London Gazette* also announced other RAF awards to 42 Squadron. They included the award of the DSO (Distinguished Service Order) to the other man who flew off without waiting for orders, Sq. Ldr Cliff, and the DFC to Pilot Officer Archer. Pilot Officer Pett was also awarded a DFC.

The *London Gazette* said, 'The King has been graciously pleased to approve the following awards in recognition of gallantry displayed in flying operations against the enemy. On the afternoon of 12 February 1942, a force of Beaufort and Hudson aircraft carried out an attack on enemy naval forces, including the *Scharnhorst* and *Gneisenau*, off the Dutch coast. In the face of harassing fire from screening destroyers, the attack was pressed home with the utmost determination at very close range. Although it has not been possible to assess the damage, owing to the extremely poor visibility, it is believed that several hits were obtained. The operation, which demanded a high degree of skill and courage, reflects the greatest credit upon the following officers and airmen who participated.

'Squadron Ldr Cliff was the leader of the formation, a squadron of Coastal Command Beaufort torpedo bombers, which delivered a formation attack on one of the two larger ships. Hudsons of the RCAF also took part in the attacks. Three Beauforts and two Hudsons were lost.

'At least two hits are believed to have been scored by Squadron Leader Cliff's squadron and the crews of the other Beauforts saw torpedoes running towards the target, as they turned away into the mist and drizzle with flak bursting round them and enemy fighters on their tails. Because of bad weather it was difficult to find the convoy and only good navigation brought them to the right spot. For some, the first indication that they had arrived came from flak bursting near them fired from unseen ships.'

There seems little doubt that to cover their own unforgivable inadequacies, Coastal Command rushed to recommend as many medals as they could to the courageous pilots.

The Navy also gave medals to its heroes. As well as the posthumous VC awarded to Lt-Cdr Esmonde, all the Swordfish survivors were decorated. The four sub-lieutenants, Brian Rose, Edgar Lee, Charles Kingsmill and 'Mac' Samples, were all given the DSO. The only surviving rating, Gunner Donald Bunce, was awarded the CGM (Conspicuous Gallantry Medal).

The five destroyer captains who took part in the action against the battleships were also given decorations.

Captain Mark Pizey of *HMS Campbell* was made a C.B. (Commander of the Bath). Captain J. P. Wright of *HMS Mackay* was given a bar to his DSO, and a DSO went to Lt-Cdr R. Alexander (*Vivacious*), Lt-Cdr W. A. Juniper (*Whitshed*) and Lt-Cdr Colin Coats (*Worcester*).

The Germans awarded medals for their side of the battle. Both Captain Hoffmann and Admiral Ciliax were awarded the Knight's Cross. One of Germany's highest awards, it is only given to someone who already has the Iron Cross, 1st and 2nd Class. Ciliax was awarded the Knight's Cross because he had been the commander of Operation Cerberus. His task was to carry out the detailed orders of Naval Group West in Paris and he had done that well. Captain Otto Fein of *Gneisenau*, who had commanded the squadron for most of the voyage, received nothing.

The sailors had no illusions about Ciliax's conduct during the battle. Someone composed a ribald song about him which was sung to a popular tune on all the ratings' mess-decks. Soon the rude song penetrated to the wardrooms.

The captains of the three ships tried to stop this song being sung. Captain Helmuth Brinkmann of the *Prinz Eugen* came out with the direct command 'This song is not to be sung'. But this was one order the well-disciplined German sailors never obeyed.

While the controversy still raged, Churchill for once remained totally out of sympathy with the British public. Although certain RAF officers like Joubert were quietly shunted aside, he refused to make any open criticism of the Navy's conduct of the battle.

This was understandable in wartime because – like *The Times* editorial – it would only add to the Germans' joy. But he consistently refused to criticize them later in either speeches or his published works.

This was obviously due to the fact that as a former First Lord of the Admiralty in both World Wars he had a special, almost blind, affection for the Royal Navy. Yet, unlike the German Führer, he was a 'sea animal', and his naval strategic sense in the long run proved better than Hitler's.

Churchill stated after the war: 'Viewed in the after-light and in its larger aspects the episode was highly advantageous to us.' His view proved to be the correct one. The battleships, effectively bottled up in German ports, meant the threat to the Atlantic which had existed so long as they remained in Brest had disappeared.

One man who agreed with him was Grand-Admiral Raeder, head of the German Navy, who commented, 'It was a tactical success but a strategic defeat.'

The Channel battle was not a total defeat for Britain. The German battleships, although they achieved victory, soon ended their careers as fighting ships.

A fortnight later Bomber Command revenged themselves by finishing off *Gneisenau*. Damaged by the mine, she was in dry dock at Kiel when the RAF made her the target of a massive attack. For three nights between 25 and 27 February bombers pounded her. On the first night 61 bombers came over, 49 arrived on the second night and on the third 68 bombers attacked. On this same night, 33 bombers also attacked *Scharnhorst* in Wilhelmshaven. She escaped unscathed, but British bombs smashed *Gneisenau*'s bows and foredecks. It was the end. Her hulk was eventually towed to Gdynia in Poland, and filled with concrete to become a blockship fort.

Ciliax was also proved right about the dangers of Norwegian waters. Just before dawn on 23 February *Prinz Eugen* was approaching Trondheim when a torpedo from *HMS Trident*, commanded by Cdr G. M. Sladen, ripped off her stern. She managed to limp into the sheltered anchorage at Aasfiord, but she never went to sea operationally again during the war. In 1948, as part of the United States Navy in the Allied share-out, she was sunk at Bikini Atoll in the atomic bomb tests.

Although *Scharnhorst* was ready for sea again after six months, her fate was to be the worst. On Boxing Day, 26 December 1943, the twilight of noon was fading to the darkness of an Arctic afternoon when she was cornered off North Cape by Admiral Sir Bruce Fraser and the Home Fleet.

She was first detected by two British cruisers, *Norfolk* and *Belfast*, who began to hold her steadily in their radar. Then Admiral Fraser aboard his flagship, *Duke of York*, picked her up on his own radar at twenty-two nautical miles.

At 4.45 p.m. the *Duke of York*'s first 14-inch salvo fired from six miles away straddled her and made one hit. *Scharnhorst* continued to steam away eastward, turning briefly at intervals to fire a broadside, then resuming headlong flight. For an hour it looked as if she would escape.

In the chase the *Duke of York* made three more hits – so did the cruisers. No Royal Naval ship received any serious damage, though the flagship was frequently straddled, and one of her masts was smashed by an 11-inch shell.

In complete darkness, five hundred miles north of the Arctic Circle, through strong winds and heavy seas, the running battle went on for two hours. At 6 p.m. *Scharnhorst*'s main battery went silent. But battered and crippled as she was, with half her crew dead or wounded, she continued to fight like a wounded shark. Her secondary armament was still firing wildly as the British ships closed in to sink her with torpedoes.

At 7 p.m. the squadron commander, Vice-Admiral Bey – the same officer who had commanded the destroyers in the Channel break-out – exchanged a last greeting with the German Admiralty and Hitler which said, 'Long live Germany and the Führer!' At 7.28 p.m. *Duke of York* fired her 77th salvo at her. Fifty-two torpedoes had already been fired but the last three – fired at 7.37 p.m. by *HMS Jamaica* from just under two miles range – finished her.

221

At 7.45 p.m. *Scharnhorst* exploded and sank in a dense cloud of smoke. Only thirty-six survivors – not one of them an officer – were recovered alive from the icy, turbulent sea. The rest of her crew of 1,940 men, including Admiral Bey, went down with her.

APPENDIX

The sister ships *Scharnhorst* and *Gneisenau* were launched within two months of each other in 1936, *Scharnhorst* at Wilhelmshaven, *Gneisenau* at Kiel. Their full load displacement was 32,000 tons. Standard displacement was 26,000 tons, and overall length 741 feet. They reached thirty-two knots on trials, and were heavily armoured with steel twelve inches thick in places. Their two armoured decks were $2\frac{1}{2}$ and $4\frac{1}{2}$ inches thick. Both carried nine 11-inch guns, twelve 5·9s, fourteen 4·1s and sixteen 1·45 A.A. guns in twin mountings. They also carried six 21-inch torpedo tubes, which had no war-heads at the time of the Brest break-out.

Prinz Eugen, a heavy cruiser of the 'Hipper' class, was launched in the summer of 1938. She had a displacement of 10,000 tons with eight 8-inch guns, twelve 4·1 A.A. guns and twelve 37-mm A.A. guns. Her armour was 5 inches thick in places, and she carried twelve 21-in. torpedo tubes. Her top speed was also thirty-two knots.

Bibliography

The following is a selected list of the books I consulted in the preparation of this work:

BUSCH, FRITZ OTTO: *The Drama of the Scharnhorst.* London: Robert Hale, 1956.

—— *The Story of the Prinz Eugen.* London: Robert Hale, 1950.

CAMERON, IAN: *Wings of the Morning.* London: Hodder and Stoughton, 1962.

CHURCHILL, WINSTON: *The Hinge of Fate.* London: Cassell, 1950.

DEMPSTER, DEREK, *and* WOOD, DEREK: *The Narrow Margin.* London: Hutchinson, 1961.

JONES, MAURICE: *History of the Coastal Artillery in the British Army.* London: R.A. Institute, 1959.

LOHMAN, WALTHER, *and* HILDEBRAND, HANS: *Der Deutsche Kriegsmarine.* Bad Nauheim: Podzun, 1956.

MARTIENSSEN, ANTHONY: *Hitler and his Admirals.* New York: Dutton, 1949.

RAEDER, ERIC: *The Struggle for the Sea.* London: Kimber, 1957.

RICHARDS, DENIS, *and* SAUNDERS, H.: *RAF in the War,* vol. 2. London: Butler and Tanner, 1961.

ROBERTSON, TERENCE: *Channel Dash.* London: Evans, 1958.

ROSKILL, STEPHEN: *The War at Sea, 1939–45,* vols 1 and 2. London: H.M.S.O., 1954–56.

ROWE, ALBERT: *One Story of Radar.* Cambridge: University Press, 1948.

RUGE, FRIEDRICH: *Sea Warfare, 1939–45: A German Viewpoint.* London: Cassell, 1957.

SCOTT, PETER: *The Battle of the Narrow Seas.* London: Country Life, 1946.

TREVOR-ROPER, HUGH (ed.): *Hitler's War Directives*. London: Sidgewick and Jackson, 1964.

VULLIEZ, ALBERT, *and* MORDAL, JACQUES: *Battleship Scharnhorst*. London: Hutchinson, 1958.

WARLIMONT, WALTER: *Inside Hitler's H.Q. 1939–45*. London: Weidenfeld and Nicolson, 1964.

Other printed sources include:

ADMIRALTY: *Führer Conferences on Naval Affairs*. Brassey's Naval Annual, 1948.

ADMIRALTY: *Report on the Escape of Scharnhorst, Gneisenau and Prinz Eugen from Brest to Germany* (The Bucknill Report). Command 6775, 1946.

JACKSON, DAVID: *In Bello in Pace Fidelis*. Blackwood's Magazine, May 1959.

SAUNDBY, AIR MARSHALL SIR ROBERT: Royal Air Force Review, September 1951–August 1952.

WARNE, WING-COMMANDER J. D.: *The Escape of the Scharnhorst, Gneisenau and Prinz Eugen*. Journal of the Royal United Service Institution, May 1952.

Index

Index

'Fritz' Lightship, 187
'Fuller', Operation, 46, 48, 75, 84,
    87, 109, 139, 142, 203, 207
Fuller-Wright, Sub-Lt, 112

Galland, Col. Adolf, 21, 23–4, 30–2,
    36, 39, 54, 79–82, 84–5, 87,
    130, 146, 173
Gamble, Lt H., 99–101, 104, 121
Gibson, Lt Paul, 99
Giessler, Helmuth, 19, 20, 26, 57,
    59, 60, 63, 77, 87, 89, 120, 131,
    173–4, 188
Gleave, Wing-Cdr Tom, 48–9, 87,
    108–11, 135–8, 140–1, 170–1
Gneisenau, 1–4, 7, 9, 10, 20, 32–3,
    36, 40–3, 50, 51, 54, 59, 62, 80–
    1, 87, 99, 104, 108, 111, 114,
    120, 126–7, 132–3, 137, 141–2,
    144, 150–7, 160, 164, 168–70,
    172, 175, 179, 181, 185–7, 190,
    200, 202, 207, 211–12, 214,
    218, 220, 223
Goode, Chief Petty Officer Willi,
    89
Gordon, Petty Officer, 163
Göring, Hermann, 8, 20, 28, 30, 214
Gosewisch, Lt-Col., 29
Gould, Lt Stewart, 99, 105
Griffiths, Chief Engineer H., 127,
    158, 162–3, 166–7, 181–2, 184–
    5
Griggs, Cpl Ernest, 94–5
Grossekurfurst, Batterie, 72

'Habo', patrol, 7, 66, 68, 75, 202
Hagan, Capt, 26
Hagger, Lt Dennis, 92
Hampdens, 9, 147–8
Harris, Air Vice-Marshal Arthur,
    139
Hathaway, Sgt, 142
Hawkinge, R.A.F. Station, 75, 80,
    82, 84, 85
Hayhoe, E. R. A., 162, 163, 172
Hedley, Pilot Officer, 145
Heinkels, 77, 148

Hehenberger, Petty Officer, 158
Hentschel, Lt-Col., 32, 65, 131
Hermann Schoemann, 146, 166,
    173–5, 177–8, 189
Heydel, Commander Hugo, 26, 131
Hillman, Sgt, 3
Hinder Buoy, 50, 126–7
Hinrichs, Lt Johann, 20
Hitler, Adolf, 8, 10, 11, 13, 16, 19,
    21–2, 24–5, 34, 41, 44, 56, 61,
    130, 204, 213–14, 220–1
Hoffman, Capt, Kurt, 1, 4, 9, 12,
    15, 35, 54, 57–9, 83, 89, 113,
    115, 120, 129, 131–4, 141, 172–
    4, 176–7, 188, 190, 219
Home Fleet, 1, 5, 6, 38, 42–3, 123,
    214–15, 221
Hood, H.M.S., 5, 156
Hornchurch, R.A.F. Station, 46,
    79, 122, 135–6, 203–4, 209,
    217
Horton, Admiral Sir Max, 41, 45–
    6, 202
Huddlestone, Major Guy, 93–4
Hudsons, 42, 66–8, 138–9, 145,
    210, 218
Hunt Class Destroyers, 50, 125–6,
    130, 147
Hughes, Flt-Lt, 143
Hurricanes, 52, 137, 211
Hutchings, Charles, 127, 152–3

Ibel, Col. Max, 31–2, 54, 65, 132,
    177, 189
Igoe, Bill, 76, 80, 86, 109, 112, 193
Ingham, Pilot Officer, 118–19
Iroise Bay, 45

Jackson, Lt D. C., 126, 148, 156,
    161, 180–1
Jaguar, 172, 189
Jamaica, H.M.S., 221
Jarvis, Wing-Cdr M., 78, 80, 82
Jasper, Cdr Paulus, 151, 153, 160
Jeanne d'Arc, 4
Jellicoe, Admiral, 43
Jeschonnek, Lt-General, 20, 22